SINGAPORE
Goes Off The Air

GILES PLAYFAIR

SINGAPORE
Goes Off The Air

by

GILES PLAYFAIR

J

JARROLDS *Publishers* LONDON *Limited*
47 Princes Gate - - - - - *S.W.*7
LONDON :: NEW YORK :: MELBOURNE

To

ERIC DAVIS

PRINTED IN
GREAT BRITAIN,
AT THE ANCHOR
PRESS, TIPTREE,
::   ESSEX   ::

CONTENTS

INTRODUCTION

I HAD my last look at Singapore on the night of February 11, 1942. Fierce fires were burning and it looked as if the whole island were in flames, as if some fearful biblical vengeance had been visited on the place where we had left behind the routine of our lives and nearly all our worldly possessions.

The small naval vessel which would carry us away to safety was moving round the harbour in circles. It sailed early next morning, while I was asleep on deck with a rice bag for a pillow and no mattress or covering of any kind.

We were exhausted, stunned and immeasurably relieved, too, for we had hardly dared hope for this chance of escape. As we watched the fires raging, turning the black moonless night into a hellish prolongation of the day that had passed, we almost wished that they could extinguish Singapore completely or that, miraculously, the island could sink into the sea so that thus the disgrace it seemed to symbolize would be submerged also and the Japanese be cheated of their triumph.

Someone standing next to me poured out a torrent of well-phrased abuse, lashing out at the perpetrators of blunders which had led to so dreadful a humiliation and in sum saying, "This needn't have happened." That was how we all felt, I imagine, though most of us were incapable of putting words to our thoughts.

For myself, I was fiercely convinced that I could never return to Singapore nor would ever wish to. To face those Asiatics who had served us and whom, in a sense, we had deserted would be impossible. Of course, unlike many others, I owed no loyalty to the place. I had lived there about nine weeks. I had arrived on the very day of the outbreak of the Pacific War, having come from England to take up an appointment with the Malaya Broadcasting Corporation. In fact, I had been longer on my way, for the journey via Jamaica, the Panama Canal, Australia and the Netherlands East Indies had taken me nearly four months.

I had enjoyed my job enormously and had been kept very busy and had learned something about the conduct of the war from the civilian end and of the mistakes which had been made. But I would have been unable to tolerate a peacetime existence in Singapore, with its petty scandals and aimlessness, its ugly indifference to the general welfare of mankind. I had a loathing, too, of my fixed idea of the average Singaporean—a vain, pleasure-loving, superficial, uncultured, slightly vulgar person—and though I had no first-hand evidence that such as he existed in any sort of abundance, I was prepared to believe in my present mood of overwhelming, unreasoning anger that he deserved the fate which had overcome him and was in part responsible for it.

More than a year has passed since the night of February 11, 1942, and in that time my outlook has changed considerably. I have an indescribable yearning to be back in Singapore, or rather to relive the weeks I spent there. I am determined to return when the war is over, or before if possible. I have an exaggerated affection for all the people who were my fellow workers and would rather be with them than with much older friends.

But that is not all.   I can no longer fit the average Singaporean into the great splodgy picture of wholesale folly, self-indulgence and ineptitude the sensationalists have painted and which public opinion both in England and the U.S.A. has apparently accepted as photographically exact.   He was the product of an outmoded system which one hopes has gone for good, though it was infinitely preferable to the Japanese substitute.   It is alleged that he was ill-prepared for war.   That is true.   It is further alleged that when the enemy marched in he was still romping around the dance floor.   That is the purest bunkum.

These two allegations, with suitable embroideries, are the sum total of a damning generalization which has commemorated the record of civilian Singapore as the most disgraceful chapter in the story of Allied reverses and in the whole course of British history.

But the generalization is both inaccurate and unfair, and should not be left unchallenged.   God knows it is impossible to laud Singapore's example, but that is no reason why it should occupy a kind of pedestal of shame.   Nor why it should be the target for the wildest sort of mud-slinging.   Allan A. Michie in his book *Retreat to Victory*, page 415, writes : "Until the day of the surrender, cars rolled up to Raffles Hotel for the afternoon tea-dances."   What crazy nonsense !   Some Londoners danced during the worst of the blitz and were considered on that account in the true Elizabethan tradition.   Had Mr. Michie danced in Singapore while the bombs fell and the shells burst and the Japs advanced I should have doffed my cap to him.   But he did nothing of the kind, because he was nowhere near at the time.   All he did was to report a bit of irresponsible hearsay.

The truth is that no tea-dances were held at Raffles in my experience, which dated from the outbreak of the Pacific War.   Furthermore, a week before the capitulation every privately owned car not being used strictly on Government service had already been requisitioned by the military.   Moreover, ten days before the capitulation a nine o'clock curfew was imposed, so that there was no dancing at night either.   Besides—but one could go on indefinitely.

I have written this book with the intent of painting a fair and faithful picture of civilian Singapore during the last nine weeks before its fall.   The bulk of it is in the form of a journal, so that as my time-to-time impressions vary so do my conclusions alter.   I had comparisons to go by because I was in London throughout the great blitz, and on my way out I saw various lands still basking in a near-peacetime luxuriance—Jamaica, Panama, Australia and Java.   By way of introduction I have described this journey in some detail.   Because of my job I had, too, a fair knowledge of the problems and difficulties peculiar to Singapore ; without consideration of these a balanced judgment of what took place is impossible.

No one need fear in the pages following a grand display of whitewash.   I have not attempted to cover up unpleasant facts, to gloss over mistakes, to withhold criticism or even to disguise my personal dislike of the European way of life in Singapore.   Indeed, it has not been my wish to thrust any particular opinion at my readers.   Much of what I have written is pure narrative and from it independent views may be formed.

It has been my purpose to modify a verdict based on the evidence of a remorseless generalization, to include in my canvas light as well as shade.   If my readers decide that there was folly, negligence, idleness, self-indulgence and even poltroonery in civilian Singapore, I hope they will agree that there was also wisdom, diligence, hard work, self-sacrifice and great bravery. If they consider that there were some persons and organizations deserving censure, I hope they will concede that there were others worthy of the highest praise. Much that happened in my experience between December 8, 1941, and February 11, 1942, was regrettable. But by no means was all of it shameful.

And now a word of explanation about the form of the book.

I left England August 25, 1941, with my wife Carol and my stepdaughter Amanda. During the long outward journey and in Singapore itself I jotted down occasional notes in a diary. These I have since elaborated into a journal.

All the extracts carry an address and a date-line, but whereas some chronicle the events of the past week or so, others, notably the later ones, deal only with a particular day.

My original notes are admittedly scanty. But they have been sufficient for my purpose, and I can honestly say that I have nowhere attributed to myself thoughts which do not belong to the time of writing. Indeed, it is because I have wanted to record accurately my impression of happenings while I was experiencing them that I have preferred a journal to a straight narrative.

To complete the story, however, I have added, by way of an epilogue, an account of my journey out of Singapore, which began three days before the capitulation and ended in Australia a little less than a month later.

GILES PLAYFAIR

PART I

ON THE WAY—AUGUST 25TH–DECEMBER, 1941

S.S. Themistocles—August 27, 1941.

WELL, here we are two days out (one day, actually. We remained stationary for the first), ploughing slowly up the coast towards Scotland, so the knowledgeable ones say, where we'll pick up the rest of the convoy.

The name of our ship was a number to us until we found a porter at the dock who immediately informed us it was the *S.S. Themistocles*. He pronounced it "Thermisstokells", which was rather confusing, but we were lucky enough to encounter a classical scholar recently down from Oxford who kindly translated.

It's a small and very shabby vessel, pre-last-war vintage, and made to look particularly woebegone by its camouflage of rusty grey. Carol, whose previous experience of the sea had been a couple of transatlantic trips to her own U.S.A. in a luxury liner, was completely downcast and went aboard most reluctantly. I felt rather the same way. But then we'd both been spoiled by our last two nights in London spent at the Savoy.

That was a very expensive farewell gesture to England. But it was worth while doing something I'd never dared even to contemplate before and probably never will again. Besides, it was instructive to observe how the very rich live in the third year of the war. Mostly I think one pays for the plumbing. The service, though it's more ornate and obsequious, has suffered just as surely as it has in our glamourized middle-class Cumberland. A desire for a whisky-and-soda can't be satisfied promptly by the mere ringing of a bell (the average waiting period is about twenty minutes). In the restaurant the prices are staggeringly high—10/6 for La Grouse Pie, 4/- for *Les Pommes Nouvelles*. But if you're bold enough to argue with the waiter you'll find that you can have more or less what you want for a fixed price of 10/6, though they've given up mentioning the fact because the choice is now too limited. Quantitively speaking, the menu is certainly pretty small. It consists chiefly of dishes which are no longer obtainable in humbler establishments. It's a make-believe fortress—this Savoy restaurant—crowded with gay-looking, smart-looking, laughing, chattering people. Most of them are regulars, bravely pretending that everything can be again as it was, and sticking to it, I suppose, even when the bombs fall. But one can make believe better still, lying in one's private sunken bath, turning on all the taps and showers just for the luxuriating fun of the thing. The plumbing really is magnificent.

After arrival at Liverpool we had time to lunch at the Adelphi. Needless to say, there are no longer any frills about the menu in the French Restaurant, where once we enjoyed such large, well-cooked meals. It's short and plain. Someone said the Adelphi had been hit, though I didn't notice it. But from my brief glimpse of Liverpool on the way to the docks it looked more battered than London—perhaps because the damage is more concentrated. Whichever way one turned one saw towering evidence of devastation.

Of course, we began our career on board with a first-class row. Carol found our cabin—spacious enough—inches thick in dust and crawling with insects (allowing for feminine exaggeration), so she made an ingratiating approach to the passage officer, who was there to look after our interests. But he wasn't having any. He didn't intend to pander to her little whims and fancies, and with superb originality reminded her that there was a war on. She countered with the sage observation that she couldn't see why the war was any excuse either for dirt or bad manners. And so it went on. Luckily the purser supported our cause. A steward was set to work and we were able to adjourn for afternoon tea shaken but victorious.

The ship, as I've said, is small, and diversions, on a wartime footing and very subordinate so far to lifeboat practice, are limited. There's a bar where drinks are extraordinarily cheap and large. Which reminds me that food is unrationed. It's a little difficult to put two lumps of sugar in one's coffee, to order bacon and eggs for breakfast, to help oneself to butter *ad lib*, without looking and feeling extremely guilty. But I suppose I shall get used to it. There's also a drawing-room with a ship's library containing nothing worth reading, and thus I've suffered a severe matrimonial defeat. Besides a vast amount of wardrobe luggage Carol insisted on bringing four packing-cases filled with household effects and an enormous suitcase with a broken lock full of books. I opposed this on the grounds that there's an outside chance we may have to leave Singapore in a hurry or not get there at all. She's convinced, or was, that probable disaster stalks us on our way and certain destruction awaits us at our destination ; but with the illogicality of her sex she was determined to be surrounded by all her possessions at the end. Particularly I opposed the books, because every morsel of printed material has to be censored before it leaves England, which meant that in the midst of all my other last-minute arrangements I had to drag the suitcase with the broken lock up five flights of stairs to the censorship office and wait patiently while elderly gentlemen scanned the pages of *The Three Musketeers*, etc. Fortunately the ordeal was somewhat lightened by the fact that the two official commissionaires—official commissionaires are usually formidable and latently sadistic—had once been members of the orchestra at my father's Lyric Theatre, Hammersmith. And now, of course, I have to admit I'm grateful for the books.

In the dining-room we sit on either side of the chief officer, a man of obvious humour but so far of few words. Carol, at her brightest, has regaled him with stories of the Royal Academy of Dramatic Art, and of greater and lesser stage celebrities. She has also for some unaccountable reason, a sign of desperate homesickness, asked him if he knows our great friend so-and-so. He contented himself with saying, "No." I must now go and have my bath. The plumbing in the cabin is poor—one cold-water tap which doesn't move. But the bathrooms are spacious. And the bath steward has an intellectual and sensitive face. I've a feeling he'd be hurt if I missed my appointment.

S.S. *Themistocles—September 3, 1941.*

I'm a little befuddled.

This morning we were bidden to celebrate in champagne the second anniversary of the war. Rather an illogical, perhaps a tasteless, procedure, it may be said. But on board this ship anything, even an obscure passenger's birthday, is a good enough excuse for a party, or rather for a break in the monotonous routine of doing nothing.

The concentration on being suitably hilarious was upset by two loud explosions. After investigation, the experts decided they were caused by depth-charges. And so we've had our first indication of the Battle of the Atlantic.

We're sailing in a fairly large convoy. It's a stately and beautiful thing. Walking the top deck in daytime, and seeing ships of all shapes and sizes moving forward unhurried and unhindered towards their destination, like a procession in a well-drilled pageant, with the destroyers and corvettes, rather self-effacing but always on guard, like policemen keeping the crowds back, one feels that one's safety is unassailable, and one's respect for the British Navy is no longer merely parrot-like. One is tempted to start singing "Rule, Britannia". It's the same thing when one goes up on deck on moonlight nights. That's really what is so wondrous about it. It's perpetual.

And yet I must confess that when I'm out of sight of it, with nothing to occupy my thoughts, when I lie in bed half-dressed, for prudence' sake, with my lifebelt very close at hand, my imagination runs riot and I'm as scared as a rabbit. Every creak and jolt seems to herald a torpedo. I sleep fitfully, and I welcome the mornings as fervently as one did during the London blitz. It's comforting to hear the purser ridicule the idea of any accident befalling the *Themistocles*. It's a lucky ship, he says. He's been with it twenty-five years. On the other hand, my next-door neighbour at table, whom Carol has christened Mephistopheles, is a confirmed pessimist. Apparently he has a passion for consulting the "old skipper", who is invariably "very worried" or "not at all happy". Carol says it's impossible for him to have won the captain's confidence so completely. But I've spied him more than once, lurking furtively by the bridge, a hungry look on his face—a vampire who feeds on bad news, though he seems to enjoy heartily the more commonplace foods served in the dining-room.

The only organized festivity, so far, was housie-housie last Saturday night. This game is surely a monument of dullness to its inventor's lifework. Hour after hour we sat in the smoke-filled bar, diligently placed counters on numbers, raised a fresh laugh every time the M.C. shouted, "Sixty-six—Clickerty-Click", and won nothing at all. Next morning, by way of counterblast to so much excitement, I took Amanda's rather unwilling hand and led her to Divine Service. We sang hymns to the accompaniment of an accordion, which never came in quite at the right time, and "God Save the King" at the end. The attendance was remarkably good, though a cynic says it will fall off when we get out of convoy. At any rate, it was quite an event in my life, though not in Amanda's, who has invented any number of diversions to amuse herself, including a daily competition in draughtsmanship, which means, as there is only one other competitor besides herself, a moral obligation on us to purchase daily from the barber both prize and consolation prize. Unfortunately, the barber has one of the best-stocked shops I have ever come across, otherwise Carol would have already cleaned him out, for she has purchased indefatigably. His prices mirror relentlessly the high rate of insurance against the current hazards of the sea.

We sighted Iceland a couple of days ago. Viewed from a distance of miles it was a mirage in white. In fact, it fulfilled exactly what its name has always conjured up in my fancy, which means that it will be useless for me to pretend that I have ever seen it. Nor have I yet seen the Northern Lights, though rumour says they have appeared on three occasions. I have always been too early or too late, gazing patiently and stupidly skyward until some kind person interrupts my vigil with, "Not due for another hour yet," or "You should have been here ten minutes ago. They were magnificent then." Seeing the Northern Lights has become more a pursuit of *amour-propre* than of aesthetic pleasure.

I haven't mentioned our fellow passengers. They depressed us excessively, of course, when we made our initial review of them. But they've improved rapidly—as they always do—even in looks. We're bosom friends with the classical scholar, who was recently invalided out of the Army and is now on his way to Panama. He was our host at the champagne celebration this morning.

We have become no part of a definite clique yet, but it looks as if we soon shall. Other cliques are already well established. We naturally disdain them. We are now heading for Greenland's coast. At least I imagine so, for it is getting increasingly cold.

S.S. *Themistocles—September 17, 1941.*

We left convoy some days ago. We are now sailing through the Caribbean Sea at an average speed of ten knots per hour. It looks as if the pleasure part of the trip has begun at last. There is a general air of summer holiday and relaxation. The officers are in white, the male passengers in shirts of various hues, and the females in summer frocks or bathing costumes. (There's no swimming-pool of course. There's a canvas affair, but it has a hole in it which the Ministry of Supply refused permission to mend on war economy grounds.) It is no longer obligatory to carry our lifebelts with us everywhere. They have been put back where we originally found them—on top of the cabin wardrobe— and are now only taken down for twice-weekly boat drill. The captain appears regularly in the dining-room and even Mephistopheles' horror tales have become very tepid. The convoy broke up at dusk. We watched the dispersal from the top deck. All the ships had their mast lights on, which seemed to my mind symbolic of the successful accomplishment of a solemn and perilous task. It was as if the ships in the convoy, after a long period of solid concentration, could now afford a little levity, and in that spirit were waving each other good-bye. Next morning we awoke to find ourselves alone in a vast expanse of sea—alone, yet nonchalantly convinced that the danger of enemy attack was more or less over.

The sun is really blazing. It's reflected in the sea by myriads of pin-pricks, giving an effect of golden rain. The ship's surgeon has warned passengers of the folly of walking about in it uncovered, and this has given me an admirable excuse to wear my topee, despite Carol's repeated remonstrances. She doesn't think it suits me. But, better still, they've put up the awning, which is not only useful but adds enormously to the gay holiday atmosphere. Combined with brightly coloured cushions and deck-chairs and iced drinks, it has transformed the tedium of doing nothing into the languid delight of a rest cure. We laze about intoxicated, so we like to think, with ultra-violet rays, yet secure against the remotest chance of death by sunstroke. As often as possible we rouse ourselves to play a round of deck golf—strictly limited to half an hour's duration because there is a general demand for the use of the two courts. I have become a real enthusiast for this game, which is spiced with unbridled malice and is said to have been the cause of as many disrupted friendships as bridge.   So too has Captain K. O. Fearon, who is on his way to Singapore to become a press censorship adviser.   But, though otherwise intelligent, he is an even less skilled exponent of deck golf than I.   Indeed, his formidable lack of prowess and his unfailing gift for missing the easiest shots, combined with his indomitable fervour and his inner confidence, provide us with our one rather innocent but enduring joke.   So that if you want to win a reputation for wit you need do no more than repeat at regular intervals, "K. O.'s in the scuppers again."   It's what music-hall comedians call "sure fire".   The ship's captain plays deck golf; but always in the same four : himself, two naval officers of fairly high rank, and the chief engineer.   They use special discs, harder and, of course, superior to the ones we are allowed, and special mallets.   While we watch these experts perform, we maintain a respectful silence, feeling like trippers from some inferior club who have come to St. Andrews for a glimpse of the champions.

Have we surrendered ourselves completely to frivolity ?   Have we forgotten there's a war on ?   Not altogether.   The chief engineer has contrived a way of putting on the wireless without endangering the ship, so that we hear the B.B.C.'s news bulletins, and are supposedly abreast of main world events.   But it's surprising how unsatisfying the radio is when there are no newspapers within reach.   For one thing, there's always the psychological urge to confirm what one has heard by seeing it in print.   Until then one can never quite believe it.   This is a superstition born of custom, of course.   But I sometimes think it's a superstition not entirely without substance.   The other day a lady spread a wild rumour that London had experienced the worst raid of the war.   We were soon imagining that all our relatives and friends had probably been killed.   But later it transpired that the lady's ears had deceived her.   It was Berlin that had been bombed by the R.A.F., not London by the Luftwaffe.   And then the B.B.C. gives us no sort of indication of the trend of public opinion.   What was the reaction to the invasion of Iran ?   Is Churchill as popular as ever ?   Is there a movement against any of his ministers ?   Is there a demand for increased aid to Russia ?   We don't know, and we want to.   Most of all, I think, one misses the smaller news items for which radio has no time, but which provide food for gossip and repetition and small talk, and, believe me, after a short time on board ship one needs food for such things.   I wonder how many opening conversational gambits have been inspired by obscure paragraphs in the press ?   It's moronic to ask your neighbour if he's heard that Kiev is threatened, because the presumption is that of course he has, and there's an end of it.   But say to him, "Have you seen that so-and-so's been arrested ?   I used to know him," and the result may be quite fruitful.

One gets a great kick from hearing, "This news bulletin comes to you from London," and undoubtedly the B.B.C.'s Overseas Service is indispensable.   But for all that, the war as mirrored by the radio seems an impersonal, almost an illusory, thing.

One gets a far more vivid reminder of it from the blackout, which is still rigidly enforced by blocking and bolting every conceivable aperture.   In the tropical heat it's no joke.   This being a British ship, coats and ties are still *de rigueur* at dinner, but they are discarded as soon as possible afterwards.   The men who patronize the bar, whatever the odds, sit perspiring in their shirt-sleeves with face towels wrapped round their necks.

Fortunately there is a bright and wondrous moon—which means that we are allowed to smoke on deck, and so spend our time in the open air without discomfort. The third-class accommodation aft is occupied by troops—mostly, I think, from a Scottish regiment. Their sleeping quarters are pretty cramped and unenviable. But they have a fair amount of deck space, which has probably saved them from going semi-demented. At any rate, they've shown no signs of being fed up with what must be for them a very long, boring and uncomfortable voyage. The other night some of them provided an impromptu alfresco entertainment. They sang Highland songs to the accompaniment of a ukulele. Their voices were not remarkable, perhaps. But they got themselves into a natural grouping which, given the setting, no producer could have bettered. The whole thing was intensely theatrical, for the moon really was luminous enough for a Midsummer Night's Dream, so that listening to the singing, isolated as it was in a gigantic auditorium of silence, and looking up occasionally to see the smoke drifting lazily from the funnel, while the ship moved serenely along in a sea which was no more than a mirror for the moon, I fell to wondering what Bailieff would have done had he been let loose with his Chauve-Souris at Drury Lane. We spent an enchanting hour.

It seems that we shall have at least one night in Kingston, Jamaica. And as the prospect is now near, there is considerable and rather acrimonious discussion as to where we ought to stay. Carol insists on the Myrtle Bank, which is the most expensive hotel, and in her view, therefore, obviously the most comfortable and luxurious—in fact the only sane choice. I favour a humbler establishment, especially as the barber's shop has already made our sea voyage more costly than I thought possible. I've overheard other matrimonial arguments on the same topic and with roughly the same line-up. It's really the purser's fault for handing out the guide book in advance. Otherwise I feel sure the husbands would have gone to the Myrtle Bank quite calmly, for they'll go in any case.

S.S. *Themistocles*—September 21, 1941.

When I looked out of my porthole, Jamaica under the early morning sun was a brightly lit green—like a picture postcard of Ireland, labelled, of course, "The Emerald Isle". That was my first and my last clearly defined impression of it. The rest is just a dream.

We had hoped against hope that Carol's brother Ted, to whom we had cabled urgently from London, would meet us in Kingston so that he could take Amanda back with him to New York. And miraculously enough, considering the difficulty of making anyone understand anything under the modern Reign of Censorship, he turned up at the quay, having spent a patient fortnight's holiday awaiting our arrival. He whipped us through the Customs formalities in no time, conjured up a porter and a taxi without the slightest difficulty and drove us to the Myrtle Bank, where he had already booked rooms. Although his triumphant organization lowered my stock still further with Carol, who has never got over my failure at Liverpool station, when the best I could find by way of a porter to cope with all our luggage and the packing-case was a small boy, it was none the less welcome. The Jamaicans are traditionally slow and lazy. But the Yanks apparently know how to get them hustling. And the Yanks are very much in evidence, though it doesn't seem so very long ago since they acquired those bases. I wasn't particularly surprised, of course, to spy American naval launches and American admirals and the *North Carolina*; but I was rather taken aback to find that the manager of the hotel was an American (a very charming one, incidentally, and an old friend of Ted), and that his clientele came almost exclusively from the United States. In fact, during our stay in Jamaica (it was a bare twenty-four hours) I can only remember hearing one English voice. Not counting our fellow passengers, of course. They all came straggling into the Myrtle Bank in the end and amusingly enough kept carefully to their little cliques. But I can't afford to scoff, for we belong firmly to a clique now, which clings together in just the same way.

I suppose if we'd bothered to break out of the Myrtle Bank we'd have heard English voices in plenty. And admittedly in the matter of research we could hardly have been less enterprising. We visited the post-office and attempted mild shopping in the early morning. In the late afternoon we hired a taxi at phenomenal cost (seemingly a Jamaican taxi-driver's minimum charge is 10/6) and drove to an exotic botanical garden, which we inspected far too casually. We drove back in the twilight (it's a lie to say that in the tropics "night falls like a blanket". The twilight is short-lived. But while it lasts it is magnificently beautiful). After a late and long dinner we tumbled into another taxi and drove to an alleged night-club called "The Glass Bucket". That was the one thing we had to do because we had been irresistibly attracted by the glamorous name and no less glamorous reputation. But we were disappointed. We found a large raised dance-floor made of polished wood. At the end was perched an enormous illuminated automatic gramophone which could be coaxed by small coins into playing last year's dance tunes. A giant "V for Victory" sign in red was emblazoned on the back wall. There were some bare wooden chairs and tables and a few rather disconsolate waiters. But otherwise the place was gloomy, and more or less deserted. We stuck it for just one hour.

And so we spent most of our precious time sleeping and eating and bathing and lounging at the Myrtle Bank which, with its many fans and complete fulfilment of the American passion for ice and prompt service, its spacious terraces and soporific chairs, its private swimming-pool at the end of a handsome garden which borders the sea, is ideally suited for such purposes. In fact it would be truer to say that we stopped at Jamaica and visited the Myrtle Bank rather than vice versa. This was probably a sad waste of opportunity. But I can't honestly pretend I regret it.

In normal circumstances we would supposedly have hastened to explore the town and as much of the island as possible. We would have remembered that this was our first sight of a tropical land and would have tried to gather impressions accordingly. In normal circumstances we might have been so shocked by the signs of native poverty and distress and disease, which you can't help noticing however rose-tinted your spectacles, that we would have felt slightly ashamed at partaking of so much plenty in the midst of so much obvious want. But the circumstances weren't normal.

When we landed at Kingston we knew that for a fleeting while we'd escaped from the war. That thought ousted all others. For the first time in two years we knew that we were completely safe from enemy action. For the first time in two years we knew that when night came we would see a town illumined by artificial light and a moon which would be no more than a lovely decoration in the sky.

If you return home after a long journey you want to sit at ease and savour old familiar things. That was how we felt. Miraculously we had been wafted back to the outset of one of those summer holidays in pre-Hitlerite times, when you arrived at a new and beautiful place and the sun was shining brightly and you were content to eat, sleep, drink and laze, and luxuriate in the fact that, though you did nothing else, you remained at peace with your own conscience. That was the prospect which Jamaica offered us. And we yielded to it. It was a continuance of the atmosphere we had found on board ship during the past week or so—only magnified a hundredfold. For whereas that had been make-shift, this was as perfect as art and nature could make it.

So Jamaica (or rather the Myrtle Bank) seems just like a dream now. Though I long to recapture it, I feel certain I should have wearied of it very soon if it had lasted.

The only practical thing I discovered is that Planter's Punch is an extremely good drink and surprisingly harmless. If you are wise you insist on old Jamaica rum, which is the real thing. It's a much lighter colour than the stuff ordinarily served up to the greenhorn.

Our return to the ship was our awakening from the dream. The passengers arrived laden with produce from the island—bottles of rum, bananas, etc. But mostly they looked very bedraggled—like Cinderellas come back from the ball. I was perhaps the sorriest sight of them all. On the previous morning I had dressed carefully in the best samples of my London-purchased tropical kit—including a grey featherweight suit from Savile Row and a pair of extraordinarily coloured shoes, which had originally been ordered by an Italian who was unfortunately interned before they were completed. As I walked down the gangway I think even my bitterest enemy would have granted me sartorial grace. But now my suit was covered in red paint acquired through sitting on a bench under the sun, and my shoes were irretrievably bespattered with black tar. In fact my plight was so obvious that it was pointed out to me at least a dozen times.

For Carol the awakening was particularly painful, because she had to say good-bye to Amanda and Ted. And here is a strange thing. While we had our feeling of renewed safety in Jamaica, Amanda was frightened for the first time since the war began. And all because of the black servants in the hotel. She has heard bombs falling and guns booming and has not betrayed so much as a tremor. But the sight of black people was something new and strange, and it inspired her with a fear which we found very hard to remove.

The poor *Themistocles* looked more down-at-heel than ever after the exotic delights of the Myrtle Bank. But though the atmosphere was depressed for a while, it has since been enlivened by a succession of farewell parties in honour, apparently, both of those who are disembarking at Panama and those who are going to Australia. As drink bought by the bottle is absurdly cheap, these parties are apt to become hilarious, not to say noisy. Last night an earnest, bespectacled young man with whom I'd had no more than a few casual words, and whom I knew only by his reputation for total abstention, tottered up to me to deliver an address: "I know you think I'm drunk, Playfair," he said (I did), "but I'm not. And in all seriousness I want to tell you . . ." What he wanted to tell me I shall probably never know, for at that moment a friend with a strongly developed paternal instinct grabbed him by the arm and forced him into his cabin. Though he broke out several times afterwards, so rumour has it, I had by that time gone to bed. And when I saw him next morning we were more or less strangers again.

We are now approaching Colon, gateway to the Canal. We shan't get in till after dark, and speculation is rife as to whether we shall be allowed ashore or not. If we are, I have agreed (and I'm very popular on that account) to finance our clique to a quick survey of Central American night life. For I am the proud possessor of fifty dollars bequeathed to me by Ted. Those less fortunate have to face the fact that nowadays pounds sterling won't buy many dollars in the Canal Zone or in the Republic of Panama.

Colon, Panama—September 23, 1941.

It is morning and I am sitting on the terrace of the Five Star Hotel, a glass of iced coca-cola by my side. Very shortly we shall bathe in a nearby swimming-pool. There is nothing else to do. In just over half an hour we have exhausted the possibilities of sightseeing in Colon.

This hotel is a cross between a vast decorated barn and a magnified boarding-house. The town itself is dusty and definitely one-horse. In its main street (and it hasn't any others to speak of) there is not a building worth looking at. The shops are exclusively stocked with cheap, mass-produced goods from the U.S.A. In fact I searched in vain for something indigenously Panamanian to take away with me. If you walk too far you come across real squalor—built-up, overcrowded shacks of a flimsy wooden construction, which are the habitation of the black people. And the population is mostly black.

Last night it was quite different. Colon, bewitched by electricity, could be imagined without the slightest difficulty as rich, dangerous and exciting. We were taken ashore by tender, and having successfully passed the U.S. Customs officials, boarded a streamlined Panamanian taxi in which we were driven to this hotel, which impressed us then as being a veritable hub of bright lights and gay, bustling activity. After seizing the opportunity to write and dispatch as many picture postcards as possible from this glamour spot, we asked in loud-throated tourist fashion to be directed to the best night club. We were answered by a native millionaire (so we thought). At any rate he was the real thing. He was short and plump; his complexion was sallow, his hair black and sleek. He wore a white suit and saddle oxfords. His tie was fastened to his shirt by an enormous jewelled pin and his fingers were encircled with diamond rings. "If it's a good floor show you want, you should go to the Florida," he said politely.

And to the Florida we were driven.

We entered a spacious bar, open to the street, and passed through double swing doors into a long, crowded, smoke-laden room. The tables were arranged in tiers, and eventually we found an empty one by a corner near the ceiling. There was such a tintinnabulation, such a saxophonous blare, such an Iberian-sounding babble that we could hardly hear ourselves speak. Through a thick haze we looked down on dark ladies with red roses in their hair and tough-looking gentlemen with coloured scarves round their necks. And we saw standing by the swing doors a posse of Panamanian police. They carried revolvers and wore shiny leather leggings, like Nazi storm troopers. Occasionally they patrolled the narrow alleyway which divided the dance floor from the lowest tier of tables.

This was the genuine native night life, we had no doubt—and spiced with danger. (We decided then and there that it would be sheer madness to walk the streets of Colon unprotected.) And to add to the illusion the band's repertoire seemed to consist entirely of the latest Latin-American tunes from Hollywood—

numbers like "Argentina". In fact our only reminder of Home and Beauty was the dear old "V for Victory" sign, which was painted on the drum and everywhere else. Nor was the illusion dispelled by the floor show. True, it was excessively long and tedious. But it contained a number of genuine strip-tease artists who, though too elderly to be exciting, were sufficiently devoted to their art to be shocking.

When it was at last over I, being a non-dancer, persuaded my friend George to come with me to the bar for a drink and a breath of fresh air. George is a young Australian professor, Anglicized by three years' experience of various English universities. He is lean and fair-haired, and not at all of this world. But he is able to enjoy mundane things, in a detached sort of way, despite a fundamental passion for philosophy.

We found that the ladies of the cabaret were now on duty as dance hostesses. A Spanish beauty approached us, and I regret to say that George treated her much as a Blimp would a Jamaican beggar. With his head turned upwards and from her (and he has a long neck) he waved his hand impatiently. "Go away, away—out, out," he hissed. This put me on my mettle. In fact, I told George he had no *savoir faire*. So when the attack was renewed—this time by a faded Californian blonde—I said blandly, "We've two wives, and very little money." Rather neat, I thought. "I'll have a sherry," she said. The regulation coloured water was produced and I handed out four dollars (£1 sterling). Shortly afterwards, Carol arrived to relieve an embarrassing lull in the conversation. (George was hopeless.) I introduced her.

"Are you really his wife?" asked the Californian.

"Yes," said Carol.

"And aren't you jealous?"

"No," said Carol.

The blonde paused a moment, then she gripped Carol's hand.

"I think you're swell," she said.

It was just like a scene from the movies.

Another of our party had unfortunately got rather romantically involved with the self-claimed leader of the troop. This meant, *noblesse oblige*, that after a short adjournment for delicious bacon and eggs at a nearby café we had to return for the second course and sit through the entire floor show again. Moreover, the lady sat with us (except when she was called for her own turn, which, of course, we applauded vociferously) and we had to ply her with coloured water at four dollars a small glass—which eventually brought us to the verge of bankruptcy. She was an Americanized Egyptian—vivacious without being pretty. When she was not doing her vamp act (that is to say, when her glass was still full of coloured water) she told me that she had turned down a big offer from M.G.M. to accept her present job. But she did not regret it. For the Panamanian Government had been "real kind" and the President of the Republic had arranged a fête in her honour which was to take place shortly. She had been born in a circus and had been in the show business all her life. She also informed me that I was now sitting in the very place where Cole Porter had written "Night and Day".

When it was time to return to the ship we rather regretted that we had not taken the opportunity to sample a rival Colon night club. But our ardour was not damped. We went to bed well satisfied that we had spent a daring evening which could not have been had anywhere outside Latin America.

Alas, the morning has brought disillusionment! It seems as if a show of night life must have been specially imported and staged for the benefit of the tourists.   Gone are the bustle and the crowd, the hints of wealth and fracas, the dark-haired ladies and the colourful gentlemen.   There is not a whisper of Spanish, not a Panamanian policeman in sight.   Even the Florida offers no enticement.   It looks like a decayed suburban picture-house.

Still, it's our own fault.   We should not have come back.   There aren't so many European towns that can stand the test of daylight.   Personally, I don't think Budapest can—at least not very well.   And even beautiful towns sometimes look more lovely at night.   Loveliest of all, perhaps, is blacked-out London under the full moon. . . .

S.S. Themistocles—September 24, 1941.

My spirits are low.

We left Panama behind late last night.   Now we face nearly five weeks of unadulterated Pacific.   I don't relish the prospect.   To be candid, I've had enough of this voyage.   The more so when I remember that the interesting part is behind and the dull part ahead.

It took us about ten hours to get through the Panama Canal.   I tried to concentrate on the passing scene of artificial beauty, though it wasn't really as impressive as I had imagined it would be.   I listened attentively while the great feats of engineering were pointed out to me.   But as I've no knowledge of, and really no interest in, engineering, I won't attempt to describe them.

What I enjoyed most was the sensation of the ship alternately mounting and subsiding in the successive giant-sized locks.   It reminded me of the one solid delight of a visit to the dentist.

What I noticed most was a thing you can't help noticing, a thing, indeed, that you are obviously intended to notice, namely that the Panama Canal is United States owned.   The words United States of America are boldly painted on every available truck, crane and engine.   There's no false modesty about the U.S. Canal Zone.

To prevent us getting into mischief on our way through a detachment of American soldiery was sent aboard to guard the ship.   They were tough, bronzed young men of the south, brim full of their native confidence.   I got into conversation with one of them.   He confided that he was longing for a war with Japan.   But he didn't think there was any hope of it, for this reason : it would take the American Navy just twenty-four hours to sink the entire Japanese Fleet, and, unfortunately, the Japanese Government was just as well aware of the fact as the United States Government.   Well, what nation would be crazy enough to risk a war knowing it hadn't a chance in hell ?

He spoke of the Japanese more in scorn than anger.   But he told me there was one class of people he really hated—the military police.   No matter what their nationality—American, English, German—they were all alike and all poison.   If ever he came across one alone he'd shoot him dead—without a moment's hesitation.   But then he never would, of course, because they always went about in twos—the lowdown swine.   That was because they knew darned well they were the scum of the earth and because they were such goddamn cowards.   Then he told me that he knew what he was talking about.   His closest buddy had been beaten to death by the military police.   Plain murder, it was.   As he said this he looked at me with so much venom that I had a sneaking fear he had decided that I was a military policeman or was the cousin or confederate of a military policeman.   The pace was getting too hot.   I cracked a feeble joke, at which he didn't smile, and made an awkward exit.

While this dramatic interlude was in enactment the other soldiers had been doing some serious drinking in the bar.   They were now, it appeared, indulging in a little mild leg-pulling and to impress the passengers were boasting of their killer instinct and were brandishing their revolvers with alarming abandon.   The more timid passengers foresaw a shooting match at any moment.   Fortunately, however, the situation did not develop.

We reached Panama about midnight, and a launch came to collect the few passengers who were due to disembark.   Among them was John, the classical scholar, who has been, perhaps, our closest friend during the voyage.   So this meant another of those unwelcome partings with which our life has been too plentifully dotted in the last month.   The mournfulness of the occasion was somewhat relieved, however, by the sight of the bespectacled total abstainer who, with an umbrella clutched in one hand and a suitcase in the other, performed the extraordinary feat of stepping off the first step of the gangway and landing upright on the bottom one.

John, a figure in immaculate white, waved and shouted good-bye.   But the launch moved swiftly towards the many lights twinkling under a great dome of darkness which was Panama.   Soon he was out of sight and hearing.   We turned sadly away.   And that, with time elongated as it is on board ship, was the end of an epoch.

S.S. *Themistocles*—*October 23, 1941.*

Will this voyage never end ?

Actually we're no more than forty-eight hours off Melbourne, and from there to Sydney is, comparatively speaking, a mere nothing.   But time has ceased to have very much significance for us.   In the past weeks—months now—our world has become so fixedly encompassed within this ship that the prospect of stepping on land again seems little more immediate or substantial than the prospect of dying some day in the dim, distant, indeterminate future.

It's a cramped and colourless world.   There have been two exciting events in its recent history—and even they take one back to the days of one's youth. The first was a prolonged sports tournament which was amusing while the sun shone but petered out when the rains came.   The second was an improvised fancy-dress ball which reached a pinnacle of natural hilarity long before it was due to begin, was suspended in mid-air while its sponsors concluded a feverish search for the missing key of the ship's panatrope, and finally collapsed at midnight after three hours of uproariously forced and alcoholic gaiety.

No need to say that it is a hideously idle world.   Indeed, I'm now so saturated in the practice of doing nothing that I'm almost too lazy to read a book.   As a matter of fact I've taken to playing chess.   That whiles away several hours each day and is no great strain on my particular mental energies. As a schoolboy chess was always a source of bitter humiliation, because it proved to me that while I was a total failure as an athlete I could lay no claim to predominance at more intellectual pursuits.   The years have not improved me. My most frequent opponent is George, who checkmates me with monotonous regularity except on those glorious occasions when he's kind enough (or weak enough) to go to sleep midway through the game and I snaffle his Queen. George, in his turn, is considered easy meat by the other chess-players on board.

Strange to say (or perhaps not so strange), there are many of our fellow passengers with whom we have still spoken no more than a few words. But those in our clique we know so well that they have no surprises left for us nor we for them. We could, metaphorically speaking, take their characters to pieces and put them together again with our eyes shut. Indeed, not speaking metaphorically, we have indulged in the first part of this exercise with such frequency that it has lost all its savour. Gone are the days when serious conversation was possible, or when it was interesting to exchange viewpoints, or when there was excitement to be had (and a long flutter of gossip) by the discovery of mutual acquaintances at home. Now our clique is like an inflated family circle whose individual members have become bored and irritated with each other through a too-close proximity over too long a period. It has occasional bursts of merriment. Sometimes it bickers; sometimes it talks inanities and sometimes it rakes at dead embers of past jokes in a hopeless effort to rekindle laughter. Quite often it just sits and drinks in unembarrassed silence.

Yes, it's hard to realize that those whose lives seem now inextricably interwoven with our own will soon be scattered over an infinitely larger world, and that we shall in all probability never see them again. But it is so. We have just returned from a grand farewell dinner at which the old dishes were served under new names (dishes of which I'm ungratefully weary), and there was an enlarged menu card on whose cover was printed in silver lettering, "Happy to meet, Sorry to part, Happy to meet again." I wonder. . . .

There's a passage from a popular song, "The Pacific Isn't Terrific", meaning, I suppose, that the Pacific isn't much fun. Oh no, it isn't. Mostly it isn't even warm. We were already back in our European clothes when we crossed the line. And now we daren't venture on deck without our overcoats.

As a passenger—of course I admit it—my complaints are merely peevish and frivolous. But what of those who, after perhaps a fortnight's break, will be homeward bound, and on arrival soon outward bound again, and then homeward bound once more and so on indefinitely? Securely ensconced on land one is apt to regard occasional effusions of praise for the men of the Merchant Navy as adequate discharge of the debt we owe them. But when one observes their work at close quarters one knows that praise is altogether insufficient. It's not merely the danger, from which there are so few and so shortlived intervals of escape (and until one has savoured that danger, one can't imagine it), it's the continual monotony and discomfort. For the officers there are obvious if small compensations. But consider what the life of a stoker must be. Even in wartime, so it seems, the ghastlier the job, the smaller the material reward. And that's a fact which is difficult to reconcile with one's faith in the present or the future. Under what system of government can a stoker be recompensed for the deadliness of his task?

My mood is a black one. The more so as I've begun to doubt the wisdom of having embarked on this journey. Some of my fellow passengers are Malayan civil servants, etc., returning from leave, and from them I've gathered odd scraps of information about my new country which I'll enumerate as follows :

A. Periods of service in Malaya, separated by regular intervals of home leave, are called tours. It's an eternal truth that during each successive tour a man looks forward to his retirement. And yet when that comes at last he is quite likely to spend the rest of his days, longing to be back—not at work—but in the East again, and quite often he does return. For the life out East has an almost mystic fascination.

B. But a man's particular job has very little bearing on his enjoyment of this life, which consists of the minimum amount of toil compatible with duty, and the maximum amount of pleasure by way of sport, dancing, bridge-playing, drinking, club carousing, etc., etc. There are, however, few if any cultural diversions such as good plays and good concerts. When I explain that (because the Malaya Broadcasting Corporation has been taken over only recently by the Government and requires rapid, pioneer development to make its purpose effective) I expect to be very busy at the outset with little more leisure than for eating and sleeping, I am given a paternal pat on the shoulder as much as to say, "You think that now. But you'll learn soon enough." For one thing, the climate in itself precludes strenuous work, though it doesn't apparently debar violent British exercise. For another—well, it's impossible to exist in Malaya outside the social whirl.

C. So far as it is within their knowledge (they left for home about eight months ago) the war in the West has had very little effect on Malayan pleasures. It's true that a five per cent income tax has been introduced and that part-time service in the Volunteers is now compulsory for most men of military age. But the bridge parties and the cocktail parties, the race meetings and the dances, go on just as usual. You need your evening clothes—oh, very definitely ! You're likely to be wearing them at least three nights a week.

D. The exchange value of the dollar is two shillings and fourpence. But its purchasing power, however, is only one shilling. A married man without children can live comfortably on anything between five hundred and eight hundred dollars a month, depending upon the amount of entertainment in which he indulges. He must have a house and two or three servants and a motor-car. If he's to have any fun at all he must join a club or so. And when he goes to his club he must be prepared to stand his whack. If he fails in this respect he will get the reputation of being "pencil shy" and will soon be ostracized.

(I've recounted this information faithfully, but I must admit it seems to me there's something screwy about it. Five hundred dollars in shillings comes to only twenty-five pounds a month. Well, how on earth do you live as a married man, householder, motor-car owner, employer of servants, non-pencil-shy member of a club or so on three hundred pounds per annum ?)

E. It is a truism to say that however much a man earns in Malaya he never saves a penny.

F. You must never—except on extraordinary occasions—say "thank you" to a native servant. You must, from the outset, establish an ascendancy over your own native servants (Malay or Chinese). You must not let them doubt that you are a masterful sort of person and know your way about. There's no need to be actively unkind or unjust or to use physical violence. (You'd very quickly get into trouble with the police if you tried anything of that nature.) But you must show them that you don't intend to stand any nonsense and you must not be afraid to let them hear the rough side of your tongue when necessary. You must in no circumstances treat them as equals—in other words, as fellow human beings —or they will despise you and rob you.

G. It is considered extremely unlikely that war will come to Malaya. Things look black at the moment, of course, but there have been scares before now and nothing has ever happened.   If by any chance the Japanese do decide to commit suicide—well, my informants want to be there when the fun starts.

H. Taking the long view, they regard—and they're certain they're voicing the general opinion in this—the Chinese as constituting a far greater potential menace to British interests in Malaya than the Japanese.   They'd prefer an A.B.D. front to an A.B.C.D. front, and though they appreciate in a vague kind of way that the practical necessity of fighting side by side with Free China may arise in the future, they definitely do not favour an immediate policy based on closer co-operation with Chiang Kai-shek.   In their view the less said about Chiang the better.   That is why no attempt has been made by the British—so far as I can gather— to rally Chinese opinion in Malaya by appealing to their sympathies for the struggle which their own countrymen are now waging against the Japanese.   In fact, the very idea of such an appeal has been discouraged, and alarm has been expressed that Chinese war charities have been more richly subscribed by the native population than British charities.

I confess that nearly all of this information has depressed me.   It may sound like bombast, but one of my chief reasons for wishing to go to Singapore was a conviction that it would bring me nearer to the war, or rather give me a chance to see more of the war.   I've no blood-lust and certainly no heroism.   As a matter of fact I think I abominate war more than most men, because, apart from my horror of the human suffering it brings, I have no interest at all in the actual mechanics of battle.   I could not master in a thousand years the elements of a military manœuvre.   The sight of an aeroplane, gun or tank produces in me no intellectual or emotional reactions whatever.   It merely leaves me befuddled.

And yet, now that this war has come, affecting, as it does, every one of us, it seems obvious to me that there is no life worth living outside of it.   Morally— and legally, of course—pacifism is still a justifiable faith.   The habit of stigmatizing registered conscientious objectors as cowards is not merely stupid but anti-social.   It is analogous to branding a man a felon who has been acquitted in a court of law.   But, practically speaking, unless its exponents are prepared to oppose the war effort by every means in their power—and this leads logically to internment—pacifism seems to me quite barren of point.   It is a mere passport to an insecure hermitage.   For all pursuits—other than those dwindling few which are purely selfish—are directly or indirectly of assistance to the belligerent cause.

In Nazi Germany and Soviet Russia even the arts are state-controlled, which means that they are fully geared to the war effort.   Millions of pounds are being spent annually on what may be roughly described as cultural propaganda.   Before I left England the same thing was gradually but surely happening.   I don't suppose the public—or even the popular Press—have much conception of the meaning of cultural propaganda.   But the existence of such national or semi-national institutions as the British Council and Committee for the Encouragement of Music and the Arts indicates that the Government has at last begun to realize the significance of the German orchestras which toured the Balkans as a kind of curtain-raiser to the military occupation of those states ; of the corps of artists following in the wake of the Russian army which entered Poland ; of the fact that in Germany actors and opera singers are exempt from military service.   In fact, those few English actors who are conscientious objectors may soon be contributing as obviously to the war effort as if their muddled thinking had not led them to obtain exemption from the Army call-up.

So it seems to me quite evident that to live life fully (and that's my very ordinary desire) one must be engaged as actively as possible in the war and in a way best suited to one's own capabilities. For that reason the prospect of being isolated from reality in a kind of socialite circus appals me. To be quite honest, I don't much care for dances and cocktail parties and bridge parties in the best of times, but after experience of the past two years in England I am certain I shall find mere contact with an existence largely made up of such things quite nauseating.

I left England pretty well convinced, as a result of talking to people and reading the newspapers, that sooner or later Japan must go to war with the democracies. In fact I had serious doubt whether I would get away in time. I was satisfied that Singapore itself would be fairly safe, apart from air raids, because of its impregnability against any invasion attempt. And I had complete faith in the power and reality of the A.B.C.D. front, which seemed to me to offer immense propagandist scope for an organization such as the Malaya Broadcasting Corporation.

One of the great advantages which the Axis nations possess in their conduct of political warfare is that they maintain the pretence, at any rate, of fighting side by side for the realization of a positive end, i.e. the establishment of the New Order. This enables them, among other things, to pool in effect their radio resources. Propaganda broadcasts from Berlin, Rome, etc., are largely consistent and supplementary, and resultant, I shouldn't be at all surprised to learn, from a system of supreme directives. The Allied nations are partners in the negative cause of smashing Hitlerism, but they have no declared peace aims in common. If they had, then the B.B.C. would be able to enter into close co-operation with the Soviet radio, and thereby increase considerably the chance of fomenting an effective revolutionary movement inside German-occupied Europe. Unfortunately, such a propaganda alliance has so far been entirely precluded by the ideological differences between the Russian and the British Governments, with the result that London and Moscow each play a lone hand so far as radio warfare is concerned.

But in the Far East it did seem to me there would be an opportunity to establish a real propaganda link-up among the A.B.C.D. Powers. I had dreams of a united radio front, with exchange broadcasts, perhaps, from Singapore and Chungking, and a planned campaign to identify in the Asiatic mind the Allied cause with the cause of Free China.

Thus I find the information that a propagandist policy based on co-operation with Chungking is frowned on in Malaya, because of the potential Chinese threat to British financial interests, excessively discouraging. Other considerations apart, it seems to me, from a practical point of view, lunatic for a Colonial Power like Britain to ignore the influence which Chiang Kai-shek's name presumably has over large sections of the Asiatic community and try instead to play an isolated game—assuming, of course, as I do, that war with Japan is inevitable. For in such a case what are the foundations of your propaganda? The benefits of British rule, I suppose. Well, I am no expert, but is that going to appeal very much to the Asiatics in Malaya? Is that going to persuade them to accept bombs as the price of freedom? Is that going to weld them into a united nation when the moment of testing arrives? Is that, in other words, going to deprive the Japanese of a Fifth Column?

It is foolish, perhaps, to set so much store by what a few people have told me. But the British community in Malaya is small and fairly well concentrated,

Everyone knows everybody else, more or less, and I am quite sure that my informants have represented to me the view of the majority. It seems to me equally certain that official policy is bound to reflect to a certain extent the opinion of this majority. So there it is.

Hotel Astra, Bondi Beach, November 23, 1941.

It was raining when we arrived in Sydney, so the beauties of its harbour, which is said to rank second only to Rio de Janeiro, were entirely obscured. One of the first things I noticed was an enormous poster urging citizens to help the war effort by eating more meat. As I write Carol is listening to the wireless. A lady is telling housewives how to win the war by making more use of eggs, butter and bacon in their cooking. Certainly there must be an abundance of food here. The streets, not only in the centre of town but in the suburbs as well, seem literally lined with grocers, fishmongers, butchers, bakers, etc., and to judge from my peerings into the shop windows, each is sufficiently well stocked to cater to a small-sized army.

I suppose the supply is greater than the demand. And the Australians are colossal eaters. I was vaguely aware of this on board ship when the ascetic-looking George worked his entire way through the menu with unfailing regularity. I am now fully aware of it. Order chicken—even if it is featured as just one item in a five-course lunch or dinner—and you'll be lucky to get away with less than a whole fowl, profusely garnished. Order a grilled steak and you'll be brought a piece of meat so vast that the plate on which it is served would fit far more appropriately as a little decoration on top. Apparently an egg unadorned is quite unknown. However emphatically you ask for *a* poached egg you will inevitably be brought two eggs, three rashers of bacon, a dish of chipped potatoes and possibly a couple of grilled tomatoes.

Before reaching Sydney we spent two nights at the Menzies Hotel in Melbourne. Carol never appears for breakfast, so on the first morning, being alone, the waiter suggested I might like to sit at the bachelors' table. I joined an elderly gentleman, who was just polishing off a plate of porridge. We fell to talking about rationing in England. I told him that though food was certainly restricted there was no question of starvation. "In fact," I said, "after one's got used to it, one begins to realize that in peacetime one probably eats too much, and one's far healthier on a lighter diet." With this opinion he agreed heartily. He added that he had recently returned from a visit to the United States, where he had been positively disgusted at the way people gorged themselves. He was expatiating on this theme when the waiter approached staggering under the weight of the largest breakfast dish I had ever seen. It proved to be a kind of giant mixed grill, consisting of two chops, two eggs, sausages, bacon, a heap of fried potatoes and miscellaneous vegetables. For a moment I thought my companion would indignantly repudiate this offering. But no, he merely murmured something about more toast, nonchalantly picked up his knife and fork and set to work.

Having a touching faith in human capacity, I'm prepared to believe that Americans eat even more than Australians. In fact—judging from a glimpse of its two largest cities—I've a feeling that Australia is about half-way between England and the United States, though I know no more about America than what I've read in books or seen in the movies or been told by Carol. So many things remind you of England here that when you come across other things that don't remind you of England at all you feel more than ever a stranger in a foreign land. During Sunday in Melbourne I went on the electric railway to a neighbouring seaside resort. I travelled in a very familiar railway carriage which had all the usual adjurations not to spit, not to lean out of the window, penalty £5, etc., etc. My first stop was Richmond, and really it might have been Richmond—I mean Richmond viewed from the Underground railway. But the next stop bore some outlandish Indian-sounding name. And when I reached my destination it wasn't a bit like an English seaside resort. It was more what I picture an American "hick" town to be. The dust was blowing up, but otherwise it was very clean and spruce, with a dead straight street, neatly labelled at intervals, "Dentist", "Beauty Parlour", "Petrol Pump", etc., like a model in an exhibition.

What is there familiar about Australia—judging it from a glimpse of its two largest towns? The Sabbath day, to begin with, though that's really Scottish in its rigidity. Everything is shut tight—not only cinemas, theatres and shops, but restaurants, bars—everything. Even the main thoroughfares are more or less deserted, and if you venture out of doors you're liable to feel you're breaking the law until the thunderous clatter of a lonely, phantom-like tram reassures you. And then the licensing restrictions which, as in England, affect the poor more than the rich. In Victoria and New South Wales public houses are closed promptly at 6 p.m. But if you are wealthy enough to patronize the larger hotels, you can apparently get a drink at any hour without the slightest difficulty. At least, that's my experience. And then the cooking—which is unmistakably English—solid, extravagant and dull. And then the slow-moving, colourless, superbly placid crowds. It's difficult to believe from experience of Sydney and Melbourne that in the whole of Australia there are only seven million souls. No matter what the time of week day, you have literally to elbow your way through the main thoroughfares; and if you want to make any speed you're forced off the pavement to dodge in and out of traffic as best you can. And then the men who even in summer—when Sydney, at any rate, has a subtropical climate—religiously go about in their city suits. I could quote other examples of such Spartan insistence on old-fashioned discomfort, which we know so well. But in this respect Australia has gone some way towards capitulation. The hotels, for example, though they are obviously not the latest things in chromium-plated modernity, have by no means rejected all the amenities of modern American civilization. And the profusion of oyster bars, milk bars and brightly lighted cafés, which stay open most of the night, is quite uncharacteristic of any English town even in peacetime. So, too, are the streamlined, high-powered taxis.

There is, for an obvious reason, though it strikes you as remarkable, a complete lack of anything approaching antiquity. If you search hard in Sydney you may come across a few houses and monuments which are as old, or nearly as old, as the town's history. But most of the buildings look to me as if they are growing up into good skyscrapers. Indeed, about both Sydney and Melbourne, in spite of their size and solidity and their evidence of being well seasoned with grime, one feels that they are not yet fully developed, that their characteristics are not finally settled. Incidentally, of the two, I prefer Melbourne. Sydney, especially when you approach its water-front, is spectacularly beautiful, but its general atmosphere is rather garish. Melbourne is quieter and more dignified.

Perhaps I'm prejudiced, for within half an hour of our arrival in Sydney I had my note-case swiped, with thirty pounds inside it.   I've heard since that Sydney's criminals are about the richest and toughest and best organized in the world. King's Cross, which is their headquarters, is allegedly a miniature Chicago, with gang warfare frequently being staged openly in the streets.

The industrial-inspired, pugnacious contempt for things of the mind (art, particularly) is, I gather, even more pronounced than it is in England.   This is explained, perhaps, by the fact that Australia has no aristocratic tradition and only a very small cultural heritage.   There are, virtually speaking, no classes, though there are, of course, owners and wage-earners.   The latter appear, comparatively speaking, well off, but there are still far too many unemployed in some of the world's most appalling slums.   Some of the former play at being café celebrities on the *Tatler* pattern.   But they are allowed no mystic claim to superiority by their less wealthy fellow countrymen.   Money can't buy the English brand of old-world deference, or obsequiousness.   You're not called "sir" by porters, taxi-drivers, shop assistants, etc.   If you want to be called "sir", your only chance is to seek out one of the imported waiters who serves in the big hotels.   Socially speaking, at any rate, all men are more or less equal.

It doesn't appear that civilian Australia is particularly war-conscious.   You come across loudspeaker recruiting vans, and a recruiting rally takes place every day in Martin Place, Sydney.   There are Government posters urging the purchase of War Savings Certificates.   And there are innumerable pictures of Churchill and "V for Victory" signs.   But otherwise life is very much on a peacetime model.   There is no rationing (except petrol), no blackout, of course, and virtually no restrictions on pleasure.   The newspapers devote columns and columns to racing, which is the national obsession.   The result of the Melbourne Cup, which was run recently, pushed the war from the front pages of the evening press and has since monopolized the cinema newsreels.

Believe it or not, the popular newspapers still carry gossip pages of the kind which went out of fashion in England with the advent of the 'thirties.   They are ludicrously vapid and they haven't even a genuine snob value, for there's not sufficient raw material available to sprinkle them liberally with titles.   In Sydney they are devoted almost exclusively to a chronicle of the dinings and winings and dancings of those who patronize the two posh restaurants—Prince's and Romano's.   What possible interest they can have for anyone who isn't a regular patron of Prince's and Romano's is beyond my imagination.

But I am wrong if I've conveyed the impression that the average Australian civilian is coldly unconcerned about the war.   On the contrary, he follows its progress very avidly in a detached sort of way.   By which I mean that while I don't think he regards the potential threat of war coming to his own shores at all seriously, I do think he's hungry for news, as detailed as possible, of what is happening overseas.   He's obviously enthusiastic about the Soviet's resistance, and he's becoming increasingly pro-Russian.   Britain's ordeal also has caught his imagination.   Wherever we go we are minutely questioned about the air raids and the rationing and so on.

A best-seller here at the moment is Quentin Reynolds' *London Diary*, which I don't remember seeing before I left England.   It might well be renamed "How Fleet Street Took It".   It is very slick, very readable, and it brings back vivid memories of the great blitz.   But it reveals nothing—nothing important, that is to say—which the average Londoner doesn't know for himself.

I enjoyed it greatly in a nostalgic sort of way, though I was also irritated not a little by it. I was irritated by its occasional but surprising inaccuracies. I wanted to answer back, then and there, when I read of the Savage Club having been completely destroyed (autumn, 1940) and of Eric Maschwitz listening to his own music. I was irritated, too, by Reynolds' full-blooded and entirely uncritical admiration for his journalist friends. Chris of the *Express*, Owen of the *Standard* are doing a very good job now, and undoubtedly, if unfortunately, it is true that what Fleet Street urges today the Government usually does tomorrow. But at the bar of history, will they, the servants of the Beaverbrook press, be able to disclaim all responsibility for the folly and inertia of those English politicians who made Hitler's war possible? Surely not. For they supported the policy of appeasement as relentlessly with their pens as the Chamberlain Government did by its actions. (One does not forget the *Express* slogan : "There will be no war this year," etc.)

But these complaints aside, Quentin Reynolds has done a very useful job with his *London Diary*. He has told the story of the air blitz on London in terms of everyday life, and he has had the courage to say some very honest things which I imagine have not added to his popularity in certain influential quarters. His tribute to the British Communists' fight for better air-raid shelters is a case in point. Most people I've come across here have an almost insatiable thirst for information about Britain under fire and about the ordinary men and women who are living their everyday lives in Britain. They want something more homely, more detailed, more actual than newspaper reports, official communiqués and propagandist radio talks. They want the kind of thing that Reynolds has given them, and they want it in abundance.

Characteristically, the Playfairs have missed the boat. When we arrived in Sydney a representative of Thomas Cook & Sons informed us that according to advice from London arrangements were being made by the High Commissioner for us to have air priority, so we allowed the first ship which carried the rest of the Malayan party—civil servants, foresters, policemen, nursing sisters and all—to sail without us. But since then nothing more has been heard of the air priority. Indeed, from inquiries I've been able to make it seems entirely beyond attainment, and short of ringing up the High Commissioner in Canberra (a course which I contemplate late at night and am too timid to adopt in the morning) I'm afraid we must abandon all hope of it. The representative of Thomas Cook, who at first treated us with deference, even awe, has now grown sick of the sight of us. Our faces are pathetically familiar to him, for we visit him religiously and hopefully every day, sometimes twice a day. But as yet he has been able to give us no definite news of when the next ship is likely to be leaving for Singapore.

It seems that we may easily be marooned here for a considerable time, especially if the situation in the Far East deteriorates further, though I try to persuade myself that it will be some while before Mr. Kurusu has reached Washington, conferred in Washington and returned from Washington and that nothing explosive can possibly happen before then. Carol is suicidal at the mere thought of spending a lifetime in Australia. Indeed, if, like Algernon in *The Importance of Being Earnest*, she were asked to choose between this world, the next world and Australia, she would, I fear, in her present mood unhesitatingly plump for the next world. As she spends most of the day and all the night asleep on her bed, and indeed seldom leaves the precincts of her hotel except to visit Cook's, I tell her that she is contemplating self-destruction without a sufficient examination of the cause. But to this unanswerable argument she merely replies that she has seen quite enough of it already.

My own feelings in the matter are not so desperate. I don't doubt that longer acquaintance would improve my liking and understanding both of the country and its people. But I'm not yet at ease. The great majority of Australians are, I'm convinced, as fiercely and defensively patriotic Britishers as they are patriotic Australians. But by contrast they are suspicious of and a little hostile to Englishmen. I think they will always be so, until they have got over their sneaking regard for the English way of life—or rather what they imagine is the English way of life (a compound of aloofness and snobbery and self-confidence)—and have decided to be unashamedly themselves. At the moment the style of living and doing things here seems to be nervously unsettled. It's like a half-way house, as I've tried to explain. And the radio is a good illustration of this. On the one hand you have your Government-controlled A.B.C., which in its style of programmes and presentation is very akin to the B.B.C., though, with its lack of facilities, it can't, of course, maintain so high a standard. And on the other hand you have your numerous commercial stations whose announcers put over high-pressure salesmanship stuff in the American manner.

After three or four nights at a large hotel in the centre we moved to Bondi Beach, which is called a suburb, though it's unlike any English suburb that I know of. In our hotel we have a double room and private bathroom and three enormous meals a day for an inclusive weekly charge of five guineas per head—that is, four guineas sterling. We could, if we desired, live a life of ease and comfort without bothering to venture further afield. For Bondi Beach has a sufficiency of shops neatly arranged in a long row, a number of oyster bars, milk bars and eating-houses, a couple of large, modern cinemas, a dance-hall and, so it is rumoured darkly, a night club or sly grog shop. It is also one of Sydney's best-favoured surf-bathing centres, with a wide sweep of sand shut in by mounting rock formations, a well-manufactured promenade, palatial changing rooms and all the usual seaside paraphernalia of ice-cream vendors, etc. On weekdays it is reasonably quiet. But on Saturday afternoons and Sundays it is invaded by swarms of health-and-rest seekers from the centre of the city, who look and behave like an English Bank Holiday crowd, though their bodies bear evidence of more frequent and consistent contact with fresh air and sun.

We had our first sight of Bondi on a Sunday afternoon. I am afraid I was too timid of the multitude to bathe, though Carol was undaunted, and came back after a while with the bather's inevitable look of glowing self-righteousness on her face. She said it was cold but marvellous, urged me to go in, and then added that she had been knocked down and nearly killed by a breaker. I spent most of the afternoon swallowing ices and listening to a loudspeaker recruiting van which was the predominant note in a cacophony. "Why fight for Britain?" a voice boomed. "Because it is through Britain's resistance that our land still belongs to us. If Britain fell you would not have your freedom, your country would be taken from you. You would not be here today to enjoy rest and peace and relaxation in these beautiful surroundings. I'm not blaming you for it. Everyone has a right to relaxation. But it's our plain duty, as Australians, to give Britain all the aid we can."

My attention was interrupted by the sudden and unexpected appearance of Ivan Menzies, whom I had not seen for many years. He's playing in a Gilbert and Sullivan opera season which is running here at the moment; and he's one of the pillars of the Oxford Group Movement. He caused a mild sensation recently by a "curtain" speech in which he seized the opportunity to pay fervent tribute to Buchman and his work.

I knew Menzies best in his younger and gayer days, and I think that whatever he may have gained in serenity by his conversion to Buchmanism, he has lost in sparkle, though I like him as much as ever. We went to see him the other night in *The Gondoliers*. If we shared his religious faith, absolute honesty would have compelled us to break the social code of behaviour on a visit behind by telling him to his face in his own dressing-room that though we'd liked his own performance well enough we had not cared for the show one scrap. For indeed it was very, very bad, and though the house was full and appreciative, I can only conclude that Sydney audiences are easily satisfied. The production was shoddy, clumsy and amateurish in the extreme, and was overladen with all manner of schoolboy buffoonery, once associated in London with the simpler types of musical comedy but long since considered inexpert and outmoded. If Gilbert's lines (which incidentally never raised a smile on their own merit) require such embellishment to make them palatable to modern playgoers it seems to me high time the Gilbert and Sullivan operas were locked up in the nearest museum.

Generally speaking, I gather the Australian theatre is in a pretty poor way. It is one hundred per cent commercialized, and even so, not good of its kind. In Melbourne we saw *Susan and God*, a play satirizing Buchmanism, curiously enough, which was an immense success in New York and has had record runs in various capital cities over here. We could not really assess its value, for it was so badly acted. The only redeeming performance came from Claude Flemming, an actor who is not well known, I fancy, to English audiences (at least I had not heard of him before) but who is obviously very accomplished. The leading lady (Gertrude Lawrence in New York) was Marjorie Gordon, a musical-comedy actress who has made a great hit in Australia. Her tricks and antics and facial contortions to gather the maximum harvest of laughs, though professional enough, bore no relation whatever to the part she was supposed to be portraying. The rest of the acting was just atrocious—well below repertory standard and not noticeably superior to vicarage theatricals. And yet, as I say, this production has drawn record audiences and has been lavishly praised. It seems to me there's a golden opportunity for some organization like the British Council to send out a first-class company to perform first-class plays in Australia.

After *The Gondoliers* Ivan Menzies invited us to a party at his flat, which is spacious and beautifully situated by the water-front. There were, of course, no hard drinks served, which did not worry me particularly. But for an awful moment I surmised that there would be no smoking either. Fortunately this proved incorrect. There wasn't the usual scramble for matches and cigarettes, but after a while an elderly gentleman showed commendable courage by being the first to light up; gratefully I followed suit. The rest of the evening passed very pleasantly for us. We ate sausage rolls, drank coffee and cream, and best of all we found an enraptured audience for all our bomb stories. In fact we weren't allowed to omit the minutest detail.

Menzies sent us away with a copy of Peter Howard's *Innocent Men*. I've since read this from cover to cover, and I'm afraid I remain unconvinced. I don't suppose A. P. Herbert is right in calling Buchmanites "canting cheats". I can't really see why Buchmanism should arouse serious hostility or be honoured with anything so complimentary as persecution. For it seems to me a purely personal and selfish creed. While it offers spiritual contentment and economic security to the wayward individual, it is apparently disinterested in the social evils which afflict the majority of mankind. I imagine that Buchmanism makes much the same appeal to the rich as well-organized philanthropy does. It's an escape from sin.

A night or two ago we went to what's called an audience-participation show at the A.B.C.'s Radio Theatre. We were invited by the compère, Wilfred Thomas, who is one of Australia's best-known broadcasters. Despite my years of association with the B.B.C. I had never before attended an audience-participation show. It was rather fun. We were given our instructions beforehand, and during the transmission a gentleman sat on the stage with two large boards, one marked "Applaud" and the other "Cheer". When he raised these we either applauded or cheered as the case might be, and when he lowered them we dutifully stopped applauding or cheering. On the whole we—the audience—played our part very well.

The show, which was called "Out of the Bag", struck me as quite a good example of radio variety, though one can never really judge the merit of a broadcast except by hearing it through a loudspeaker. At any rate it obviously pleased the audience. A new edition of this programme goes on the air every Monday at 8.30 p.m. It's an hour show, and according to Wilfred Thomas, who is a very intelligent and keen radio man, it's only during this time that the A.B.C. has the majority of the listening public. Generally speaking, the commercial stations are predominant, and the more serious A.B.C. programmes —talks, concerts, plays, etc.—have only a very small audience. This state of affairs seems to me a good argument in favour of the monopoly broadcasting system. There is no doubt that the B.B.C., by its rigid adherence to a policy of educating as well as entertaining, has raised and broadened popular taste in a way which would never have been possible if it had had to contend with competition from industrial advertisers. In wartime particularly it seems to me essential that radio should be government controlled. I can't see how Australian broadcasting is ever going to function effectively as a propaganda weapon when so much of it is dependent on commercial interests.

Incidentally, we feel very much on the outskirts of Singapore here, although it seemed that we were going a crazily long way round when we left England. Apparently a rule came into force recently debarring English employees in Malaya from returning home for their long leave. So a lot of them have come to Australia instead. If one goes into any of the fashionable bars one's almost certain to see a crowd of boisterous, opulent-looking people shouting for "stengahs" and arranging to meet each other for "tiffin". In fact it was remarkable that our fellow Malaya-bound passengers, like caged animals released, substituted stengah for whisky-and-soda and tiffin for lunch the moment they set foot on Australian soil. We haven't yet followed their example, and Carol is determined that we never shall. Personally I think I may be able to manage stengah as a joke among friends, for it has a nice colonel-like sound, if the last syllable is accentuated. But I'm afraid tiffin, which is an expressionless word and not so easy to make fun of, will have to remain permanently stuck in my throat.

And then, of course, one's not allowed to forget that Aussie troops have been sent to Singapore to defend Australia's near north. The newspapers carry daily columns about them and their new surroundings; one gathers that on the whole they are dissatisfied with conditions and are fed up with doing nothing and are longing for action.

The telephone is ringing and I must answer it.

C

I have done so. It was our old friend the representative of Thomas Cook. We are actually leaving on a Dutch ship tomorrow morning.

Hotel des Indes, Batavia, N.E.I.—December 5, 1941.

We arrived here this morning. It is our fifth and last port of call since Sydney. The others were Bowen, Sumbawa, Surabaya and Cheribon. To-morrow we trans-ship and all being well will reach Singapore in the early hours of December 8.

After coaling at Bowen, a small country town on the Queensland coast which might well have provided the setting for one of Tom Mix's silent films, we had our first sight of the East when we put in at the tiny Dutch Island of Sumbawa. It turned out to be a rather protracted one, for though we were only supposed to tarry a couple of hours to load a cargo of cattle, a slight navigational error caused us to remain there three days. The ship had collided with a coral reef, where it stuck fast, and the combined power of two hastily summoned rescue vessels was needed to pull it clear again. I'm afraid we saw too much of Sumbawa from the same angle for me to write of it as glowingly and romantically as doubtless I would have done if we'd seen as little of it as the K.P.M. time-table intended that we should. We went ashore on arrival, and the shipping agent drove us a couple of miles down a leafy road to the capital. It was a formless scattered village built round four sides of a patch of green field, which much to my surprise had been turned into a football ground, and consisted of a school, a few houses, a couple of native shops and the Sultan's palace. Having inspected and admired the place, there was nothing else to do short of calling on the Sultan, to whom we had no introduction; and as the local flies were insistent on giving us an embarrassingly effusive welcome, we decided to return forthwith. By twilight that evening Sumbawa, green, thickly wooded, mountainous, looked really rather beautiful, so that comfortably sipping my preprandial glass of Bohls and anticipating our departure at any moment, I told Carol, who was lamenting the fate of the shipping agent, that I wouldn't mind being in his place at all. That was shameful affectation, the worst kind of romantic hypocrisy. At any rate no one suggested a return visit during the subsequent days. Certainly not I.

Fortunately, however, life aboard passed pleasantly enough. We found the ship small, only 6000 tons, but very clean, very comfortable and possessed of an excellent and enterprising cuisine. The Dutch officers were a gay, friendly and exuberantly cheerful crowd. The chief steward—there was no purser—was indefatigable in organizing sweepstakes, dances both indoors and under the moonlight, bridge drives, whist drives and, of course, the inevitable housie-housie. His colleagues, too, from the captain down, seemed equally determined to make the trip as carefree as possible. The senior ones joined enthusiastically in games of dice, ping-pong, deck tennis and table football. The junior ones, who were normally debarred from mixing with the passengers, flirted gallantly if surreptitiously with the girls. Incidentally, there was one very pretty girl—an aesthetic pleasure traditionally associated with sea voyages but unfortunately lacking from Liverpool to Sydney. Another tradition—the captain's bumper dinner—is forbidden in wartime. But the K.P.M. took the opportunity to hand out farewell presents, bottles of scent for the ladies and note-cases for the men. We thought that the K.P.M. could well afford this luxurious gesture of generosity, for it has a large fleet and the prices it charges in the bar are noticeably ruinous. But its gifts were none the less flattering. The weather was often excessively hot, but fortunately the blackout restrictions were not too zealously enforced. Besides, it was possible to spend most of one's time on deck. There were occasional showers, but there was never a suspicion of a roll or a pitch. Sometimes the sea looked smooth and quite black, like a great expanse of treacle.

We made several good friends, notably and pre-eminently Carey Foster, a young veterinary surgeon who has a lucrative job in Malaya with the Race-course Association, and is on his way back to Singapore from a long leave in Australia. Carey loves horses and dogs and indeed all animals. But he's equally well disposed, I think, to the majority of human beings. At any rate, he's one of those rare people upon whom one can unload all one's worries without the least compunction or embarrassment.

Our friendship with him really began with the discovery that he and I have, or had, a mutual godmother in Mrs. Patrick Campbell. We immediately began to swap stories about her, as people who mention Mrs. Pat inevitably do whether or not they were her godsons.

What a magnificent person she was; by far the most impressive woman I have ever met, and among actresses the only genius. Of course she was impossible, her own worst enemy, a sinking ship firing at her rescuers, as Alexander Woollcott put it. And her magnificent egotism and huge caprices led her into shameful betrayals of her art. I remember going to see her in one of the last plays she did in England (it wasn't *The Matriach*, that was the very last). I noticed—it must have been obvious to everyone in the audience—that throughout the evening she kept her eyes rigidly averted from her leading man—in love scenes and all. Afterwards I learned the explanation from Mrs. Campbell herself. "What a dreadful creature!" she said. "Why does he want to be an actor? He's so ugly, I can't look at him." And yet, when she chose to try, as she did on the afternoon I saw her in *The Matriach*, she was to my mind peerless. And surely no stage personality of today approaches her stature or has even begun to fashion a legend comparable with the one which she has left behind. That legend places her among the immortals.

Her personality swept everything before it. It was so grandly overpowering that somehow it lifted her above all the abuse, cacklings and shakings of heads, however justified, in which mere managers and critics and players indulged. I remember once, when she was still alive, sitting with a group of fairly celebrated actors who were amusing themselves by exchanging gibes at her expense. I said nothing. But I thought to myself, "If Mrs. Campbell were to walk into this room now, you would all collapse like a pack of cards." And so they would have done.

Before her death Mrs. Pat inspired that veneration and awe which are usually reserved only for the great departed. The most exhausting day of my life was one Sunday in 1929 when my parents, with amazing temerity, invited Mrs. Campbell to lunch and Tallulah Bankhead to tea. Mrs. Campbell was then fat, elderly, jobless and pretty well impecunious. Had she been in any sense an ordinary woman the coupling of her name with Miss Bankhead's might well have prompted one to ponder on the old story of the fallen star and the star in the ascendant. But, of course, one did nothing of the kind. Her very presence forbade such a vulgar thought. Without a suspicion of rancour she called Tallulah, who has a far stronger personality than most of us mortals, Talluloo, and somehow it seemed quite right and logical that she should. I've a feeling that in the celestial world to which she has now gone she is following with casual interest the careers of Peggy Ashhedge and Margaret Roarings.

She may have been malicious, even cruel, though personally I never found her so. But there was certainly nothing mean or petty or spiteful about her. She was superbly profligate in everything. If you sent her a wire on one of her first nights, she always thanked you in a wire. And she had no regard for telegraphese. Her telegrams to me began *Dear Giles* and ended *loving God-mother, Stella Patrick Campbell.*

Shortly after her death I reread her autobiography, which is a bad and rather dishonest book and doesn't do her justice. But it reveals, I think, the secret of her life, namely that she was a great actress in spite of herself. Like Fanny Kemble, she hated the stage, and was ashamed of her calling. Essentially she was a snob, in a very big way of course, and the theatre, which was her bread-and-butter, clashed violently with her snobbery, so that she despised herself. Undoubtedly she would have won fame even if she had never stepped behind the footlights, though she would have done so by those very methods which are now considered the cause of her failure. For she had all the equipment to be what she really wanted to be—a grande dame—save for one thing: an independent income. That was at once her tragedy and art's inestimable gain.

When she died, the present war had already begun. And yet surely her life and work deserved more space, more glowing tribute than the British press allowed them. *The Times* in a very short obituary notice referred to her as a lady "who had been a distinguished actress in her time". The popular newspapers were content merely to recall her famous correspondence with Mr. Shaw. Only one critic, so far as I know, paid her the homage which was her due—James Agate. He wrote, if I remember aright, that he had seen three great actresses in his time and three only—one of them was Mrs. Patrick Campbell.

Carey has given me several good reasons why he doesn't think I'll like Singapore, and they confirm more or less my worst fears. In his view Malaya is ill-prepared for war, both materially and psychologically, and he's not at all confident of the issue if the balloon does go up.

We were sitting with him a short while ago in the big red-carpeted enclosure which is the lounge of the Hotel des Indes. We did not feel inclined to explore the town, for the heat, to which we are not yet accustomed, is intense. We were content to laze comfortably in the shade, to sip cooling drinks and watch the busy, assorted crowd moving along the canal-lined, sun-scorched street—the poorer natives on foot, the richer ones in little horse-drawn or pedal-propelled vehicles and the Europeans in taxis or large private cars. In an hour or so we shall meet again in the lounge. By then the sun will have set, and the electric lights will be blazing. We'll have some more drinks and toy with what is called "*kechil Makan*"—little plates of cheese, olives, straw potatoes and delicious hot meat balls. We'll then meander into the alfresco dining-room and sit down to a very rich and lengthy dinner, for the Dutch, though their diet is different, eat as prodigiously as the Australians. Afterwards we'll spend an hour or so, I dare say, in the ballroom, and perhaps we'll finish the evening by sampling the flavour of the famous Chat Noir night club. After all, we've only one night in Batavia, so we might as well make the most of it. And yet I know that for my part I shall be haunted the whole time by a morbid question mark. How long can this illusion of peacetime life and luxury last? How long will it be before Batavia is a blacked-out city, and a raided city? How long indeed before the Hotel des Indes itself is shattered by bombs?

The news at the moment is pretty grim, so grim that I'd rather keep my eyes tightly closed until I reach Singapore. But by contrast one still hears the parrot-cry that the Japanese will never go to war, or that if they do they won't attack Malaya. It's remarkable that of our fellow passengers bound for Singapore at least fifty per cent are women. A few have definite jobs to do. But most are wives returning to their husbands; some are mothers with small children attached. They're all quite confident that they've nothing to worry about. I hope they're right. But I'm none the less glad we haven't got Amanda with us.

I remember they used to sing at one of the Oxford University Dramatic Society smokers a little ditty which went something like this:

> Out in the sun
> Having such fun,
> All in our nice pyjama.
> That's the way
> We spend each day
> In Java.

In my youthful mind it conjured up an idyllic picture of decadent life in the tropics. But the very last thing you really want to do is to sit in the sun, and personally I've given up wearing pyjamas even at night.

Actually I don't suppose we've spent more than forty-eight hours in Java all told. But I've done my best to absorb some of its atmosphere. From Surabaya we made a two-hour journey by car, past miles of tea plantations and rice-fields, to a very civilized hill station, where we enjoyed an excellent lunch and a bathe in a large swimming-pool which is built in an artificially fashioned hollow, with tiers of verdant terraces rising above it. The colours on the way looked hard and bright and distinct compared with the soft blendings of the English countryside. I was struck by the swift change from unbearable heat to pleasurable warmth, and I noticed, too, the phenomenon of torrential showers which cease as suddenly as they begin. We drove through the sordidly picturesque Arab quarter of Surabaya. And at Cheribon I ate Rijstafel.

This performance brought back those qualms of conscience which first assailed me when I found that rationing was no more. I've grown used to helping myself to as much butter and sugar as I want, and to enjoying again the refinements of unrestricted eating. But Rijstafel is no gourmet's meal. It is just an essay in gluttony, with assorted meats, fish, eggs, poultry, vegetables and condiments piled indiscriminately on top of a rice basis. I'm told that, though you may help yourself as lavishly as you please from each successive dish, etiquette does not oblige you to swallow all that your eye has chosen. However, the Scottish in me forbade my taking advantage of this Dutch prerogative. So I ploughed right through and at the end felt much as if I'd drunk a gallon of beer. My one desire was to totter to sleep. Some people, I believe, eat Rijstafel for lunch—or its equivalent in quantity—every day of their lives. How they do this and contrive to remain healthy-looking and awake and at work during the afternoons is beyond my comprehension.

A thing which has surprised me about Java is that it seems more like an independent country than a colony. This may be because the Dutch have no other home now that Holland is occupied. But among so vast a number of

Asiatics the Dutch are as rare as aborigines in Australia, and one does feel somehow that the whole Javanese population—whites, Asiatics, Eurasians— have been welded into a kind of national community.   In other words, that in fact as well as in name there is such a person as a Javanese.

This is only an impression, of course.   And by contrast Java must be an ideal place to become rich quickly, if you can use labour as you like.   Proverbially it is a wealthy land, but unlike other wealthy lands I've seen, it looks it.   It sparkles at you, jewel-like.   And it appears, at the visitor's casual glance, to have no flaws.   The Dutch see to that.

Every suitable inch of soil is cultivated or industrialized.   Nothing potentially useful is wasted.   No honest means of making money, whether indigenous or imported, is overlooked.   Even the tourist trade, which must now be infinitesimal, is still catered to.   When we arrived at Surabaya we were all handed illustrated booklets suggesting various excursions we might care to make— dependent, of course, on our length of stay.   An agent then appeared on board and it was with him that we arranged our drive to the hill station.   Eight of us went and we were charged six guilders a head, which, considering that the lunch and bathe were thrown in, was quite reasonable.   But prices generally are fabulously high.   It cost me the equivalent of 3/6 to have my hair cut the other day.

Though the natives understand only Malay, it's remarkable that all the Dutchmen we've encountered—and we've encountered quite a few in the simple pursuit of finding our way about—speak fluent English.   This supposedly betokens strong British influence in the N.E.I.   In fact, it leads one to conclude that the Dutch are only colonizers by the grace of Britain, which is unquestionably true in the sense that if it were not for Singapore they would be stripped of their possessions in no time.   Put in a friendlier way, they are obviously good and active allies.   "V for Victory" signs and pictures of Mr. Churchill are as common as pictures of Queen Wilhelmina.   Both at Surabaya and Cheribon the authorities provided free entertainment for the Australian and New Zealand servicemen who are our fellow voyagers to Singapore.   Moreover, I should say that though the Dutch have no illusions about their situation, they are unflurried and quite prepared to face war if it comes.   Civilian life, it is true, is still fashioned very much on a peacetime model.   But you see plenty of green-uniformed soldiers in the streets, and at the approaches to the harbours of Surabaya and Batavia, which are mined, great seaplanes soar and swoop like wild birds in a vast aviary.   These seaplanes were our first visible reminder of the realities of war since we broke convoy in the Atlantic.

I am writing in the comfortably furnished private terrace outside our bedroom for the night at the Hotel des Indes.   But the sun is sinking and the time has come for me to prepare for the evening's festivities.

Even the best-appointed houses in Java possess no full-length baths.   But I must now explore the possibilities of getting clean and polished in our spacious tiled washroom, which has a drain, a shower, a jug and a large stone vessel filled with cold water.

S.S. *Plancius—December 6, 1941.*

It's nearly 5 p.m., and as dusk will soon be falling, and we've got to get through the minefields before dark, I imagine we're due to sail in a few minutes.

At any rate I've wearied of leaning over the rail and looking at the white, dusty Batavian docks and the long line of K.P.M. ships and the tattered bunches of perspiring coolies loading cargo.

Compared with our other two this is a monster vessel.   There's an impressive amount of deck space, and at last we've been assigned a cabin which is big enough to allow us both to dress and undress, pack and unpack at the same time.

Our fellow passengers from Sydney are now just a small bunch of friends in a great new gathering of strangers—men, women and children of various nationalities, including Chinese.   In the writing-room just now I happened on some fairly recent back numbers of the Singapore press.   From one paper I learned that my arrival is shortly expected (I'm described as "the British author", which is somewhat flattering considering my total literary output).   In another I read a two-column editorial attack on the M.B.C., which I must confess amused rather than alarmed me, for it is hysterically abusive.   At least there's nothing reasonable about it and it's written in the style of a woman scorned.   I gather there is some long-term grievance, but the immediate cause of upset is that a music director and orchestra are being sent out from London to Singapore. Apparently *The Straits Times* thinks there is no need for a big and powerful radio station in Malaya ; is convinced that recorded programmes are just as good as "live" programmes, and considers it "scandalous" that "a violinist" (Thomas Matthews, ex-leader of the London Philharmonic, who was recently appointed M.B.C. Music Director) should be allowed to take up valuable shipping space in wartime !   There are so many good answers to this kind of nonsense that I feel tempted to write them now.   But I must hold my peace until I know more of the situation, especially as I've already gathered from odd conversation with people that the M.B.C. is not popular.

The cranes are silent, and a Malay steward is going the rounds beating a gong. So I presume we really are about to sail, and I must not miss a last, sentimental sight of Batavia.   In thirty-six hours we shall be at the end of our journey, which will have taken us just fifteen weeks to complete.   To Singapore—in 105 days. I hope the reward will be worth while.

PART II

"IN SINGAPORE"

Raffles Hotel—December 9, 1941.

WE were up early yesterday morning. Carey heard the news, and knocked at our cabin door about 6 a.m., like a postman with bad tidings. When we got down we found confirmation chalked on a large blackboard: "Japan has declared war on Britain and America."

Little knots of passengers gathered round the blackboard, looked at the notice in a dazed sort of way, and walked down to the dining-room without a word. Breakfast passed almost in silence. There were no speculations, no exclamations. The thing was too big to talk about just yet, too sudden for realization, too tragic for comment. And it had created so many problems which were purely personal. A mother with a child aged six had intended to join her husband in Bangkok. She had been looking forward to a happy family reunion and had been quite convinced that she'd risked nothing by leaving the sanctuary of Australia. What was she going to do now? For nearly everyone it meant a complete readjustment of attitude. Singapore was no longer a peaceful place in the sun. It was a threatened citadel. The dream of returning to the old, luxuriant, sheltered way of life was quite shattered.

So for a while the passengers hugged their thoughts to themselves, and it was not until after we'd drawn alongside and the Customs officials had come aboard that tongues began to wag and a small volume of alarming stories to circulate. We didn't believe them (Carol and I) at first. We said they were just scare rumours. But it turned out that most of them were accurate. Leaning over the rails, I saw a smiling British officer in kilts, who'd apparently come to meet his wife. "We were bombed here last night," he said, as if he was proud of the fact; as if the show for which he'd been waiting had at last begun. That confirmed one of the stories. Later we learned all the shameful details. The alarm wasn't sounded until the raid was over. The city lights remained ablaze throughout. No precautionary blackout had been ordered. No A.R.P. services were at the ready. I could only ask why, and remember what Carey and others had already told me about Singapore. Presumably, as war hadn't actually been declared, there was still an obstinate belief that war would never come.

We sat in the writing-room awaiting passport examination. Someone had got hold of a newspaper. It didn't tell us much, but what shocked me most was the report that the Japs had already landed in Malaya. The bombing didn't surprise me particularly, though it had started sooner and more suddenly than I'd expected. But this landing in Malaya, which must presumably be intended as the prelude to a land assault on Singapore, was something I'd been led to believe could never happen, would never even be tried. Therefore it alarmed me considerably. I must say no one else seemed to attach particular importance to it, so perhaps I was being unreasonably anxious. But having no knowledge of military matters I'm inclined to base my opinions on superstition. I couldn't help remembering Britain during the invasion scare when we based our best hopes not on beating the Germans if they did land in force, but on preventing them from landing at all. Neither could I forget that so far in this war, whenever the enemy has attempted to do something which our own experts have assured us is impossible, he's always achieved complete success.

Before the passport examination was over the air-raid alarm sounded, and we were bundled down to the dining-room. Though most of our fellow passengers were English, with one or two exceptions none had been in England during the blitz, and this was their first experience of a modern air raid. To begin with there was a tense atmosphere, but very little evidence of open nervousness and absolutely no panic. Then boredom set in, for after ten minutes it became pretty obvious that nothing was going to happen. But we sat there stolidly for more than an hour. There wasn't much else we could do, for we weren't allowed on shore or on deck, and the bar had been closed tight. So far as Carol and I were concerned we couldn't help feeling rather let down. Though we were afraid with the rest, we couldn't share their excitement at something new. All we had by way of compensation was a sense of superiority which I suppose people who are wise in experience—even of unpleasant events—inevitably feel. This was something we knew all about. It was as unwelcomely familiar to us as the trenches to the soldiers of the last war.

Nevertheless, it seemed to us that after fifteen weeks of travel we'd succeeded in turning full circle. We'd glimpsed the lights of Jamaica and Panama, of Australia and Java, and now at the end of our journey were back amidst the familiar realities of darkness and war. The sirens sounded exactly like the London ones. Now we had lost all our eager anticipation at seeing a new country and a new town. We were just going back to the war.

And yet, it's no use pretending that I was altogether sorry. I couldn't indulge in much self-pity. It might have been fun, perhaps, to have had a brief taste of Malaya's peacetime life, but I was never attracted to it, and would have been tortured by conscience if I'd had to endure it for very long. Now, I concluded, the mecca of pleasure and ease, which had so often been painted for me, was suddenly gone and we had even less reason to feel isolated from danger and discomfort than the friends we'd left behind in England. That was a salutary thought.

Our eventual entry into Singapore could hardly have been less luxurious. To begin with, the M.B.C. car which had been sent to meet us apparently grew weary of waiting and departed before we had finished having our passports stamped and had arranged for our heavy baggage to be transported to Raffles Hotel, where Carol, loyal as always to her American instincts, insisted on spending at least the first night. When we did get ashore there wasn't a taxi in sight, and to add to our difficulties the sirens began to wail again, which effectively brought all the usual facilities offered to the traveller to an abrupt halt. The sun was blazing and we were extremely hot, tired and irritable, but there was nothing to do but carry our own suitcases to the Customs office a few hundred yards down the road. Even if we'd felt like taking cover, the only available shelter was a tin-roofed shed, which wouldn't have provided much better protection, we decided, than the open air. Actually the Alert didn't last long on this occasion, and as soon as the All Clear had sounded Carey got busy on the telephone, pleading with every garage proprietor of his acquaintance for some kind of conveyance. But his efforts were unavailing. All Singapore's taxi-drivers had disappeared— at any rate, for the time being.

I estimate that in normal circumstances one allows ten minutes for the journey from the quayside to Raffles Hotel. It took us almost two hours. We made our way partly on foot, partly by lifts in private cars, and partly by bus. (Incidentally, in pre-war days it was definitely not done for Europeans to make use of the public transport service. Carey, though he's spent six years in Malaya, had never boarded a Singapore bus before. This, perhaps, was the thin end of the wedge, for I surmise that in present circumstances many of the European's most zealously guarded privileges and conventions will have to be abandoned, just as in England increasing enemy pressure has wrought, almost imperceptibly, a semi-revolution.)

It's true we paused for half an hour at the Cricket Club, where Carey gave us a drink and renewed his telephone attack. This was my first contact with Malaya club life, and I noticed none of that noisy bar-propping and dice-shaking and sizzling jocularity traditionally associated with it. We sat in a large lounge which was empty except for ourselves and a fat lady at the other end of the room scanning back numbers of the *Tatler* and one Asiatic waiter who ambled up to take our order. Had I been, as Carey was, a wanderer returned, I feel I should have exclaimed, "Where is everyone?" For the streets outside were likewise strangely quiet and almost barren of people and traffic. I concluded that the first blow of war must obviously have had a big effect, though it was too early to judge of what kind. And yet in itself the first blow, apart from its suddenness and apparent unexpectedness, was not particularly shattering, for I've discovered since that the unheralded bombing attack was in no sense a parallel to the onslaught on Pearl Harbour. The only evidence of it is in and around Raffles Square, where some buildings have been partially demolished and some Arab houses destroyed and the glass blasted out of the front of a large department store.

We got to Raffles eventually about 12.30. It also looked deserted and strikingly unexotic. When Carol and I sat down to a *tête-à-tête* lunch with avenues of empty tables all around us we were quite gloomy, and thought that after fifteen weeks of travel we'd had a pretty poor welcome. In fact, we began to entertain an uncomfortable suspicion that there was no point at all in our having come to Singapore.

However, Aubrey Herbert, the M.B.C. Director of Programmes, turned up shoftly afterwards to reassure us. He apologized for not meeting me at the quay, though that's what he'd promised to do when we said good-bye in England last June and the prospect of actually being together in Singapore seemed about as remote as the next world. He explained that he'd been too busy and then announced rather dramatically that he needed my help urgently but would give me the rest of the afternoon and the next day to settle down. I replied with fervour that I was sick to death of idleness; that I never wanted a holiday again and the sooner I got going the better. So he volunteered to show me round while Carol was left to unpack.

The main M.B.C. studios are five miles away at Thomson Road, but the offices are in the Cathay, a miniature skyscraper a few hundred yards from here which dominates Singapore city as the Eiffel Tower dominates Paris. It's a modern steel-and-concrete building erected on two separate levels. The lower structure comprises a cinema, milk bar, restaurant and roof garden. The upper one, eight storeys high, is composed of flats, though some of these have been turned into offices for Government departments, like the Ministry of Information and the Ministry of Economic Warfare, as well as for the M.B.C. Actually it was built very recently and its first two floors are not yet completed. Nor are its basement rooms, which will eventually be M.B.C. studios.

I found Aubrey tired but excited. He'd hurried from his bed to the office shortly after 4 a.m. and had been on the job ever since. Of course, it was difficult for me to appreciate the full dramatic flavour of the situation. I'd come in, as it were, just a few minutes too late. Drama, after all, is a matter of contrasts, and when I arrived the storm had already broken. I'd no personal experience of its suddenness. So far as I was concerned Singapore might always have been just as it was today—with its empty streets and its dazed atmosphere, its deserted bars and its unprocurable taxis. For me there was none of that swift transformation which made London seem unreal and incredible on September 3, 1939.

Apparently the M.B.C. is still very short-handed, and the war has resulted in a sudden and complete reorganization of programmes. (By the war I mean, of course, the Japanese attack. That is the war so far as we are concerned out here. Apparently the other war, which has been going on since September, '39, has had hardly any effect at all on Malaya.) Many more news bulletins, both in English and the Asiatic languages, have had to be fitted in, and in addition the military are making use of the microphones for code messages. Programmes are frequently interrupted for no apparent reason by a gramophone record of "Keep the Home Fires Burning", and at regular intervals listeners are being informed that a car in Raffles Square was robbed yesterday of certain valuable papers !

The chairman of the M.B.C., Eric Davis, whom I've never met, left for London a couple of months ago, and is there now. I gather that he intended to recruit more staff, but I imagine he'll have to abandon all hope of that in present circumstances.

It seems a bit doubtful if he'll be able to get back himself.

Aubrey has asked me to become a relief announcer for the time being (he's one himself), so it looks as if I shall be tied to the microphone at odd hours in the evenings and early mornings. During the daytime I must get my own job organized. I haven't discovered yet what its exact scope is going to be, but I do know it offers opportunity for real pioneer work. The intention is (there've been occasional announcements about it in the press) to make the M.B.C. the Empire's biggest and most powerful radio station outside Britain. But the process of development is by no means complete, and broadcasting here is still very much in its infancy. That means that the M.B.C. has now been shouldered with a very important and responsible task ahead of schedule. It's got to be the voice of Britain in the Far Eastern war. It's got to be a first-class agency of offensive propaganda. It's got to sustain morale. It's got to instruct. In moments of severe stress it's got to preserve an illusion of normalcy. In the event of severe raids, it's got to be the sole provider of entertainment just as the B.B.C. was during the worst days of the London blitz. In short, it's got to fulfil all those functions, both of attack and defence, which make a well-equipped radio station essential in the conduct of modern warfare. That's the aim, as I see it, and because the M.B.C. is still so small an organization one feels one will have a personal responsibility in helping to make the aim a reality. I start tomorrow, and I'm looking forward to it.

The remainder of yesterday passed raid-free. We anticipated there'd be an Alert after dark for certain, and sure enough the sirens wailed in the early hours of this morning. But nothing happened—there wasn't the murmur of a gun or a 'plane—and personally I don't think anything *will* happen for a while at any rate. The nearest land base which the Japs can use is still many hundreds of miles away, and it doesn't seem to me they're likely to risk an aircraft carrier. That first bombing attack—carried out by naval 'planes, so I'm assured—was presumably just a bellicose flourish which could safely be indulged considering we were entirely unprepared for it.

Officially a brownout has been introduced. This is a vague, indeterminate term which no one seems able to interpret accurately. Roughly speaking, it allows you to show some light but not much. When the warning goes an immediate blackout comes into force, which means, of course, that you can't show any light at all.

But brownout or blackout makes the evenings pretty good torture. Admittedly it's not so easy a matter to imprison the light as it was in England, for it's a question of covering not only windows but great balconies and verandas and in some cases whole façades. But no preparations of any kind were made in advance, and the Raffles management is thus far showing little inclination to begin now. The result is that except for the dining-room, which happens to be suitably encased, the whole hotel is plunged into semi-darkness during the brownout and complete darkness during the blackout.

Last night after dinner we sat for a while in the large front veranda, which is wide open to the street outside. The lights were so dimmed that we couldn't even distinguish the writing on the chit which we signed for our dinners. A small dance band on a raised dais was gallantly swinging out-of-date tunes, and a few straggling couples were groping their way round the floor. It was rather a pathetic sight—the last kick, I suppose, of the East's famous pleasure ground.

But we've made no arrangements to leave Raffles. Singapore is very full, and from what I gather a dwelling of any kind will not easily be obtainable. Even if it is, Carol has set her heart against housekeeping in present circumstances, and I rather sympathize with her. The future is too unpredictable. Yesterday there were confident stories that the Japs had been driven back into the sea. But from today's newspapers it's fairly obvious they're still very much in Malaya, while our own troops, on the other hand, are engaged in a strategic withdrawal. Certainly the tradespeople—European and Chinese—do not seem in the least confident of the issue. I'd always heard that in Singapore one could live on the fat of credit as in no other place in the world. But this morning when I went to order my tropical kit it was made very plain that I would be required to pay C.O.D. for everything; and this in spite of the fact that Carey took me to shops where he's a regular and favoured customer and offered to guarantee my account. Carol had a similar experience. The dressmakers told her frankly that because of the present emergency they'd withdrawn all credit facilities.

Of course, we can't afford to stay here indefinitely, though it's not as ruinous as I'd been led to believe. At the moment we have an enormous room and bathroom for an all-in charge of twenty-two dollars. Worked out at the correct exchange value of 2/4 (and I'm determined to reject the theory of the dollar being worth only a shilling), that comes to roughly 25/- per head, which is less than one would expect to pay at the Savoy if one could get *en pension* terms and about the same as we paid in the most expensive Sydney hotel. As a matter of fact, in my limited experience I haven't found Singapore prices at all staggering. Clothes are cheaper than in England. Drinks purchased in hotel bars are about the same, though I'm told if you buy them by the retail bottle they don't cost so much. The average wage paid to native servants, including chauffeurs, is thirty dollars a month (i.e. £42 per annum), and that, I should imagine, is rather less than the average earnings of domestic servants at home. It's too early to be dogmatic, but I'm beginning to believe the story about the dollar having a purchasing power of only a shilling is purely fictional and was invented to salve the consciences of those Europeans who live right up to their phenomenally high salaries and boast of their inability to save a cent. If I'm right in this, it's extraordinary how wide a belief the fiction has gained. Even the Crown agents warn applicants for civil service jobs that the purchasing power of the dollar is considerably less than its exchange value.

None the less, I think we are paying much too much for our board and lodging. The trouble is that Raffles, in spite of its world-wide reputation, is pretty mediocre. Certainly it's not a patch on the Hotel des Indes, and it doesn't even look in the first flight. Granted its tropical distinctiveness, it's like a second-rate station hotel—big enough, but dirty and much trampled. The food in its dining-room is not noticeably above boarding-house standard, and so far we've been offered nothing remotely native—only a dreary procession of English dishes from cold storage numbered 1, 2, 3, 4, etc. The purpose of this number-ing is to enable customers to order either by pointing or by speaking the appro-priate numeral in Malay. Actually I attempted to learn a few Malay words on the voyage from Sydney. But I find that from a strictly practical point of view my efforts seem at the moment to have been rather wasted. If I say "*satu*" the table boy politely answers "one", and if I say "one" he goes off murmuring "*satu*". In fact he's just as bilingual as I am, and it's obvious that so far as hotel life is concerned one can make oneself perfectly well understood in English. Doubtless a thorough knowledge of the language will be extremely valuable. But at the moment I can't see how I'm going to find sufficient time for study, for it's obvious, thank heavens, that I shall be pretty busy during the next weeks, and I can't yet contemplate a thereafter.

We've kept in touch during the past twenty-four hours with several of our fellow passengers whose plans have been completely disrupted by the war. I must confess they've adjusted themselves swiftly and courageously to the new situation. Three of them are nursing sisters. In peacetime it's a pretty good job to be in the Malayan Nursing Service, for the pay is good (far better than in England) and the duties fairly light and the prospects of marrying out of it rosy. But now it's obviously going to be hard and tough. Our nursing sisters are not certain of their plans yet. Normally they would be sent to hospitals on the Malay Peninsula. But in the present precarious circumstances, with travel services thrown out of joint, they imagine that they'll probably be stationed in Singapore for the time being. Carey is leaving in the morning for Kuala Lumpur, where he has a house which must be disposed of. But he's applied for a commission in the Army and hopes to be stationed in Singapore. Another man with whom we spent quite a lot of time—Mac by name—is also joining up. In normal circumstances he would have gone on to Malacca, where he's manager of a rubber plantation. And then one of the older men, who's a chartered accountant during the day, has been whisked off for duty with the special constabulary by night. He's hardly had a moment of leisure since he landed. His wife is rather a nervous lady, and because she hates being left alone Carol has volunteered to spend tonight in her house. On board ship she used to tell us how uncomfortable she found her cabin, etc., how she had disliked Australia because of its lack of "service", how glad she was her husband's leave was over, and how much she was looking forward to being in Singapore again with its abundance of native service. Sad awakening! I'm dining with the Herberts, who are staying at the Seaview Hotel. My role is to cheer them up, for they tell me that during brownouts and blackouts the Seaview is even gloomier than Raffles.

From all I hear and from my own observation, civilian Singapore was psychologically ill-prepared for war. And yet obviously the great majority of its Europeans were already committed to some kind of war service when the events of yesterday happened. All the younger ones, in non-essential jobs, have been called up for full-time military duty with the Volunteers. And most of the older ones, in addition to carrying on with their ordinary jobs, are either members of the L.D.C. or one of the passive defence services. So it looks as if some kind of war organization was ready even in those days—only just passed—when oysters and strawberries were still being specially flown over from Australia. And that makes the story of the appalling muddle in the early hours of December 8, which is apparently quite true, even harder to understand.

Raffles Hotel—Singapore, December 27, 1941.

We've now been here nearly three weeks, and let me record before anything that on the whole I'm enjoying myself hugely. I've never worked so hard, and quite honestly I've never felt so well. The climate seems to suit me. I may, of course, be hurtling towards a catastrophic breakdown in health ; but I don't think so. In fact, in my present mood I'm ready to swear that all the talk about the vital necessity of plenty of exercise, relaxation, rest, etc., is pure bunkum.

The first day or two, when I was a relief announcer, wasn't much fun, because then I hardly got any sleep at all. I was on duty at the Cathay until midnight. Getting back from there to Raffles, though actually within easy walking distance, was hellish, as I was unfamiliar with the way, for the so-called brownout in the streets outdoes any blackout in my experience. There's not a glimmer of light to be seen anywhere, except for the screened lamps of passing traffic. I had to be up again at 5 a.m., and walk through the half-light of dawn to our small improvised studio among the great Government buildings at Empress Place. I remained there till nine and then, after a hurried breakfast, had to get back to the Cathay again for the day's work.

Now, thank goodness, I've been taken off relief announcing and am free to organize my own job, the scope of which, incidentally, is much wider than I anticipated. I'm looking after drama, features and music productions as well as talks. It keeps me busy all day and most evenings, Saturdays and Sundays included. That isn't a boast, it's a thanksgiving. There's not much fun to be had out of living in Singapore, apart from one's work. And I think the majority of our programme staff average about a seventy-hour week. Carol feels the same way as I do. She's exuberantly well and has got herself a job at the naval base which keeps her occupied most of the day.

The only snag is the future. I still can't contemplate it with any confidence. My common sense tells me that short of a miracle this place is doomed. The military position is obviously bad. It's probably worse than most people imagine, for the official communiqués are invariably varnished by omission and at least twenty-four hours out of date. But that's not all. It's a current saying that in modern warfare human courage is no good without machines to back it up. Well, from all I gather there aren't nearly enough machines here. But what's worse, there is a deficiency of courage, or of determination at any rate, among the civilian population.

At least that's my impression. Admittedly, I haven't encountered actual panic. But, on the other hand, I've noticed none of that popular spirit of defiance, none of that placid determination to take the worst that's coming, none of that blind refusal to contemplate capitulation, which was so characteristic of London during the great blitz. My private bet is that if Singapore has to face a prolonged siege, civilian morale will crack.

It's palpably unfair to compare this place with London, I know. But that doesn't alter the fact that the ordeal it's got to face is likely to be even more formidable.

Singapore is British, but the vast majority of its population are British only in name. They are Asiatics—Chinese, Malays, Indians, Arabs—who mostly dislike the whites and, what is more alarming, dislike each other. There is no spirit of one for all and all for one here. There is no national feeling. The Chinese don't show the least inclination to fight for the Malays, nor the Malays for the Chinese, nor the Arabs for anyone.

Comparatively speaking, the Europeans are a mere handful. But in a state of society which is semi-feudal they are the chiefs. On them devolves the essential task of welding this turbulent, heterogeneous population into a compact and spirited community. For years they have had the pleasure of exploiting, now they have the responsibility of leading. It's for them to set an example of cheerfulness and calm in the face of danger. It's for them to guide and inspire. It's for them to show that resistance, whatever its cost, is worth while. Above all, it's for them to prove that Singapore, and indeed the rest of Malaya, is a country commanding equal and undivided allegiance from all its peoples, whether white or coloured.

The problem is admittedly prodigious. But before there can be any hope of Singapore withstanding a long siege it's got to be solved. And since a siege of some kind now looks inevitable, there can be no justifiable delay in making an all-out attempt to solve it.

Unfortunately, however, there is worse than delay. There are no signs yet that an effective attempt is even being prepared. In fact I should surmise that at the moment civilian morale is worsening rather than improving. And the causes of this are various. To begin with a great many of the British-born civilians have been called up into the Volunteers (which, in spite of its name, is largely a conscripted force) or for full-time service with the Local Defence Corps. Who was responsible for thus disrupting the commercial and administrative life of the country in return for a small army unit of extremely doubtful value I am not quite sure, though I fancy it was the military authorities. A well-equipped L.D.C., trained on the British Home Guard model, might well be useful if there were an intention (and there is no indication of it) to defend Malaya inch by inch, town by town, street by street and house by house. But to deplete the already thin ranks of the British residents who are urgently needed in the task of leading the native community and who presumably have the knowledge and experience to do it, by turning large numbers of them into full time, ill-equipped and half-trained private soldiers, seems to me an act of pure folly.

The majority of those Europeans who are exempt from conscription by reason either of birth date, job or nationality are working far harder than was their custom in the halcyon days of peace and are doing all that can be expected of them in an orthodox sort of way.   With few exceptions, I think they were more or less unprepared for this war, though they are certainly throwing themselves into it wholeheartedly now that it has come.   Whether they have a full appreciation of the imminence of the danger, or of the magnitude of the task which must be accomplished if failure is to be averted, it's hard to say.   They make devastating cricitisms about the way things are being run here at the moment, and deplore the trend of events.   But at the same time they indulge in a lot of chest-slapping and parrot-cries that Singapore can't possibly fall, even though they acknowledge their inability to put forward a single common-sense reason why it shouldn't.

In any case their efforts, though perfectly creditable in themselves, are unavailing against two very severe handicaps.   The first of these is represented by a minority of Europeans who are worse than useless.   They regard the war as an unwarranted intrusion on their pleasures, and they go about moaning and groaning, making preparations to leave as soon as possible and meanwhile clinging selfishly to their old way of life, which is futile enough.   Of course, a similar minority existed in England—may still exist, for all I know.   But in Singapore its influence and the harm it is doing is out of all proportion to its size, for the simple reason that while the total European population is extremely small, civilian morale depends entirely on the example which it sets.   In Britain, with its great and closely united population, you can afford a few hundred or a few thousand idlers and ratters.   But among Singapore's European community you can't afford one.   So this minority, small though it is, is doing a lot of harm, and is overshadowing the record of the majority.   In it, I think, women predominate.   Facts and figures would prove, I've no doubt, that most of the women in Singapore are prepared to conduct themselves just as gallantly as the women of London did during the blitz.   The girls in our office, for instance, work a minimum of fifty-two hours a week, and since the M.B.C. officially is recognized as an essential war service, they have no moral obligation to do any more.   But without compunction nearly all of them have volunteered for some kind of passive defence job in their spare time—nursing, ambulance driving, etc.   And their example is by no means unique.   But there remain, unfortunately, a few women in Singapore who are convinced either that they have a kind of divine right to run away now that things look like getting tough, or that they are sufficiently discharging their obligation by some token war work—e.g. an hour a day winding bandages—and can devote the rest of their time to the old rounds of ease and pleasure.   The trouble with these women is that they haven't the stamina or the reserves of character to adapt themselves to the realism of the present.   They have possessed (and still possess) all the advantages of wealth and position but have apparently never been trained in the responsibilities—such as leadership and courageous example—which under a system of capitalist society are usually supposed to justify the existence of a ruling or privileged class ; and with the working class represented by the excessively under-educated, underpaid and under-developed bulk of the Asiatic community, society in British Malaya is, as I've said, semi-feudal.   Their lush standard of living, now so seriously menaced, was always artificial because, I suspect, they are mostly recruited from the English or Scottish suburban class and have been uprooted from the environment in which they were originally bred.   Had they remained at home they would probably be spending their time sweeping and cooking and sewing in a four-roomed villa. Instead they have come out here to lead a life of complete and luxurious idleness at the expense of a husband's inflated salary. Because of their comparative rarity they have been encouraged to regard themselves as very smart and very beautiful. They have been pampered and admired out of all proportion to their deserts in an open market. They have been driven around in large cars. They have even had removed from them the responsibility of looking after their own children. In short, they have been spoiled and their native worth has been undermined. For them—and in a lesser degree for their menfolk—Singapore isn't an island to which they owe particular allegiance, it isn't even a British Colony in whose administration they take much pride. It's simply a means of wish fulfilment—a place in the East where they can imitate the ways and manners of the idle rich. Therefore they are incapable of making the kind of sacrifices for it which they'd probably be willing to make for England. Either they want to be out of the way until the soldiers of the Empire have refashioned their dream world for them, or they want to keep their eyes closed and make believe that there is no real cause to wake up. The latter attitude exists in varying degrees, and I came across one rather mild example shortly after my arrival. Carol, in common with the other European women who have jobs at the naval base, is driven to work every morning in a large Admiralty car. On her first morning one of her colleagues complained bitterly in a loud Cockney voice that the car was now overcrowded because they had to sit three in the back! The same lady subsequently refused to work on Saturday mornings on the grounds that this would rob her of her only opportunity of meeting her friends at tiffin! Other women of her kind are even more insistent on doing as little as possible, and there are some who aren't engaged in war work of any sort.

The women who want to get away from Singapore spend their time besieging the shipping offices, and many of them have not yet succeeded in booking a passage. Mothers with children are being given priority and it's right that they should go. But the others, in my view, have no excuse, for running out. It's through their own choice and their own folly that the war has caught up with them. They wouldn't be in their present predicament if they had listened to official warnings and advice.

Admittedly the problem is a difficult one. Because of general ill-preparedness in civilian Singapore, most women (I'm speaking of the majority as well as the minority now) haven't had much training in war work, and it doesn't look as if there will be time to get them sufficiently organized before the test comes. Obviously, as events have turned out, with the threat of siege growing daily more imminent, they should have been compulsorily evacuated months ago. But it is too late now. Wisely and inevitably the Governor has pledged his word that there will be no discrimination between Europeans and Asiatics, which means, in effect, that an organized evacuation of any kind is out of the question. In the circumstances, therefore, every European woman has a clear duty to remain where she is as long as she can be of service. If she uses her privileged position to escape, while the going is still good, she is contributing immeasurably to a general lowering of morale, which just can't be afforded. The Japs know this perfectly well. That is why their propagandists have been at such pains to emphasize that white women who are captured will suffer "a fate worse than death". It's conveniently forgotten, on both sides, that hundreds of Chinese women have already suffered that fate.

The other handicap of which I spoke is the lamentable lack of leadership at the top. After the fall of France, Britain had Churchill to rally and personify the will of the nation. There's no one comparable here. Indeed, it is a pity that Churchill can't find time to pay a flying visit to Singapore or, better still, Chiang Kai-shek. Whether through his own fault or not (I'm not in a position yet to judge), the Governor's prestige is about nil. Brooke-Popham was completely discredited, and though Pownhall's appointment has been excitedly hailed as the best news of the war, there's a good deal of antagonism between the military and the civilians. The military blame the civilians for failure to co-operate before the Japanese attack, and the civilians blame the military for the shattering series of disasters which have succeeded it. Most people, I think, fix their best hopes on Duff Cooper. But his position is ill-defined, and in the public mind, at any rate, there's no certainty as to how far his authority runs or what his exact functions are.

I don't know whether the responsibility for clogging the wheels of good government belongs to one man or several men : nor who he or they may be. One hears all sorts of conflicting stories. However, the administration seems quite palsied. It's got neither energy nor drive. It's making no really great efforts and doing nothing sweeping to organize for the siege which now seems inevitable.

Nearly three weeks have passed since the outbreak of the Pacific War, and those weeks have been comparatively peaceful, for we've had no air raids, and apart from the news, which gets progressively worse, of the fighting in Malaya, we've enjoyed quite a sense of security, however false, and the general nervousness, at first apparent, has calmed down a good deal. But the opportunity thus presented for grand-scale preparations has been ignored. In spite of the obvious need to conserve food stocks, no scheme of strict rationing has been introduced. Although it is no longer possible to buy limitless meals in hotels à la carte there has been hardly any restrictions imposed on the sale of ordinary foodstuffs and commodities. In spite of the obvious necessity of making Singapore as bombproof as possible, no plan for building deep or surface shelters has been formulated. And in spite of the labour shortage, which is already acute as a result of the first and only air raid, no noticeable attempt has been made to rally public opinion and to impress upon it the urgency of the situation. In short, the administration is displaying so little vigour that the Asiatics are entirely uninspired and there's an atmosphere of apathy—almost of resignation—about the whole place. One can't resist the conclusion that the average citizen has little confidence that Singapore will hold—or even that the British intend to put up much of a fight for it. Why else should the tradespeople have stopped all credit facilities ?

Everything that has happened so far has tended to undermine Asiatic faith. I was in our news-room when the story of the sinking of the two battleships came through. I overheard one of the sub-editors dictating to a typist : "The Board of Admiralty regrets to announce that H.M.S. *Prince of Wales* and H.M.S. *Repulse* . . ." Well, that was the Navy gone, and one should realize that rumours too insistent to be doubted had already convinced us that we were, virtually speaking, without an air force or a properly equipped army. It was a stunning blow. Someone mentioned June, 1940. But I felt worse than I did then. I'd always had an instinctive conviction (most people had, I think) that we would survive the fall of France. Now I had no such belief.

Shortly afterwards, Duff Cooper came to the microphone. Personally, I think he's a good broadcaster. In fact, among Cabinet Ministers I rank him second only to Churchill, for he has the supreme merit of being literate and is no disher-out of badly delivered *clichés*. But his speech was extremely reminiscent of his B.B.C. *apologias* as Minister of Information and consequently entirely unsuited to a Malayan audience. The Asiatics aren't impressed by talk of the British showing their greatest qualities in times of crisis, etc. They want to be told that what looks like a disaster isn't really a disaster at all. Indeed, so far as I've gathered from our Asiatic programme organizers, our propaganda is hopelessly handicapped by the failure of the authors of official communiqués and so on to appreciate or even consider the Asiatic mind. The British may like to hear that their enemies fought with skill and daring. But if you tell a Chinese anything of the kind he immediately jumps to the conclusion that his enemy is irresistible. In short, there's far too great a tendency to run this war on the false assumption that the whole population is English to the core.

Then there was the wretched and disgraceful story of Penang. The evacuation of the white population, which looked like a clear violation of the Governor's pledge, enraged many Europeans here as much as it did the Asiatics. It has since been partly explained away, but the damage it wrought has by no means been undone.

I have seen next to nothing in the newspapers about the Penang Radio being captured intact. This was an amateur station; neither the military nor the civilian authorities made any attempt to blow it up before leaving. The Japanese are now using it for propaganda purposes with devastating effect. Rumours spread far more widely and quickly here and gain far greater credence than they do in Europe. Penang Radio was just a ready-made rumour factory and, so far as I can gather, it was put into full production within a couple of days of the Japanese taking over. As a matter of fact, I first heard of it on Christmas Day, when I learned from our Asiatic programme organizers that it was having an excessively damaging influence on their own listeners. I've since discovered that even the military authorities are perturbed, for they've already run up against a huge Fifth Column in Malaya and I suppose they've at last begun to realize that radio is not just a new-fangled luxury but one of the chief ways Fifth Columns are recruited and enlarged. I went up to Command Headquarters the other day to try to get some material for a counter-campaign. I was received very courteously by a high-ranking staff officer who made a lot of intelligent promises which so far haven't been fulfilled. Meanwhile, we've had to fall back on the usual defensive line: "potential Allied resources", "the Japanese are liars", "partners in crime of the Germans", etc., etc. That's all right in Britain. And it's all right here, I suppose, so far as it goes. But what's really wanted is something far more positive and offensive. I doubt if we shall get it unless and until the urgent need of paying special regard to Asiatic requirements is generally realized. At the moment we're fighting this war as if Malaya were a province of the United Kingdom.

One hears a good deal of dismal speculation about how the Asiatics will stand up to heavy air raids. I should imagine this largely depends on the European example and on the measures taken for the protection of life and property, particularly A.R.P. measures, which are inadequate at the moment. One of my first jobs was to initiate a series of talks on A.R.P. I was lucky enough to get hold of a rubber man, C. E. Hudson, who's a spare-time divisional warden. He's very forthright and very intelligent; a natural broadcaster, with a voice and manner extremely reminiscent of the B.B.C.'s Mr. Middleton. I anticipate he'll become really popular and will succeed in building up a large

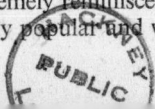

and regular audience. But his task is pretty difficult, because there are many things he'd like to say but can't. He's precluded, for example, from mentioning shelters. The plain fact is there aren't any shelters in Singapore. So far as the Asiatic community is concerned, the authorities are relying on a scheme of dispersal which, when one remembers that every part of this small island is equally vulnerable to air attack, doesn't look like working out in practice. The excuse for not having built surface shelters or underground shelters is the dampness of the subsoil. Hudson (and there are others who agree with him) doesn't think this explanation good enough. But so far, as I've said, there is no indication that anything is going to be done to improve the situation.

Broadcasting here is pioneer work indeed. For one thing, our equipment is still extremely primitive, and though the M.B.C. is scheduled to be one of the Empire's largest and most powerful stations, and we are already operating four simultaneous transmissions in thirteen languages, we haven't got the facilities we need, and which will eventually be ours. For another thing, we've little knowledge of the nature and extent of our listening public. Obviously it's grown since the Pacific War began and will continue to grow, for nothing fosters the stay-at-home habit better than blackouts and air raids. Even those Europeans who had little time for radio and who disliked the M.B.C. particularly, because they regarded it as an unwarrantable charge on the Malayan Exchequer, are now having to resort to the practice of listening-in. My own idea is to seize this opportunity to popularize the station by improved programmes and the introduction of as high a percentage of "live" entertainment as possible. Once we've established public confidence we'll have the chance to be a really effective propaganda organization. But time is desperately short.

I'm putting on a fair number of plays, and I've got Marie Ney to help me with these. She rejoined her husband in Malaya some months ago after a theatrical tour of Australia and now she's taken on a permanent job with the M.B.C. She really is a wonderful worker, and I'm lost in admiration of the energy and enthusiasm she's showing under conditions which are very rough and ready, to say the least. We have to rely on amateur casts mainly, though fortunately there are a few professionals whom the war has brought to Singapore by chance. Jane Cobb is here with her actor husband Jack McNaughton, who's serving now as a lieutenant in the Loyals.

We've seen quite a lot of the McNaughtons—we spend the majority of our free evenings with them—and I fancy their views on things in general are much the same as ours. We haven't yet contemplated the idea of joining a club, and though *Pahit* parties may be in full swing for all I know, we haven't been invited to one or heard of one being held. As a matter of fact, the opportunities for leading a gay and rollicking social life are extremely restricted, apart from the demands of work. For one thing, transport is a major problem, and a taxi after 10 p.m. is virtually unprocurable. For another, only a few places of public diversion have survived the war. Most of the cinemas are still open, but amateur theatricals and similar festivities, which used to abound, have all been cancelled. Singapore's night club, the Coconut Grove, is no more, and two of the famous Worlds, where the taxi girls are to be found, have closed down. The remaining one shuts its doors promptly at 10 p.m. The dance-band at the swimming-club, which used to play until the early morning, has packed up for the duration. That leaves the restaurant at the Cathay and Raffles veranda, where dances are held nightly from 8 p.m. until midnight. The latter has now been so effectively screened that it can be lit up and is usually crowded. A fair sprinkling of the men one sees there are in uniform—soldiers and sailors on short leave. At Christmastide the ladies of Singapore put up quite a peace-time show. They arrived in full regalia and made entrances in the fashion of stage stars, which was more comic than impressive, for most of them looked plain and *passé* and excessively unsmart. But otherwise I've noticed very few civilians in evening dress. A minute or so before midnight the band plays "God Save the King" and then drinks are swept off the tables and lights are turned out; so there's nothing for it but to go home to bed. You can indulge in precisely the same kind of reckless hilarity at the Cathay Restaurant, which has no windows and is air-conditioned. I've only been there once and that was on the night I was announcing, when it was literally empty except for myself and a colleague drinking glasses of milk, though the band played undauntedly. I hear it has since regained its patronage, and that nowadys tables have to be booked in advance. On the whole, however, there's probably less public pleasure-making in wartime Singapore than there was in London at the height of the blitz. Certainly the facilities for it are fewer.

Rumour says that the famous Tanglin Club is shortly to be commandeered by the military. Personally, I don't think it will be any great loss. It has a nice swimming-pool, but that's about all. Otherwise it's one of those terrifying get-together-over-the-bar places which is my idea of everything a club should not be.

Carey and Mac are now comrades-in-arms. They're both lieutenants in the same regiment. They call in at Raffles occasionally (we're still there, by the way. It's dirty, uncomfortable and too expensive for us, but we haven't yet been able to face the prospect of moving). They contrive to remain cheerful in a philosophic sort of way. But their predictions of the future could hardly be more gloomy.

On Christmas Eve or thereabout, Allan Rose, the M.B.C.'s senior announcer, who arrived from England shortly after we did, introduced me to Martin Agronsky; he's one of the N.B.C.'s star correspondents and made a name for himself through his broadcast dispatches from Ankara. He's a tall fellow with dark hair and a pale complexion. I don't know whether his face was whiter than usual, but he seemed so strung up with nerves he could hardly speak. I got the impression that he regarded his assignment to Singapore as a passport to certain death.

By contrast was my meeting with Duff Cooper. I happened to be at the station when he broadcast after his recent appointment as Minister for Far Eastern Affairs. Much to my surprise and pleasure, he recognized me, for he'd only set eyes on me once before at an Oxford Union debate ten years ago. An invitation to lunch followed last Sunday. There were about four other guests besides myself, and the conversation was smooth and easy and unflurried and in no way mirrored approaching catastrophe. Indeed, apart from the orthodox Malayan meal of curried chicken and Gula Malacca, and the fact that the party broke up immediately lunch was over, the whole thing reminded me of the sunny placidity of a summer afternoon spent at an English country house. I came away feeling faintly hopeful of the future for the first time since my arrival in Singapore.

The moon is ominously large, and we expect the night raids to be launched any time now. Last evening at Raffles we ran into Mephistopheles (the Mephistopheles of *Themistocles* fame). He came out here as an aircraft technician, but was whipped into the Air Force the moment he arrived. His travelling companion, who sat next to him in the ship's dining-room, fell an early casualty to the Japanese. He was killed by a bomb at Ipoh. Uncharacteristically, Mephistopheles had something optimistic to say. Apparently fifty Hurricane fighters have just arrived. It'll take about a week to assemble them, and then we'll be considerably better off than we are now with only a hundred or so American Buffaloes to send into the air.

I wonder how well the English newspapers are in touch with events here. I've read something about a *Daily Express* attack on "whisky-swilling planters". Well, I must confess I've swilled considerably more whisky in Singapore than is my custom ; but as to this, it must be remembered first that because of the climate the swallowing of a great many pints of liquid of some kind is a medical necessity ; and, secondly, that you can drink more alcohol than is probably good for you without feeling any ill effects—again because of the climate. I can't pretend I've noticed any drunkenness in Singapore so far.

I've also read something of a leader writer's pronouncement that the Malay is the world's best soldier, and condemnation of the Government for not having built up a huge Malay army. This, I am afraid, is the sensational vapouring of an ignoramus. The majority of the Malays are, at the moment, unrecruitable. They're idle by nature, and they are loyal only to their Sultans. The best of them, from our point of view, are sufficiently pro-British to stand by and do nothing. The worst are actually helping the Japanese. So, short of a really effective propaganda campaign, which in my view should be pre-eminently directed to putting the fear of almighty British vengeance into any actual or potential Fifth Columnist, I don't think we can expect much assistance from the bulk of the Malays. We can, on the other hand, expect considerable hindrance from them.

Raffles Hotel—January 1, 1942.

On Monday night (December 28th) we had our first Japanese air raid. We half expected it, for the moon was full, and the full moon over Singapore is so luminous you can almost read by it.

Carol and I were sitting in the Raffles dining-room. I suppose because our ears are accustomed to such things, we made no mistake that the guns were in action a minute or so before the actual warning sounded, though our fellow diners were apparently in blissful ignorance of the fact. At the first note of the wailing sirens, however, they jumped to their feet, pushed back their chairs and literally ran to the shelter, which in reality is a sort of pathetic tin-roofed hut and incapable, I hazard, of withstanding the shock of more than a small anti-aircraft splinter. The Asiatic "boys" (waiters, cooks, kitchen assistants, etc.) naturally followed in the wake of the fleeing Europeans. Then all the lights in the hotel were turned out.

By the beam of a torch we discovered that with the exception of the head waiter and four Army officers, we were alone in the dining-room, which a few minutes ago had been full. Frankly, we were both angry and disgusted, particularly as there was absolutely no cause for alarm, let alone panic. At the time the sirens sounded the guns had already ceased firing and there wasn't even the noise of an aeroplane in the sky. The head waiter shared our view ; he argued that life would become quite impossible if everyone ran to ground the moment there was an air-raid warning. And I fancy he thought, though he did not say as much, that the Europeans were largely to blame in this instance for setting so craven an example.

Admittedly, we are acclimatized to air raids, whereas our fellow diners were presumably not. But even so, the whole scene contrasted very poorly with my memory of the first London warning (not counting the three false alarms at the very beginning of the war). It was about six o'clock one evening in August, 1940, if I remember aright. I was standing in the crowded bar of the Thermionic Club. There were a lot of women as well as men, some young, some middle-aged. But the dreaded sirens, which we had been keyed up to expect ever since the fall of France, caused hardly any sensation. A few people murmured, "That's the air-raid warning." But no one moved or seemed in the least bit upset. The barman put up protective shutters across the bar and continued to serve drinks behind them. That was really all that happened. And, of course, Londoners had more immediate grounds for fear at the time than Singaporeans have today. The Channel ports are considerably closer to the heart of Britain than the nearest Japanese base is to Singapore.

But whatever our feelings, there was nothing for it but to sit in the darkness until the All Clear sounded. Fortunately for our patience, it came quite soon and we were then enabled to finish our interrupted meal in peace.

I was committed to working on a script that evening with two of our pro-gramme assistants, Peggie Broadhead and Eric Robertson. So after dinner I went round to the Cathay, where Peggie has a flat on the eighth floor above the M.B.C. offices. The script, scheduled for production on New Year's Eve, was boldly entitled, "1941—A Radio Flashback", and was intended, when written, to be a dramatic reconstruction on the B.B.C. pattern of the main events of the past year. But I'm afraid we didn't make much progress with it that evening, for there were two more air raids before midnight. The first was more or less quiescent. During the second, however, we heard a good deal of gunfire and one or two distant bombs.

Though the Cathay is a magnificent target, it's one of Singapore's very few safe buildings, inasmuch as it's made of steel and concrete and has a large base-ment. I'm glad to say its inhabitants (flatholders, servants, late office workers, etc.) behaved with infinitely more decorum than the Raffles Hotel clientele. A few people naturally sought shelter and some of the Chinese amahs looked really scared. But there was no wild scurrying down the stairs at the first note of the siren.

The M.B.C. has one studio in the Cathay from which various news bulletins, commentaries and recorded programmes are broadcast. It's a converted out-side room on the fifth floor of the building. It isn't even soundproof and it doesn't afford the faintest illusion of safety. But as our total studio accom-modation is extremely limited there was no thought of closing it down when the raids came. Thus the Asiatic control engineers as well as a European announcer had to remain there whatever happened. They did so without question, which indicates to my mind that Asiatics are psychologically just as capable of standing up to aerial bombardment as white men, provided they are given the right lead. Possibly I was unfortunate to have been at Raffles when the first alarm went and thereby got a false impression. Nevertheless, I've heard no other reports of panic among the Europeans. Mine must have been a particularly poor lot.

I fancy that neither Peggie nor Eric had had any previous experience of being bombed. They seemed more elated than cowed, which was possibly the way their nerves took them; for I'm convinced that no one but an unimaginative dolt can go through a raid without being frightened, and I won't accuse the spirited part authors of "1941—A Radio Flashback" of being unimaginative dolts.

We watched the second act from the flat balcony. A direct hit was scored on an oil-tank, causing a fire large enough to be an island beacon. The ack-ack, from its noise and consistency, was quite impressive, though I've heard nothing glowing yet about its accuracy. But if you're an amateur in such things you derive great comfort, I think, from the mere sound of ack-ack fire. I remember in the early days of the London blitz how I longed for our guns to reply more frequently to the continual threatening buzz of the Nazi bombers overhead.

There has been an average of three raids every night this week. Compared with the German mass efforts they are mere pinpricks. For one thing, they are shortlived, seldom lasting more than an hour, so that there's never any danger of your going without sleep. For another, they are apparently aimed exclusively at military objectives. In spite of their blood-curdling threats over the radio, the Japanese have so far not attempted anything in the nature of a terror raid. And it's remarkable how much store they set by the moon. Indeed, one is able to predict the night's programme pretty accurately by a mere knowledge of the times when the moon rises and sinks. It looks from this as if the bomber crews have strict orders to guard against hitting anything but specified targets.

The only alarming thing is that we can't, of course, be certain that the Japanese won't suddenly decide to bomb indiscriminately. If they ever do we shall feel like rabbits without a hole. For in and around Raffles there's no shelter worthy of the name.

Though the raids are not yet particularly frightening they are excessively inconvenient. Everything stops for the warning—every noticeable public service, that is to say, except the radio. Lights are extinguished, bars and restaurants are closed, transport comes to a complete standstill. You can't get a meal; you can't get a drink, you can't get a taxi. You're just a prisoner in the darkness. A night or so ago, during another dinner at Raffles, Carol found the position so intolerable that she took the law into her own hands. By the light of a torch she groped her way into the kitchen and pilfered. It was her only alternative to going hungry for an indefinite period.

Broadcasting under these air-raid conditions is apt to be both a trying and a thankless task. By strict orders of the military, we have to close down our medium-wave transmission the moment there's a "yellow". We continue our programme on the two alternative short waves, but I imagine the change-over robs us of a good many listeners.

I've mentioned the studio on the fifth floor of the Cathay. Well, our main studios at Thomson Road, from which all the English talks, plays and features are given, seem to me even less secure. They're housed in a sort of flimsy bungalow affair and they're neither blastproof nor soundproof. Moreover, with public transportation at a standstill during air raids, Thomson Road is virtually cut off from the town after dark, and short of cadging a lift from a long-suffering colleague your only certain means of turning up at the studios for an evening's broadcast is to arrive before sunset. You then hang about for a few hours until your programme is due and pray for a miracle in the shape of an empty seat in a private car or a really adventurous taxi-driver to get you home again. I suppose I should shoulder the white man's burden of buying a car of my own. But with the future so apparently gloomy (the Japanese are steadily advancing) I haven't yet been able to face the very great hazard of wasting a lot of money thereby.

That enterprising programme, "1941—A Radio Flashback", was eventually completed in rehearsal five minutes or so before it was due on the air. Transmission at 10 p.m. neatly coincided with the evening's second air raid. Two narrators, a news-reader and myself, playing all the Cameos, tried to work up our listeners (though in the circumstances we couldn't feel at all certain we had any) into a pitch of sustained excitement over the dramatic events of last year, while outside the guns boomed and occasional explosions made the studio shake like a jellyfish. In my celebrated impersonation of Hitler, which I render on the smallest encouragement, I had a kind of running fight with the ack-ack boys. I made a great noise, though I can't swear I succeeded in drowning their efforts completely.

The All Clear sounded as soon as the programme was over—that invariably happens—and we then made our way to a New Year's Eve party given by Jane Davis, the chairman's wife.

The chairman has a most impressive house on Mount Rosie, a mile or so from Thomson Road and a few miles out of the town. It was originally built by a German and it was once the official residence of the commander-in-chief. It has an enormous room running the whole length of the building, which is big enough for a museum and looks rather like one. And it has a spacious balcony overlooking a large and beautifully decked garden, with a great, sloping lawn. In peacetime this could have been the setting for a New Year's party to dream about. But as it was the inside of the house had to be effectively blacked out and so was blocked from the balcony and garden, and all hope of an alfresco night's entertainment under the tropical moon was gone. Carol rang up shortly after my arrival and admitted her failure to find a conveyance, so she had to celebrate the advent of 1942 on her own at Raffles. I imagine a similar fate overtook many others, for we guests who did turn up were so few that we were completely absorbed in the vastness of the room. When midnight struck we stood in a shy little circle and sang "Auld Lang Syne" while great oceans of space gaped all around us and our voices drifted feebly away into nothingness.

Afterwards the gramophone encouraged a few couples to take the floor, and there was some eating, drinking, and conversation, and at least one romance was coming to rapid and fullest bloom. At 2 a.m. there was launched the inevitable discussion about how we were going to get home. Eric Robertson offered me a lift, but as he was already committed to taking Peggie to the American mess, it was conditional on my accompanying them there first. Eric has an alarming-looking car—open and battered and shabby, but long, powerful and snorting. He drives murderously by day and like Jehu by night, and to beg for mercy is merely to encourage him to greater feats of daring. To drive with him, in short, is to experience the giddy sensations of the giant switchback but with a hundred-fold the reality of danger.

We had great difficulty in finding the American mess, and soon enough Eric admitted, as is his invariable custom, that his petrol-tank was nearly empty and that he had no coupons left and that all four of his tyres were liable to explode at any moment. When we arrived at length, the party was in that determined stage of hilarity which is the last kick before the finish. I remember a small, smoke-clouded room with a long sort of high table at the far end which was graced by a row of rather frighteningly impressive members. I remember a phenomenally loud gramophone and some prancing on the dance-floor. I remember being served with a plate of bacon and eggs, hot coffee and iced whisky by a charming host. I remember another short air-raid alarm. I don't remember how we contrived to stay there for nearly two hours. But we did. I got back to Raffles at 4 a.m.

Thus I saw the dawn of 1942 in Singapore. I wonder if I shall still be here when the time comes to celebrate next New Year's Eve. I wish I could believe so.

Raffles Hotel—January 11, 1942.

There's been a lull.

The night raids have more or less petered out, and the bombers only come now (if at all) in the early hours of the morning when there's still some moonlight left.   One result of this is that we're extremely busy rebroadcasting programmes which were spoiled in transmission and which in our vanity we suppose are worthy of a full-sized listening public.

On Tuesday last, for example, we crammed three major productions into one evening's programme. The first was a revival of the "Radio Flashback", the second a play about Florence Nightingale designed to rouse the courage of the women of Malaya, and the third a weekly musical feature called "International Blackout".   This doesn't sound remarkable by B.B.C. standards, I know, but our standards aren't and can't be B.B.C. Indeed, our facilities, human and mechanical, are so limited it's really quite an achievement to put on a "live" production of any kind.   For example, it's only possible to have studio rehearsals between 2 and 5 in the afternoon, when the transmitters are off the air.   But as most of our actors are amateurs with jobs of their own to do, they're not free to attend during weekdays.   As a matter of fact, I think it's a tribute to their spirit of service that they help us at all, for they get paid only a token fee for sacrificing their leisure, and there's not much kudos to be had out of taking part in a broadcast play.

Anyway, the result is that almost everything in the way of preparation has to be done at weekends. Furthermore, our studio accommodation is woefully primitive and we have nothing so grand as a dramatic control panel or even a "talk back". We have to rely exclusively on the main control-board to which the gramophone turntables are attached and which is operated by one of the Asiatic control engineers. So that rehearsing a play, apart from any mental strain involved, is apt to be an exhausting business. After you've given your preliminary instructions as carefully and thoroughly as possible, all you can do is to sit hopefully by a loudspeaker in one of the offices and whenever anything goes wrong either in the control-room or the studio, run as fast as your legs can carry you to put it right.

But modesty won't prevent me from saying that, all things considered, I think the M.B.C.'s output of "live" material is really quite creditable. Owing to the complete revision of the programme schedules, we started from scratch at the beginning of the war. We're now keeping up an average of two plays a week, three musical features, one ordinary feature and various talks and readings. So at least we've made progress, and it's a satisfaction to know that the bombs have not been allowed to interfere with it.   I fancy, too, that we've succeeded in making the public a little more radio-conscious. Hudson, who gives the A.R.P.

talks, is an undoubted success, as I predicted he would be. Judging from the mail which comes in for him daily, he already has a large following, and because he is particularly honest and outspoken he'll be able to exert the right kind of influence on civilian morale when the time comes. The other day he was praised for his broadcasts in the *Straits Times*—a remarkable fact, because the *Straits Times* has been consistently and violently hostile to the M.B.C. (There was the hysterical leader about Matthews and the orchestra, for example.) I met Seabridge, the editor, shortly after my arrival here at a luncheon party given by Marie Ney. He wouldn't be drawn out on the subject of the M.B.C. except to say that he had to write about something, and as a matter of fact he hasn't returned to the attack since then. Whether his attitude was ever dictated by a conviction that a fully equipped broadcasting service in Malaya is a waste of money I'm not sure, though I rather gather there was something more deep-rooted behind it. But in any case, the argument that a wartime radio pro-gramme should consist entirely of news bulletins interspaced by a succession of bunged-on gramophone records, though plausible enough, has always struck me as being plain ridiculous. (I don't forget the British public's reaction when the B.B.C. tried it in the early days of September, 1939.) Apart from the intrinsic propagandist value of first-class entertainment, which can and should be considerable, entertainment is the means through which you "sell" your station, the means through which you build up confidence in your news and propaganda services. Ideally, I think, news, propaganda and entertainment should be closely interrelated and should be separated by no rigid department-alism.

Hudson himself is fairly typical of the hard-working majority of Europeans, though he's probably more critical, more aggressive, more fearless than most of them—more determined to push the administration into some kind of action or to assume the responsibilities of leadership himself. To my mind he's one of the men whose names shouldn't be forgotten when this war is over, and whatever the eventual fate of Singapore he deserves praise and recognition. I imagine he allows himself hardly any leisure at all. He's got his own job to do, which is concerned with rubber and is obviously important to the war effort. In addition, he's an extremely active divisional warden and he provides us with two broadcasts a week for which he refuses to accept any reward. On Wednesdays he gives a straight talk on some specific A.R.P. topic. On Fridays he answers questions from listeners, which are put to him by a young American named Al Larson. Most of the letters he receives come from Chinese, who are patently dissatisfied with the A.R.P. position, though they have obvious faith in Hudson's integrity. There are, of course, a great many English-speaking Asiatics in Singapore, and it's a remarkable thing that our English programmes carry more weight with them than the programmes broadcast in their own languages. They suspect that what is said in English is more likely to be true than what is said in Chinese, Malay or Tamil !

I'm always being asked, particularly by representatives of the Services, who are obviously sickened by the state of affairs here and are violently and unreason-ably antipathetic to the civilians, why we don't increase our output of straight propaganda material in the English programmes. One answer is that propa-ganda of any kind is valueless without an assured listening public, and our first task is to popularize the station, which is what we're trying to do now. But another answer is that a broadcasting organization cannot, or at any rate should not, manufacture propaganda of its own. It should merely be concerned with the task of putting out ready-made propaganda in a palatable form. In other words, it should be the kitchen to which raw material is sent for cooking and serving up.

My own relations with the Ministry of Information here have not been particularly fruitful—or, rather, they've been virtually non-existent. I don't think the men in charge have much appreciation or understanding of the potential propagandist value of radio entertainment, or, indeed, of the necessities of an effective broadcast service. So far as they are concerned, the news is all that matters, and the rest can go hang. Consequently, apart from occasional material for short informative talks of local interest only, I haven't received more than one directive of any kind from them—let alone a guidance on general policy. As a matter of fact, I found myself in sharp disagreement with the only positive instruction I have had. It was to broadcast a talk written by the wife of one of the American correspondents here. This lady gave an account of her visit to an island near Singapore where Japanese women are interned. She called the island a "home", described in glowing terms the comfortable, pleasant, luxurious and even privileged conditions of living there, and mentioned, *inter alia*, the wives of one or two distinguished Britishers in Government service who had apparently been doing welfare work on the island. When I pointed out that this talk was almost certain to cause keen resentment, particularly among the Chinese community, I was informed by a Ministry of Information official that its purpose was to refute charges of ill-treatment of internees and thus persuade the Japanese to give British prisoners a better deal. I voiced my feelings as strongly as I dared, but eventually was compelled to make arrangements for the broadcast. The result was inevitable. Judging from the letters we received, the Chinese were enraged, and I don't think the Europeans were well pleased. It remains to be seen whether the Japanese will now decide to behave like little gentlemen !

By contrast, certain officials of the Malayan Government (the Ministry of Information or Far Eastern Bureau, as it is called, is a mission from the Imperial Government) show a keen interest in all the work the M.B.C. is doing and appear to be genuinely good friends of broadcasting. The Governor himself is passionately addicted to the microphone, and goes on the air at every possible opportunity. Jones, the Colonial Secretary, is a keen, regular listener, and he has 'phoned me more than once to praise or criticize certain of our productions. By his own request he is sent advance copies of all Hudson's scripts for approval before transmission. From our point of view this is more a matter of courtesy than obligation, and I don't think we are bound to recognize his right of censorship. However, up to now such minor deletions and alterations as he has made have been wise and fair.

Our Asiatic propaganda, though the programme organizers are doing an admirable job within prescribed limits, is still woefully restricted—not only for reasons which I've already mentioned, but because of the apparent reluctance of the majority of prominent and influential Asiatic citizens to commit themselves in front of a microphone. They're obviously waiting to see which way the cat jumps, and they're not at all anxious to get in wrong with the Japanese in the present precarious situation. I'm more than ever convinced that no real progress can be made unless and until there is a complete reorientation of outlook and policy. That doesn't look like happening.

Another result of the lull is a resurgence of limited merrymaking. The Raffles dance floor was empty during the worst of the night raids, but now it's full again, and one still sees those occasional couples in evening dress trying to forget that Singapore is no longer what it was.

The town is packed with refugees from up country who have had to leave their homes and nearly all their possessions behind. The Singaporeans have been very good to them, and have given shelter to those who need it. Most of the men have joined the L.D.C. or A.R.P. services and their womenfolk have got war jobs of some kind. But one hears complaints that a few are behaving very badly—making impossible demands on private hospitality, sitting around doing nothing, complaining and bewailing and altogether behaving with a complete lack of graciousness and courage. The other day I met a lady who was so palpably sorry for herself that I couldn't feel any sympathy with her at all. She'd just arrived from Kuala Lumpur. Her face was as white as a sheet and lined with worry and she could hardly get her words out. She told me that she and her friends had been infuriated by a recent broadcast of Lady Thomas (the Governor's wife). "What right had Lady Thomas to talk of hardships?" she asked. "You people in Singapore don't know what war means. You've no idea of the ordeal we had to face in Kuala Lumpur. How dare Lady Thomas tell *us* what to do?"

I didn't have the temerity to inform her that Lady Thomas's broadcast appeal to the women of Malaya had been at my suggestion because I considered a reminder of the courageous example set by the women of London and Chungking timely. Indeed, I concluded that there might be some reason in what she said until I learned that the "ordeal" the Europeans of Kuala Lumpur had had to face was one stick of bombs dropped along the main street. Carey has just returned from a flying visit there. He found it quite deserted—a city of the dead—but unscathed except for slight damage to Government buildings.

Of course, these European refugees have had their roots cruelly hacked away, and one shouldn't, I know, minimize or discount the tragedy that has overtaken them. And yet one can't forget, however much they may have lost, that they are lucky to be alive and free. The Asiatics in Malaya haven't fared so well. There has been no escape, no evacuation for them. They have been left behind to their fate, which in the case of the Chinese doesn't bear thinking of. To be fair, the majority of the Europeans realize this perfectly well. I've heard several of them admit that parting with their Asiatic servants was the hardest thing of all to bear. When the moment came they had to do it. But morally and sentimentally it was irreconcilable with their consciences.

We've been doing slightly more lately in the social line. Wherever one goes the war (our war) is the only recurring topic of conversation. One hears bitter criticisms both of the civilian and military authorities, dissatisfaction with the present, recriminations about the immediate past. One hears scare rumours and scandalous revelations. One hears lively, intelligent comments and suggestions. But one hears very little complacent talk. The only optimistic point to which most people stick, gluelike, is that miraculously Singapore will hold.

Last Saturday we gave a cocktail party on the veranda of our room at Raffles. We raked together about a score of guests, including some of my colleagues, some of Carol's, Martin Agronsky and his friend George Weller, who's correspondent for the Chicago *Daily News*. After a few hours we adjourned to the Cathay Restaurant for dinner and finally to the flat of our guardian angel at the Hongkong and Shanghai Bank, Johnny Raikes. There we squatted in semidarkness and listened to samples of Johnny's large and impressive selection of gramophone records. The semi-darkness wasn't an atmospheric device. It's a necessity in all Singapore's dwellings at night-time unless you're prepared to face the alternative of suffocation which the brownout entails.

And then on Friday night, because we felt we must while there was still an opportunity, we went to the New World. It's the only one of the Worlds which has remained open, and even so it closes promptly at ten. Admittedly, we sampled it under bad conditions, for the brownout has not only plunged it into semi-darkness but has made it unbearably stuffy, in spite of its prodigious size. It struck me as being rather like a Messrs. Lyons' conception of a vast Asiatic Palais de Danse. Messrs. Lyons couldn't improve on the Chinese decorations. They would improve, I fancy, on the food and service, and perhaps on the taxi girls, who were rather tatty, it seemed to me. The doleful band playing out-of-date European dance tunes was well up to Lyons Corner House standard. However, it's not fair to judge Singapore's high spots in present circumstances. It's really something of an effort to go gay.

I've been on several occasions to see the Aubrey Herberts at the Seaview Hotel, which is about five miles out and is the great social rendezvous on Sunday mornings. From 11 to 1 an orchestra plays in the Pavilion Lounge and invariably ends its programme with "There'll Always Be An England". The guests join in the vocal chorus, of course. Jane McNaughton (Bunty to her friends) has suggested it's time we broadcast a slightly revised version of this song under the new and inspiring title, "There'll Always Be A Singapore".

Last Sunday morning, by way of a change, Aubrey took me to the swimming-club, which is next door to the airport. In the palmy days before the war it had a dance-band of its own and was the recognized last post of a night's whoopee. All that is over now, of course, but it is still a very engaging place to spend an hour or so of the daytime while the bombers are not around.

As we paddled about in the lukewarm water (we're neither of us particularly athletic swimmers and felt pretty small fish when we saw George Weller diving from the top rung) Aubrey began to speculate on what would befall the M.B.C. if Singapore became untenable. He was speaking more than half in jest, for he is an incurable optimist, and I remember he rubbed his hands in glee when the Germans made the "fatal mistake" of attacking Norway. But as a matter of fact the ugly word "evacuation" is already in the air. Carol's department at the Naval Base was closed down some days ago and the majority of it packed off to Colombo. She and her colleague Bunty have now got jobs in another Admiralty department at Kranji. I rather wish Aubrey had refrained from dragging me into the morbid future, for this visit to the swimming-club was by far the most refreshing experience since my arrival in Singapore. The pool is large and clean and was remarkably uncrowded. The dressing-room accommodation is spacious and well-equipped. And there are little shaded tables at which you can sit and savour something of the atmosphere of peace. I'm seriously thinking of becoming a member, and I'm told there won't be any difficulty about this provided I can satisfy the committee that not a drop of Asiatic blood flows through my veins.

What a gesture it would be to throw open a few of Singapore's famous clubs to Asiatic membership! That's an extravagant thought, perhaps. But I deplore the traditional attitude on the Asiatic question to which too many hard-boiled Malayan Europeans still cling, though the sands are running so perilously low. In my experience it's entirely unnecessary to shout at or bully-rag native servants, and the White Raj manner strikes me as being more ill-bred than sensible. The other day, when the Raffles veranda was crowded out before lunch, a group of ladies grew quite hysterical because they couldn't obtain immediate attention for their order. Finally they got hold of one of the boys by his coat-sleeves and bellowed at him. That sort of behaviour is not only disgusting, it's excessively short-sighted in the present circumstances.

For, make no mistake, the sands *are* running perilously low. We know it in our hearts, though most of us won't admit it in so many words. Mac, who's a born pessimist, says quite openly that Singapore hasn't got a chance. Carey feels instinctively that Singapore will hold, though he's not better than anyone else at arguing rationally about it. Cecil Brown has been banned from the microphone for plain speaking—and quite rightly, I think. The London news-papers have been making a great fuss about it, which shows how badly out of touch they are. I don't doubt that what Brown has been saying is the truth, and possibly there's no harm in his American audience hearing it. But unfortunately his broadcasts can also be picked up by Singapore listeners, and that just isn't allowable in present circumstances. I can't imagine the Russians letting Cecil Brown loose at one of their microphones.

There's been a lull. But I anticipate that it's very nearly over. So far the Japanese have attempted only token air raids by daylight, but now that they've captured Kuantan and Ipoh and Kuala Lumpur they'll presumably be able to send over large forces of fighter-escorted bombers. Whether we'll be able to repeat the Battle of Britain here I don't know, though rumour has it that we've at last got some Hurricanes to send into the air. Personally, I don't relish the prospect of mass daytime air raids.

While I write, Carol is busily packing in the bedroom. We've at length summoned up the courage and the energy to move from Raffles, having been driven out as much by the cockroaches and the poor service, which grows steadily worse every day owing to shortage of staff, as by the expense. We've acquired a self-contained flat in a bungalow annexe of the Goodwood Park Hotel, to which we were introduced by the McNaughtons, who have lived in the main building for some while. We've agreed on an inclusive charge of $434 a month, which is huge enough in all conscience and nearly as much as the $500 we're paying here. But Singapore is now even fuller than it was at the beginning of the war because of the large number of refugees from up country, and, as landlords are un-scrupulously intent on making profits while there's still a chance, prices have shot up in consequence. The flat, I'm bound to confess, is delightful. It's comfortably and lightly furnished and, unlike so many of Singapore's European dwellings, which for some unaccountable reason are darkly and gloomily coloured, is decorated in cream and pale green. It is on the upper floor and it has two bedrooms, two bathrooms and a large veranda sitting-room overlooking the gravel drive, which leads to the bungalow, and the hillocks and banks of grass, the massive leafy trees, the thick bushes, and the clusters of tropical flowers which are all part of the private grounds of the Goodwood Park Hotel. On the whole, I think we are very lucky to have found it.

I'm hoping against hope that we may be allowed to make some kind of home there. I'm sick to death of moving, and I've no desire to leave Singapore. On the contrary, the Japanese threat to this island's future already has a personal significance for me. There are so many things I like about it. I like the climate. It suits me. I feel well here and I never felt well in England. I like the hot sun which makes an eternal summer and the occasional thunderstorms and tor-rential showers. I like the unchangeableness of the days and the seasons. I like the clothes one wears, the cool white trousers and palm-beach coats and the featherweight suits. I like the hodgepodge variety in style and architecture and atmosphere of the town itself, the inharmonious blendings of civilizations, the crazy transitions from cleanliness to dirt, from luxury to squalor, from monumental dignity to exotic grandiloquence, from British Government buildings to oriental palaces, from suburbia to Chinatown—West perpetually sightseeing East, and East, West. I like the tropical beauty of the island scene, though I haven't explored nearly as much of it as I would wish. I like my colleagues at the M.B.C. I like most of the Asiatics with whom I have come in contact and some of the Europeans. Above all, I like my job, which keeps me occupied with my first love, entertainment, but does not bind me exclusively to it. For me, it is one job in a million.

There are many things I don't like. But if coming events rob me of the particular joy of living I've found in Singapore I shall have an eternal regret.

Goodwood Park Hotel—January 25, 1942.

The news could hardly be worse. But I've bought a car at last. It's a very old Vauxhall, and Carol, in spite of a long and sentimental attachment to Vauxhalls, refuses to ride in it, which is very snobbish and very timid of her and makes me afraid she's getting pre-war Singaporitis. Admittedly, it doesn't look much. Its leather upholstery is peeling badly, two of its wings are battered, and it has a number of old bottles and tin cans in the back which I haven't the heart to remove. But buried beneath its doughty bonnet, I'm convinced, is a heart of gold. Its previous owner confided in me that though he himself had acquired it second-hand, he had come to love it as his own child. He went into raptures over its "pick-up" and its "compression", and unfolded a veritable saga about its "distributor". He admitted that its petrol gauge no longer worked, but claimed that this flaw in an otherwise perfect specimen mattered less than I might imagine, for the engine was altogether so extraordinary that it could almost be said to run without petrol. He was on the point of tears when I agreed to the purchase, but was comforted by the thought that his dear one was at least falling into good hands. Indeed, he flattered me with the gratuitous information that it was for that reason he had refused several more lucrative offers.

I have since discovered other exceptional qualities in the car about which he evidently knew nothing. To begin with, it can be driven without brakes. It can't be driven any other way. And then its self-starter, which never works, is superfluous for the reason that its ignition-key has the curious habit of turning round and round in its socket without producing any effect on the engine whatsoever, which means, of course, that the motor is kept running night and day and is thus the first-known example of perpetual motion.

I sometimes think that my flair for buying cars is one of the few gifts I've inherited from my father. He began shortly after the last war (I'm not counting the auto-wheel he acquired in 1917 and which exploded in the same year) with a Singer. This dainty, second-hand open four-seater had a temperamental steering-wheel which was attracted to ditches as by a magnet. After it had found its last resting-place in a rural hollow somewhere between Maidenhead and Oxford, my father became a pioneer in the purchase of the Galloway—a Scottish make which has, I fancy, since deserted the market. Passing over the De Dion Bouton, which kept up a remarkable average of ten punctures a week, and the red Citroën, whose radiator was magically transformed into a hot-water spring, he bought in his latter years a small but speedy sports model to celebrate his début as a film star. This purchase really represented the climacteric of his achievements, for the engine developed a complaint so chronic that it could only be temporarily relieved by blowing down the petrol-tank and so eccentric that even the original makers at Coventry were avowedly unable to diagnose it.

Though I don't doubt my choice is a good one, I sometimes wonder why I've bought a car at all, especially since the market value of cars has reached a record low and the largest and most powerful models can be picked up for a song. But the truth is, it's impossible to live and do one's work without one, for buses run infrequently and seldom if ever in the right direction and taxis are now completely unprocurable. As a matter of fact, I first became aware of the hopelessness of my situation without a car of my own on the day we moved into our new flat at Goodwood Park. We gave a housewarming cocktail party that evening, and as I had a broadcast later, Carey drove me up to Thomson Road. The arrangement was that he and Carol would pick me up again after the programme at 10 p.m.

It was raining cats and dogs and I wasn't altogether surprised when they didn't turn up at the time agreed, especially as I'd had a message earlier to the effect that Carey had got waterlogged on his way back to Goodwood Park. But by 11 p.m. I was anxious; by midnight I was frantic; by 1 a.m. I was desperate; and by 2 a.m. I was so sorry for myself that I could hardly listen to Carol, who told me over the telephone, in a voice choked with emotion, that they'd met with a serious accident. Here was I forced to spend the remainder of the night sitting upright in an office chair while mosquitoes dive-bombed me ceaselessly and relentlessly from every conceivable angle. And to make matters worse, I was wearing my best suit—that same suit which had already come disastrously in contact with the red paint at Jamaica and had only recently been cleansed of it.

Next morning Arthur Jeffries, one of our most enterprising and kindest-hearted engineers, came to my rescue with an offer of a lift to Goodwood Park, otherwise I see no reason why I shouldn't have been stuck at Thomson Road indefinitely. After breakfast I felt better disposed to listen to Carol's story, and I had to admit—to myself, though not to her—that she'd had a worse time than I. Apparently Carey lost his way in the storm and took the wrong turning. The car then burst into flames and they eventually came to a halt on the lawn of a private house. The owners of the house—European husband and wife—behaved with excessive discourtesy. They couldn't (or wouldn't) provide any water with which to extinguish the flames. They couldn't (or wouldn't) offer Carol and Carey even temporary shelter. And they added insult to injury by saying that while they didn't mind the Japanese, they really were not prepared to put up with "this sort of thing". As if by way of excuse, the wife explained that her nerves were very much on edge because she'd just been evacuated, and that though she'd been two days in the house she didn't know where the kitchen was. "Oh !" exclaimed Carol, all sympathy in a flash, "I'm so sorry. Were you in Penang or Hongkong ?" "No," she replied. "We've come from the Seaview Hotel." The Seaview Hotel, mark you—which is just five miles from Raffles and which still houses Aubrey Herbert and his wife and three children and doubtless many other gallant ladies and gentlemen ! The end of the story was that Carey and Carol had to abandon the car, which was by then virtually burnt out, and make their way back to Goodwood Park through the torrential rain.

In the last fortnight our routine of life has been transformed. We are now

E

living under real blitz conditions. True, there is still no very noticeable shortage of essential commodities, and such rationing as has been introduced is of the mildest kind. True again, the so-called martial law which was recently proclaimed has had hardly any apparent effect and the military seem strangely shy to use the powers now vested in them. But none the less the enemy is approaching very close to our gates and he reminds us with monotonous regularity of his dangerous proximity.

Unless weather conditions are exceptionally bad, one can look forward to at least three raids during the daylight hours as a certainty. Mostly they take place in the mornings, and for some reason which I don't pretend to understand we're usually allowed to spend our afternoons in peace. Apparently the Japanese have a kind of a bombers' timetable, and they vary it very little.

It's difficult to assess the effect which the raids are having on one's stamina. Superficially, one has little cause to be worried by them, for so far there's been nothing approaching an indiscriminate attack, and on only one occasion have bombs, which were quite evidently intended for Government House, fallen in the European residential quarter. The Japanese are concentrating more or less exclusively on military objectives. It looks as if they've definitely set their hearts against causing any unnecessary destruction. Indeed, one can't resist the conclusion that they're quite confident of capturing Singapore and want the prize as little damaged as possible. At any rate, their 'planes do not buzz relentlessly overhead, they do not hover in the sky or drop incendiaries and high explosives in haphazard fashion. They fly over in perfect formation, make straight for their targets, discharge their load, which is usually made up of pretty small stuff, and then make off. The result is that one's moments of acute alarm, though concentrated, are comparatively rare and shortlived.

And yet the very fact that the bombers are able to employ such tactics is extremely demoralizing. It's proof that they can do, practically speaking, as they choose, and it's a warning that at any moment they can blast Singapore and its inhabitants off the face of the earth.

Our defences are pathetically weak. There was considerable excitement when the first Hurricanes were spotted in the air, but the promise which they seemed to portend has not been fulfilled.

It was a big fillip to morale when the news came through that thirteen Jap 'planes had been destroyed in one morning. It produced hopes that we might eventually be able to beat back the bombers. Certainly it seemed as if some progress had at length been made, for it was a major victory in comparison with anything that had gone before. But it didn't look quite so good next day when the official communiqué reported that of the thirteen 'planes brought down, nine were accounted for by ack-ack fire and only four by our fighters. And, in fact, it was an isolated record which has not since been improved upon or even maintained. The plain truth is that the small number of Jap 'planes destroyed each day—not invariably without loss to ourselves—is an insufficient deterrent, and one has no good grounds for hoping that the raids will slacken or peter out. On the contrary, one has every reason for believing that they will get progressively worse. And thus one is apparently condemned to grope through a tunnel which may collapse at any moment, but which has no end.

Meanwhile, the Government is doing nothing to tackle the urgent question of air-raid shelters, with the result that the labour shortage is getting more and more acute. Even a token gesture would be better than the present policy of ignoring the problem completely. It's easy to criticize the Asiatic workmen who have deserted their posts and cannot be persuaded to return, but what better can be expected from them when their families are in such obvious jeopardy and have no more solid protection than the street-side drains or their own flimsy dwellings? The situation is lamentable, and an illustration of it is the passage leading from a side entrance of the Cathay to the cinema building, which is now the equivalent of one of London's tube-station shelters. Day and night it's cluttered up with poor, ill-clad, pathetic-looking Asiatics, huddled together like frightened animals, lost to all feelings but the instinct for self-preservation. They eat and sleep there and presumably find it so much safer than any other bolt-hole to which they have access that for them it's a natural fortress. They daren't leave it even when the All Clear has sounded. And yet this passage is at ground level. It can't really be classed as a good surface shelter even. A small bomb falling outside would blast it into a death-trap.

Shelters apart, the A.R.P. organization, though its individual members both Asiatic and European are said to be doing admirable and courageous work, is considered by no means adequate; and the failure to make it so is only one of the charges against the Malayan Government, which is now virtually discredited and is being openly assailed on all sides. A scapegoat had to be found, and the choice has fallen on Jones, the Colonial Secretary. From all I gather, this dismissal of Jones was a rather clumsy political move which has deceived few people here, and has certainly done nothing to bolster up public confidence. In the small amount of business which I had personally with the Colonial Secretary, I found him both helpful and considerate and a staunch and appreciative friend of broadcasting. I have also heard that he was one of the only men in authority to foresee the size and imminence of the danger ahead. Had he been allowed his way, Malaya would have been emptied of its European women and children months before the Japanese attacked. And what an inestimably wise move that would have been! Instead, the choice of stay or go, return or remain away, was left to the individual, and as the attitude of blind refusal to contemplate the possibility of war, so characteristic of civilian Malaya, prevailed in most cases, the result today is an insoluble evacuation problem.

In the Cathay (and in most offices, I think) the Alert is no longer the signal to take cover, for a Jim Crow system has been introduced and a buzzer informs us when we're in real danger. But restaurants, shops, etc., still close down the moment the warning sounds, and taxis mysteriously disappear from the streets. On the day the raids first started in earnest I had to do without lunch and breakfast, and now I've adopted the procedure of taking a packet of sandwiches with me to the office every morning in order to make certain of getting something to eat.

Though one is forced to realize from such outside evidence as the labour shortage that on the whole the Asiatics are standing up badly to the air raids, I can't report from personal observation that a craven spirit is by any means common to them all. So far as our own staff is concerned, there hasn't been a single case of desertion of duty—and this goes for the drivers, messenger boys, etc., as well as for the top men, such as control engineers.

Admittedly, there is a noticeable lack of ebullience even among the Europeans and there is little of that capacity to laugh and jest which is usually so characteristic of the Britisher in times of crisis. But of course we've no reason for optimism. We've virtually no faith left in the future. We're not in the mood to dig ourselves in, as it were, for we don't honestly feel we've got the time to do it. Events are moving too rapidly upon us, and there's no let-up at all in the news, which gets worse and worse.   Any day now we must expect air raids to be supplemented by bombardment.

If one thinks about the situation, planning ahead is a painful process.   In the M.B.C. office nowadays it seems just an extravagant waste of time to decide on what programmes one is going to broadcast next week, or the week after. So the only solution is not to think about the situation—to ignore it, or at any rate to isolate it from one's work.   As a matter of fact, we're actually increasing our radio output and have got so far organized that we now have projected arrangements a month in advance.   But one really couldn't be bothered to write out a schedule of productions for the last week in February if one allowed one's mind too much preoccupation with the military position!

But perhaps I'm too bound up with my mood of the moment.   With happenings so crowded, and with the situation for ever changing and changing so swiftly, a week or even a day ago is apt to seem like an age.   I feel that I have been in Singapore a lifetime, or rather that the part of my life I have spent here is quite separate from the rest, has no connection with it.   And I feel, too, that the good friends I have made here are lifetime friends.   And I feel that all my memories of trivial things—gay and cheerful and dissociated with the war—and all the esoteric jokes at which I've laughed and at which others have laughed with me, are imperishable.   These memories and these jokes cannot be recorded.   And yet for us who have shared them, if we survive, what an immeasurably rich harvest of "do you remembers" they will provide!

How little Carol and I really know of Singapore!   We're still strangers in the town and we've hardly explored the island.   We've done very few of the things a conscientious visitor in peacetime was presumably intent on doing. We've stayed at Raffles, we've drunk stengahs (at the Tanglin Club), we've been to the New World, we've eaten curry tiffin (once), we've ridden in rickshas— and that's about all.   (Incidentally, I always feel rather barbaric when I ride in a ricksha, and to salve my conscience usually pay the coolie more than I would a taxi-driver.   But often there's no alternative.)

Every morning Carol and her three girl friends—Bunty McNaughton, Joan Tanner, and Joan Reid—drive off to Kranji, a military objective.   Once or twice they've been caught *en route* and have had to lie flat in a ditch, and seemingly they spend a good part of their working hours sheltering under the office table. But they carry on.

Every morning I chug down in my Vauxhall to the Cathay, hoping I'll arrive before the morning's first Alert.   We just haven't had the time or the opportunity to familiarize ourselves with the place where we intended to spend three years, or with its ways and customs which we thought we were going to dislike so heartily.   And yet if fate should send us away tomorrow, Singapore would mean more to us than to the most thorough-minded tourist.   We would remember vividly every little thing that was said or done, everything which amused or irritated us, made us cheerful or depressed, the gay things and the sad things, big events and small.   For us the significance of the few weeks we've spent here would be historic.

I cannot help feeling a little proud that our ordinary broadcast programmes, sandwiched in between the news bulletins, which grow daily more ominous, continue undismayed, thus preserving an atmosphere of normality in an otherwise abnormal existence.

Courageously and optimistically, a man named Carter flew from Australia at the beginning of this month to join our programme staff. Carter is a "strip writer" by profession. A strip, for the benefit of the uninformed (admittedly it was a new one on me), is a dramatized news item. And Carter is entirely devoted to his art. Come bombs, come thunder, he sits all day long banging out strips on his typewriter, only emerging at irregular intervals, when the excitement is too much for him, to tell us that he's just polished off a "peach of a strip", or that he's about to embark on a "beauty of a strip", or that he's in the middle of a strip which is "a hundred per cent". He's now responsible for a weekly feature called "Malayan Newsreel", which is largely made up of strips. It's acted by a group of three or four enthusiasts (including the author in person), who transform themselves from Nazi *gauleiters* to British majors, from Chinese *amahs* to lady diplomats with amazing dexterity and verve. The Malayan in the title is unfortunately something of a hyperbole, for even Carter can't conjure up sufficient "local news" to fill a three-quarter-hour bill. Too often he has to fall back on out-of-date overseas items gleaned from what I shrewdly suspect, though cannot prove, is a strip-writer's manual.

I admire Carter's imperturbability. And I admire Marie Ney's too. Seemingly, nothing can upset her singleness of purpose ; and with her great assistance we've now embarked on a schedule of plays which ranges from Shakespeare to Crazy Comedy. Only the other day we cabled Bernard Shaw for permission to present the "Trial Scene" from *Saint Joan*, and when the answer came back agreeing to a fee of fifteen pounds it gave me momentary confidence that I wasn't, after all, completely isolated from the outside world.

I sometimes think that the stage is one of the best possible trainings in self-discipline. Marie Ney is an unusually nervous woman, and when she first arrived in Singapore she didn't attempt to disguise her dread of air raids. But now she never betrays so much as a tremor. To all appearances she's a model of calm and self-possession. She'd make an ideal shelter marshal, and I've noticed occasions when her example has had an obviously soothing influence on some of the more excitable Asiatics. Perhaps her only rival in this respect is my secretary Miss Glazebrook, who has an unaccountable but irresistible inclination to watch the Japanese 'planes fly over in formation instead of taking cover when the buzzers go. But Miss Glazebrook arrived in Singapore with a ready-made reputation. It was her habit to ride about London on a bicycle when the bombs fell in the autumn of 1940.

Incidentally, there is a good deal of resentment at the moment (justified, I think) at the disproportionate amount of publicity given to the Australian troops. But the streamer headlines which greeted the news that they'd gone into action, when compared with the consistent official silence about the doings of the British troops, have hardly been justified by events, for in fact the Australians seem to be staging the fastest retreat of the entire campaign. Maybe the odds have been weighted too heavily against them. Maybe they have fought with great gallantry. But so, too, have our own men, and their ordeal has been measurably longer. Why not pay at least equal attention to the Argylls and Sutherlands, for example, who have fought their way heroically right down the peninsula? Or to the Loyals, who went into action some weeks ago and who, according to rumours that have trickled through, were very badly mauled. Jack McNaughton was with the Loyals. And Jack is now missing.

Perhaps the habit of focusing the limelight exclusively on Australian troops is a matter of fixed policy. It seems persistent enough in all conscience. But in the present state of the war such a policy, so it seems to me, has clearly outlived whatever uses it may once have had. At the shortest-sighted view the defence of Malaya is just as vital to Australia as it is to Britain, and presumably Australians are quite aware that they are serving their own interests by taking part in it, and need no special wooing from us. A policy of recruitment by flattery is, therefore, unnecessary, and, for the rest, it merely results in misunderstanding, ill-will and, incidentally, telling shots for Axis propaganda.

Now that Jack's missing (the report came in a day or two ago) I think of the number of evenings I sat with him and Bunty in their darkened bed-sitting-room at Goodwood Park. We were exiles together then. We were at ease as only people who share the same point of view can be, and we had much to criticize, much to bemoan, and also much to laugh at. The very word "stengah" was an enduring joke. Jack had no more love for the European way of life out here than your average newspaper correspondent. He owed no loyalty to Singapore; he hated the place. But he has fought for it and maybe died for it, or, at any rate, has sacrificed his freedom. I hope that his reward, and the reward of many others like him, will be something better than oblivion.

Carey went to the front the other day, though we're not quite certain what that means now. The most optimistic reports put the front seventy miles away, but I gather twenty would be nearer the mark. It's strange to remember how often one's tried to imagine the feelings of people living in the shadow of an enemy advance and now to realize that one's experiencing the actual thing. As a matter of truth one can't realize it, or rather one won't allow oneself to do so. Read in the newspapers that the Germans are twenty miles from Moscow and the distance seems infinitesimal; know that the Japanese are twenty miles from Singapore and the distance seems infinite.

The air-raid alarm has just sounded. In the Cathay I wait for the buzzer and then sit on the stone stairs or wander down to the basement shelter. In the flat, where I am now, I wait for the sound of the guns and then move to one of the slit trenches with which the grounds of Goodwood Park are plentifully provided.

It's a beautiful morning—one of Singapore's best. The venetian blinds are drawn and I can lean over my balcony and gaze out at the mounting sweep of garden under a sky which is a vast canopy of blue. Faced with so lovely and tranquil a scene, one gets a glimpse of eternity, and one is comforted by the thought that though the Japs may blast the works of mankind and gain by violence temporary possession of all that is now ours, they can do no more than ruffle Nature.

But the illusion of peace is over. The guns are booming and I must be off to the trench.

Goodwood Park Hotel,
Friday, January 29, 1942.

It's another of those beautiful mornings, and Carol is busy packing. She's leaving Singapore this afternoon.

The Admiralty have made all the arrangements, for she's being sent away so that she can carry on with her job elsewhere. She's not sure where she is going yet (she hasn't been and she doesn't think she will be told), but she guesses Java.

It happened very suddenly. On Wednesday night we entertained her boss to dinner and he was refreshingly cheerful. He refused to admit any cause for alarm or despondency, and talked of the urgent need of boosting morale and the folly and shame of prevailing defeatism. Yesterday morning, however, when Carol arrived at the office she found there was no work for her to do. She spent the day in idleness while she watched papers being burned and obvious preparations being made to close down.

Last night I brought Eric and Peggie back with me to Goodwood Park for a drink. We'd been doing a broadcast at Thomson Road together, and afterwards had had supper with Marie Ney and her husband. We'd spent quite a carefree evening and had laughed a good deal. We hadn't thought much about the war or of coming events, and there'd only been one brief air raid to remind us of them.

We found Carey with Carol. He'd turned up unexpectedly from the front. They both looked rather solemn, and I guessed at once that something must have happened to make their mood out of key with ours. That's how it goes nowadays. Then Carol broke the news to me she'd received instructions an hour or so ago to be ready to leave Singapore tomorrow afternoon. I was jerked so painfully back to reality that for a while I thought I wanted no one near. However, if this was our last evening together, it was like many others we had spent with a few friends in the blue-lit balcony flat at Goodwood Park. And so we lay comfortably back and drank and talked until it was time to go to bed.

I won't attempt to describe my feelings now that I know Carol is actually going and that I may never see her again. But it's really happened very fortunately. There had been some dispute between the four girls of Kranji, who've been friends and colleagues now since the early days of the war—how long ago that seems! They were all obstinately determined to stay until the end. But whereas Bunty and Joan Reid were free agents in the matter, Joan Tanner's husband had insisted on her leaving, and I'd already made up my mind that I must send Carol away; in fact, I had arranged to get her off on an American evacuee ship. Now the issue is settled.

Did I once say that it was the clear duty of every European woman to remain in Singapore so long as she could be of service? Well, it's easy enough to think and talk like that from a purely objective point of view. But when the issue is personal and pressing, one regards it very differently. In any case, it seems obvious now that, with the exception of trained nurses, women in Singapore will be much more of a hindrance than a help. The siege is upon us. We may hold out for days, weeks, even months. No one supposes we can hold out indefinitely and no one supposes that life is going to be anything but unmitigated hell.

Of course, the Asiatics lose still more faith in British honour and British omnipotence when they see shiploads of European evacuees scurrying out of Singapore harbour, especially since they are aware that immigration laws make it impossible for more than a handful of their own kind to get away. But on balance it's too late to worry any longer about Asiatic morale. That, in my judgment, has already been destroyed beyond repair by two recent events emanating from London. The first was the recall of Duff Cooper and the second was Churchill's triumphant House of Commons speech in which the Prime Minister admitted that the Japanese were sweeping through Johore and that worse news must be expected. What else could the simple mind deduce but that Singapore was already given up for lost? From the beginning the Japanese have tried by insidious propaganda to spread the belief that the British were preparing to abandon Malaya and Singapore. Regrettably, they have been aided in this task by certain actions and speeches of Allied statesmen, notably Australia's Mr. Curtin. Churchill, so it seems to me, must have been very badly advised of the situation here to have spoken as he did.

It's pretty awful for Bunty, as there's still no news of Jack, and it's ten days now since he was reported missing. The remnants of the Loyals are back in Singapore. From what Bunty has been able to gather, there are good grounds for believing that Jack is alive, though it seems likely that he's been taken prisoner. I think she understands that there's no point in her hanging on here any longer.

I went down to the bank with her earlier this morning. It was feverishly crowded, and but for Johnny Raikes, who came to our rescue, we should have been hours cashing our cheques and arranging for letters of credit. Indeed, all appearances point to the beginnings of a general exodus. It's rumoured that at least three big ships are due to sail today. I can't avoid the rather frightening feeling of being left behind. Carol and Bunty are leaving, and so are several of the women members of the M.B.C. staff. Moreover, it looks as if Singapore will soon be depleted of the majority of its newspaper correspondents, which is a bad enough sign in all conscience. Outside the bank I met George Weller, who told me he was off to Java this afternoon and bade me a fond farewell. Martin Agronsky has already gone.

I wish I could believe there was a real chance of this place holding. But I can't. Carey, who's just back from the front, says the game is up. According to him, we haven't got a serviceable airfield left on Singapore Island. His predictions have been gloomy throughout. But unfortunately they've been pretty well accurate.

I must, however, record one arrival amidst all the departures. Eric Davis, the M.B.C. chairman, flew from England just after Christmas and got back to Singapore yesterday afternoon. I haven't met him yet. To be honest, I'm not looking forward to the encounter. I've heard so many stories whispered against him by people who were here when he first came out. It's alleged that he's tactless and that he's largely responsible for the unpopularity of the M.B.C. The stories may be malicious or senseless—they very possibly are. But nevertheless they've made me fearful that I may not like Davis, or at any rate may not be able to accord him that respect which one should have for one's chief if one wants to be at all comfortable in a job.

And yet, in spite of my prejudice, I've already one solid reason for admiring him. It must have been obvious to him, unless he's the blindest fool, that to come back to Singapore was to gamble very heavily with his life, or at any rate with his freedom. He had every excuse for not showing up at so late and so hopeless an hour. He was urged by cable to stay put in India, whither his wife had already gone, and later was urged to stay in Batavia. But he has ignored the pleas and warnings. He has disregarded the excuse to avoid a perilous adventure which can have no reward. He has returned to join his staff in beleaguered Singapore. And that, I'm persuaded, is an act of considerable courage.

Later.

It's only a matter of hours since my last entry, but I think that every minute has impressed itself indelibly on my memory.

The day that's passed has been the hottest of my experience in Singapore—so hot that it was impossible to wear even a palm beach coat with any comfort. We left Goodwood Park shortly after lunch, though I don't remember that we actually ate anything. We were in something of a daze, hardly realizing what we were about.

We strapped Carol's huge cabin trunk on the carrier of the Vauxhall, which held it, much to my surprise, for the trunk is phenomenally heavy and on our journey out I had seen tough, strong-armed Australians wince and pale and stagger under its weight. Even so, Carol was not able to take away with her more than a portion of her belongings, and some of her dresses, which she will never see again, still hang limply and sadly in the closets of our bedroom.

Carey agreed to drive, and as we were already late it was necessary to travel as swiftly as possible. We stopped at the bank on the way to pick up the draft which I'd arranged for that morning. Johnny Raikes came out for a moment to say good-bye. He was amazingly calm and cheerful, and parted from Carol as if she were just off for a holiday and would soon be back. The banks have done a splendid job in the last few days of crisis. They have remained open throughout the air raids and have coped with a mountain of extra work efficiently. Indeed, on reflection, I wonder if I've been grossly unfair in thinking ill of Singapore's Europeans. When I remember men like Johnny Raikes I think that I have. Or is it, perhaps, that Singapore has at last been purged of all its feeble elements?

Near the docks we ran into a phalanx of cars, four and five deep—cars of all shapes and sizes. Carey stormed and hooted and wheedled us through the entrance. But for him I don't think we should have ever made it. Left to my own devices, I doubt if I'd have even found the way.

When he'd got us safely parked in a definite line, and there was nothing for it but to wait our turn patiently, he said a hurried good-bye and I took the wheel. He had to get back to his unit. We moved along slowly—stop, go—foot by foot more or less. I had plenty of time to look around, and I recognized several acquaintances. There, sitting in the back of a milk-van with her small son, was the woman who had travelled with us to Singapore eight weeks ago and had been convinced that war in the East was impossible. I suppose that with the dearth of taxis a milk-van was the only conveyance she could find.

It was only a question of getting a porter to carry the luggage from the car. There were no formalities to be gone through—no Customs examination, no passport control, no ticket supervision. This was an evacuee ship. It was a great grey monster, American owned, I fancy, and far larger and more imposing than any we had known on our outward journey. I told Carol she'd better embark at once so as to make sure of getting some kind of accommodation. I would have her trunk carried down to the hold and would stand sentinel by the rest of her luggage until she rejoined me and could let me know what she wanted done with it. Alas, we were very innocent, for though this might have been a good enough arrangement in peacetime it was certainly far too refined to be practical in the present brutal circumstances of war and defeat.

Besides the vast concourse of women and children there were, much to my surprise, quite a number of troops travelling and some R.A.F. personnel. Army lorries filled with the men's equipment trundled recklessly on to the quay, and Carol's little pile of luggage—three small suitcases, two large sun-hats and a picture-frame containing George Belcher's *Punch* drawing of my father—was in their way, so I had to shift it.   I moved it again—under the projecting tin roof of one of the Customs sheds—when the rain started to trickle down, but I was still not very far away from the spot where we'd agreed to meet and I thought that Carol could not fail to find me.   Fortunately, there was no tropical storm, else luggage and I would have been drenched.   The rain ceased and the sweltering heat continued.

After half an hour I grew impaient.   I paced up and down the length of the ship.   I joined the fringe of the milling throng by the gangway and strained my eyes in vain for sight of Carol or one of her friends.   With the continual surge of people going upwards, I imagined it would be impossible for anyone to come down for a long while yet.   I paced the quay again, occasionally looking up at the top deck in the hope of seeing Carol among the passengers who were clustered there.   I sat down on an empty trolley, still searching.   I returned to the gangway.   The crowd was no smaller, and it looked as if the procession upwards would never dwindle or cease.   I began to realize what I should have known from the beginning—that, once aboard, Carol would not be allowed off again.

And so the wretched, anxious business of pacing the quay, standing by the gangway, and sitting on the trolley continued.   At one period there was a short-lived air-raid alarm.   The workers on the quayside disappeared into the bowels of the ship, though embarkation, so far as I could judge, went on without a pause, for the throng by the gangway remained.   It occurred to me I was perilously close to a likely target, but as I couldn't persuade myself to take cover and was, anyway, convinced in my present mood that I didn't much care what happened, I just walked round in little nervous circles.

The All Clear sounded and the noisy, heartless, bustling activity of the quayside was resumed.   After another hour and a half I felt pretty desperate.   I encountered two soldiers who told me they'd been diverted to Singapore on their way to Egypt and now had no idea whither they were bound.   When I informed them of my predicament they offered to take the rest of Carol's luggage aboard, and that seemed the only sensible thing to be done now, for I'd long ago given up hope that she'd be able to come ashore again herself.

It seemed a long while before they returned.   They said they'd put the luggage in a safe place, but could find no trace of Carol.   I urged them to accept a tip, but they refused.   They were glad to do anything they could to help.   We were all in this thing together.

I continued to hang around—foolishly and hopelessly now.   I felt very conscious of my presence and of being out of place, with nothing to do and no point in remaining where I was.   I couldn't bear to leave until the ship had actually sailed, and yet I was sure I was wasting my time by staying.

I was sitting on the trolley, when someone shouted in my ear, "There's a lady asking for you."   I turned round and saw Carol standing at the head of the gangway, an agonized expression on her face.   I dashed along the quayside, edged my way through the crowd, ducked under the rope, and was by her side, looking up at her.   The ship's officer supervising embarkation told her she'd have to move.   She was blocking the passageway.   I don't think she heard him. Anyway, she took no notice.   "I thought I'd never see you again," she said.   "I thought I wouldn't see you to say good-bye."   There was time to say good-bye now, and that was all. The ship's officer turned to her again. "Break it up," he said—or words to that effect. "There are hundreds of others who feel just as badly as you do." He was quite right, of course.

I hate partings, anyway, and I've had to endure a good many in the last few months. But this was by far the worst of my life. I'd no idea where Carol was going or if and when I should see her again, and I've none now. She thought Batavia, but from what I gathered at the quay her ship was bound direct for Colombo. I rather hope she gives up her job and goes on to the United States, where she'll be with her own family. It doesn't seem there's much chance of our meeting again until the war's over. How long will that be? How old will we be by then?

I walked away from the quay so depressed I thought myself without ambition to go anywhere. But my mood soon changed to one of intense, frenzied irritation. I couldn't find the Vauxhall. It wasn't where I'd left it. After I'd walked up and down the car park at least half a dozen times without seeing a trace of it I reluctantly, unbelievingly, came to the conclusion that it had gone for good. Then I noticed a couple of soldiers tinkering with the lock of a car which obviously didn't belong to them, and this reminded me of something I ought to have done a day or two ago and hadn't. Miss Glazebrook had given me a bit of paper which bore the printed inscription, "On Government Service, Not To Be Requisitioned". She'd urged me to paste it on my windscreen at once, for she said that otherwise the car was likely to be requisitioned without notice or warning. Like a fool, I thought she was just telling me a fairy story— at least I felt confident the Army would have to be pretty hard up for transport before it considered taking over my Vauxhall.

As a matter of fact, I'm still far from certain that the Army has taken it, for the order allowing the military to requisition has resulted in an outbreak of wholesale theft, and an unattended car, whether or not it bears the "On Government Service" notice, is now liable to be driven away at the whim of any passing soldier or even civilian. Probably my Vauxhall was just stolen.

Needless to say, there was no taxi to be had, and walking more than a few yards was out of the question in the heat. So in desperation I begged a lift from a complete stranger. He was an L.D.C. man, and he happened to be going the same way as I—to the Cathay, which has recently become the headquarters of the L.D.C. During the drive, for want of something better to say, I told him of my misfortune. He said he was sorry to hear about it, and then asked me quite casually, "Would you like this car?" I said, "Yes," rather feebly, because I thought I hadn't heard him aright or that he was joking. But without any prompting from me he repeated his offer, explaining that he had another larger car parked outside the Cathay and that as he didn't really need two I might just as well have this one. All he wanted in return was a couple of my petrol coupons as soon as the new issue came in on Monday. When we drew up at the Cathay he wrote down my name, collected his few belongings from the back, handed over the keys and left me in full possession.

So now I've got a newish Morris Eight. It's in far better condition than the Vauxhall and uses much less petrol. In fact, it's a very good exchange.

When I arrived at the office I had a comic story to tell as well as a sad story to hide. But I found Aubrey looking very grave. He said that in present circumstances we'd have to postpone *Saint Joan*, which was scheduled for production on Sunday, and he asked me to apologize to the company who'd been called to rehearsal. Though it was already late, only two of them had turned up—A. B. Cross, an elderly solicitor, who's done a lot of work for us, and Carl Lawson, a professional actor who's lived for years in the East. I explained the situation to them in a few, rather hastily chosen words, which I tried to make as soothing and unalarming as possible. They looked a bit dejected, but said they quite understood and departed without protest and a casual good evening. I wonder what will happen to them in the coming days. I wonder whether I shall ever meet them again—here or elsewhere.

The *Saint Joan* broadcast was doomed in any event, for Marie Ney is no longer with us. Apparently her husband made up his mind suddenly that she must go and packed her off at a couple of hours' notice. She had no time to say good-bye to anyone. She was working in the office this morning. Her desk is still littered with papers and scripts scheduled for future production. They are dead things now.

Several other women members of the staff have gone, and I hear that an M.B.C. unit is leaving shortly to operate an emergency service from Batavia. Eric Davis apparently made arrangements for this on his way here. It's not been decided yet how many members of the staff will comprise the unit or who they will be exactly, but Aubrey tells me it's certain that neither he nor I will be among them.

Phyllis Herbert was in Aubrey's room when I got back. She has consistently resisted any suggestion that she should "run away", as she calls it. And she's only agreed to do so at last with almost bitter reluctance. But she couldn't have chosen otherwise. She has three children to consider, and though you can't argue rationally why European children should go when thousands of Asiatic children have no alternative but to remain, instinct tells you now it's against nature to keep them here. So Phyllis came to say good-bye. She's leaving with her children tomorrow on a Java-bound ship. Aubrey and I will be grass widowers together.

Eric Davis looked in for a moment. It was my first meeting with him. We only exchanged a few words, but he shook hands with great cordiality, and I had the impression that I would get on well with him. He's tall, lean and rather gaunt. He has prematurely grey hair brushed back from his forehead and wears powerful glasses which give him rather a schoolmasterly look. But he has an active, sensitive face, and a manner earthy and alive. He didn't seem at all downcast or conscious of the fact that he had rejoined a sinking ship. On the contrary, he appeared like one who had returned, after a long absence, to lead a booming concern into new and even more fruitful ventures. I envied him his business and his enthusiasm. For my part I was on the point of despair. My job, I thought, was virtually finished, and with Carol gone too I felt an overwhelming sense of loneliness.

But there was work to be done at the Thomson Road studios. The evening's bill—with one slight alteration—still stood, and part of it read :

"8.15 p.m.—A.R.P. and You. Divisional Warden C. E. Hudson answers listeners' questions brought to him by Al Larson. 8.30—B.B.C. News from London. 8.45—'Stage Panorama', a musically illustrated programme about London theatres and London shows compiled and presented by Giles Playfair."

The slight alteration, not as yet divulged to the public, was caused by the fact that Al Larson had dropped out from the broadcast with Hudson. He'd informed Peggie this morning, who looks after the A.R.P. talks, that he wouldn't be available, and as it was too late to get hold of anyone else outside the office I'd agreed to deputize for him.

I drove Peggie up to Thomson Road in my newly, miraculously acquired Morris Eight. It goes like a bird. In the interim between rehearsal and transmission I argued rather acrimoniously with the P.A. on duty. (Every evening one of the women programme assistants sits in the Thomson Road office to keep a log of broadcasts, telephone calls, etc.) I was a little surprised to see this particular lady still in Singapore, and was frankly shocked to learn that she had made no arrangements to leave, for she has a small son with her. I told her she must understand there was a strong likelihood of Singapore falling and an absolute certainty of siege with the hellish accompaniments of famine, bombardment, etc.; that it was her duty to get her child away at the first possible opportunity. She told me that I was an alarmist and a defeatist; that there wasn't the remotest chance of Singapore falling; that the Japs would soon be pushed back; that there was no real danger; that all her sensible friends felt exactly as she did, and that she intended to stay on with her child until things got worse—which they wouldn't. Magnificent obstinacy? A lost hangover from civilian Singapore's chronic refusal to face up to reality?

Hudson began his broadcast: "Al Larson can't be here tonight, so I've asked John English to come along instead." (John English is my fourth radio pseudonym in Singapore. I've also been Anthony Boston (compère and actor), Brian Golding (commentator) and Mark Caffyn (writer and producer).) I tried to make John English a creditable person, getting him to halt, stutter, um, er, and be affectedly casual in the best B.B.C. manner. Perhaps this was a mistake. Peggie said afterwards he wasn't a patch on Al Larson. I'm afraid she was right.

A wave of acute depression overcame me during the "Stage Panorama" broadcast. I didn't think the programme was good in any case, for the records had not been well chosen and the script had been too hastily put together. But, good or bad, it somehow seemed so inappropriate to the moment, so useless, such a waste of time and effort. Hadn't I once said that it was radio's job in wartime to sustain morale and to preserve at all costs an atmosphere of normality? Yes, indeed. But that was all very well a fortnight ago, a week ago, yesterday even. This evening was different. Suddenly events had come to the boil, and I myself had been scalded by them. I didn't believe that anyone could possibly be interested at the present in a light and nostalgic programme about Drury Lane Theatre or that there could be more of such programmes broadcast from Singapore. I felt like a tired runner who has been left yards behind, but must still continue his hopeless race until one of his opponents far ahead reaches the winning-post.

In between bits of narrative, while the records were being played, my mind wandered back to the docks and the ship and saying good-bye to Carol, so that when the light cues came to speak again I was not on the alert. My voice faltered and was weak and hesitant when it should have been strong and forceful and lively.

At the end I thought I was due for a measure of well-deserved censure from Peggie, who had been listening in the control-room. Instead I was summoned to the telephone: "Hello, is that you, Playfair? Eric Davis here. Look, I'm sorry we didn't have time for a longer meeting this afternoon. I want to congratulate you on your programme. Excellent. Just the sort of stuff we need at the moment. See you tomorrow." I was immeasurably cheered. I wished, of course, that Davis could have heard a better specimen of the broadcasts I've been doing during the past two months. But I didn't doubt the sincerity of his appreciation, and by the very fact of his bothering to listen and ring up he'd imparted to me something of his own courageous attitude. He'd lifted me right out of my despairing mood. Now I felt I had been wrong to give way to depression, that my job was not over but merely required reorganizing, that there was still worth-while work for me to do in Singapore.

I went back to supper with Peggie in her flat on the eighth floor of the Cathay. W. R. Reid, M.B.C.'s chief executive officer and deputy chairman, came in for a few minutes afterwards. He's staying in one of the Cathay flats himself, for his own house was suddenly requisitioned by the military this afternoon. He talked to Peggie about the move to Batavia. Apparently she's likely to go, though the unit will mainly consist of news staff and announcers.

I persuaded Eric Robertson to stay the night with me at Goodwood Park. I couldn't face the prospect of sleeping there alone.

On our way to the flat we looked in at the McNaughtons' room, for Bunty had asked me to pack up Jack's civilian clothes. She hadn't had time to do it herself this afternoon. Jack's golf clubs and an assortment of hats and coats were hanging in the lobby outside. The room itself bore several signs that it had been vacated only recently and very hurriedly. Recognizably, it was the skeleton of the living body it had been a few hours before. Magazines were spread out on the table (I remembered those magazines very well), and a bottle of white wine was there too. We thought we might purloin the wine for a nightcap, but then decided that perhaps it had been purposely left out for sentiment's sake. However, the main job of packing had already been done—supposedly by the Chinese boy. And so after a casual look round, as one might inspect a small museum, we took our leave. I still have a faint belief that Jack will return. If he does I hope someone tells him that Bunty has gone before he enters that strange spectre of a home.

Goodwood Park, Saturday, January 31, 1942.

In the early morning there was a terrific explosion. I'm a heavy sleeper, but this was enough to awaken the dead, and when I'd recovered sufficient conscious- ness to be alarmed I got out of bed and went into the sitting-room. I found Eric crouching beside a cupboard. I asked him what on earth he was doing. "Taking cover," he answered rather obviously. "Didn't you hear the explosion?" "That," I said, "was the blowing up of the causeway." I was only guessing, but Eric thought I was probably right. We hung about a bit to make sure there weren't going to be any more unaccountable bangs, and then we went off to bath and shave.

During breakfast there was an Alert, which was disturbing because it was well ahead of schedule. Usually the first air raid of the day takes place about nine o'clock. The guns started booming and we had to make for the trench. Nothing much happened, however, and after about a quarter of an hour we returned to our coffee (now a little tepid) and the remains of our bacon and eggs (quite cold).

I did a very poor morning's work at the office. Everything was confusion and speculation about the move to Batavia. Some people had been informed they were likely to go, others had been ignored, no one had been told anything definite. Apparently a list had been prepared, but whose names were on it and whose were not was a matter of pure guesswork. Miss Glazebrook seemed rather worried—she didn't know whether to pack or not—so I went along to see Davis. He told me he'd secured facilities for an emergency programme to be broadcast from Batavia on the Singapore wavelength in the event of our own transmitters being put out of action. Accordingly, he was sending a skeleton M.B.C. staff to operate the scheme and was trying to arrange for its departure as soon as possible—perhaps today, perhaps tomorrow. News bulletins were the most important consideration—in fact, the unit would take over certain of our news bulletins on arrival. But in addition to news staff it was also essential to include representative announcers and engineers. Reid had consented to go as administrative head of the unit, though very reluctantly, and only on the understanding that he would be enabled to return to Singapore as soon as he had got things running smoothly. "In fact," said Davis, "we shall probably have to hit him over the head and carry him to the boat."

Though Davis didn't admit as much, I shrewdly suspect him of intent to make the Batavia unit far larger than is necessary from a strictly practical point of view. His main motive, no doubt, is to ensure M.B.C. listeners a broad-casting service of some kind whatever disasters may happen in the next week or so. But I think he has the definite—if subsidiary—purpose of removing as many members of the staff from Singapore as possible—particularly women members of the staff. When I asked him if Miss Glazebrook was going he said that was an excellent idea, because Miss Glazebrook had once worked in the B.B.C. newsroom and would be very useful on that account.

There are all manner of formalities to be gone through before a unit of any kind can leave, and its size and personnel really depend on Davis's success in securing priorities, visas, etc., at short notice. The rush for passages at the moment is naturally prodigious. But Davis was just off to the shipping agents when I left him, and he seemed superbly confident that he would get exactly his own way. He has the grand manner and a sort of mischievous delight in his ability to make powerful use of it.

Next week's programme schedule will obviously need drastic alteration, but in the prevailing uncertainty and excitement, somewhat reminiscent of the last days of a school term, it was impossible to work on it. However, I had to do something about the ten minutes' poetry reading which Marie Ney was due to broadcast tonight at 10.50. It could reasonably have been cut, of course, for poetry readings aren't at all popular and I've no doubt the majority of our listeners would prefer an extra ten minutes of recorded music. But I was deter-mined not to cut it for two reasons. First, I'm opposed on principle to sacrific-ing more than the absolute minimum of our "live" output, otherwise it looks as if we've been driven by panic into broadcasting a second-rate, makeshift pro-gramme, and that's tantamount to a major defeat. Secondly, this poetry read-ing provided an opportunity to put a white woman on the air, and in the midst of the present great exodus of European women and children, which many Asiatics doubtless regard as wholesale European desertion, I thought it would have a somewhat reassuring effect for a white woman's voice to be heard again in Singapore.

So I asked Mrs. Robinson, who runs the general office, to undertake the job, and she agreed without my having to do a lot of persuading, which both sur-prised and gratified me. I didn't know whether she had any particular qualifica-tions for reading poetry—one can't bother about that sort of thing any longer.

As a matter of fact, I hadn't spoken with her more than once or twice before because she's been away ill most of this month. But I remembered that Marie Ney had often expressed both liking and admiration for her, and she's young and rather pretty and has an attractive voice and looks more like an actress than anyone else in the office. From now on an actress she's got to be.

Eric Robertson and I had lunch in Peggie's flat. Eric, like myself, is a dead certainty not to be going with the unit to Batavia. But he's concerned about ways and means of escape if worse comes to worst. Apparently he's talked to Davis and Reid, and has got himself appointed unofficial organizer of N.B.C. evacuation. He's very mysterious and secretive—dramatically so—but I gather he's working on several alternative plans, one of which involves the chartering of a whole fleet of sampans. He impressed on me the urgent necessity, which I couldn't take quite seriously, of getting a rucksack ready packed and of keeping it always by me in case of a hurried departure. I should include, so he told me, a simple change of clothing, a thermos of water, a sarong (for I may have to leave disguised as a native) and iron rations. Peggie also fancies herself as some-thing of an expert on the rough life—days and nights in an open boat, days and nights in the jungle, etc.—and there was a dispute between them on the question of iron rations. Peggie favoured a tin of canned meat (it was conveniently in her store cupboard) but Eric ridiculed the suggestion and stated emphatically that hard biscuits and chocolate were the maximum fare allowable. After lunch Eric went off on some undisclosed mission to do with sampans, and Peggie returned with me to Goodwood Park to supervise the packing of my rucksack.

Under her watchful eye I proceeded to collect from drawers and cupboards a number of odd, half-forgotten possessions which seemed to me of little practical value in any circumstances and of no possible service in a civilized existence. Indeed, I was on the point of protest when it came to filling up precious space, at the expense of shirts, shoes, suits, socks, etc., with a roll of cotton, a knife, a flashlamp, a silk scarf and a fake oriental dressing-gown (transformable into a sarong). However, I was a child in her hands, and in the end I did exactly as I was told. Now the rucksack stands ready packed in a corner. It is prodigiously heavy and it is stuffed full of objects upon which I can only hope my well-being will never depend.

Carey turned up at tea-time with a fellow officer. I don't know what they'd been doing, but they were both black with grime, and I suspect they'd come as much for a bath as to see me. Anyway, they had a bath. Carey was exuber-antly cheerful. Now that things are obviously about as bad as they can be, he seems more amused than alarmed. (That's the way it's taken most of us.)

"Do you think we're finished?" I asked him, half in jest.

"I shouldn't be surprised," he said, "but you can answer that better than I can. Quite honestly, I haven't the faintest idea what is happening. All I know is we've stopped fighting in Malaya. We've got all our troops back on the island."

"Yes, we've blown the causeway."

"Have we? I hadn't heard. It's amazing. When one's in the Army one's never told anything."

Eric Robertson reappeared, looking more mysterious than ever and clutching an odd sort of map which, according to him, revealed secret channels through the minefields off Singapore.

Carey was interested in this, because he is determined to have a shot at escaping in the event of capitulation; and after he and Eric had studied it closely we discussed in conspiratorial solemnity a specific plan for reaching Sumatra, which is excellent in theory but involves the previous acquisition of a number of tommy-guns and a fast motor-launch. We hadn't sufficient time to work out the practical details of how and where the tommy-guns and the fast motor-launch can be obtained, for Carey had to return to barracks before nightfall. But he's promised to get in touch with me again tomorrow. Of course, he really hasn't the vaguest idea what he'll be doing tomorrow. Neither has any of us.

Back at the Cathay we listened to the Governor's broadcast. It began with an announcement that the causeway had been "successfully breached", which confirmed a rumour I'd heard this morning. It's obvious now that the causeway has not been destroyed, but has merely had a small section blown out of it. Apparently the military consider this good enough, for the Governor gave no hint that they were dissatisfied with their work or intended to do any more about it. Maybe they are right. I'm not expert enough to argue. But I must say I'm disappointed and not a little alarmed, for I imagined that preparations for the complete destruction of the causeway had been made weeks ago. They seemed to me an elementary precaution.

The rest of the speech was stereotyped: "We're all together on Singapore island, cut off from the rest of Malaya. We've got to work hard, stand shoulder to shoulder. Chungking took it, London took it, Malta took it, Moscow took it, we've got to show we can take it . . . Singapore must stand. It shall stand. . . ." I'm afraid this sort of thing won't have cut much ice.

I had dinner with Margaret Robinson. She has a flat in the Cathay which she shares with a Mrs. Nixon, whose husband is serving with the Volunteers. She knew Mrs. Nixon in Kuala Lumpur before the war. Mrs. Nixon was librarian there and came to Singapore a day or two before its fall. She's in her early fifties now, and I feel very sorry for her. She's lost everything, and so has her husband, who left his lifework behind in Kuala Lumpur and has no recognizable future. However, she's one of the people whom disaster has made neither plaintive nor cowardly. She's behaving courageously. She's got herself a temporary job with the M.B.C., and her husband has joined the L.D.C. Seemingly her only worry is a guilty feeling that she and other Europeans in Malaya failed in their duty to the Asiatic population. She says that whatever happens there will be no more evacuations for her.

Both Margaret and Mrs. Nixon were a little critical of some of the women who have left in the last day or two, and, ironically enough, I found myself defending them. I chose Marie Ney as an example, and reminded them that in her case it was not her own decision but her husband's that she should leave. I said that no one had behaved more courageously and that personally I could never forget what a splendid job she had done for the M.B.C. I told them how, in spite of her inherent fear, which was so apparent when she heard the alarm for the first time, she had steeled herself to be impervious to air raids and had calmly remained in her office while most of us were taking shelter. I told them how imperturbable she had been during transmissions when the guns outside were almost loud enough to drown her voice and the flimsy studio at Thomson Road was being shaken by explosions. And I told them I didn't know another actress of her standing who would have worked so tirelessly and without fuss in such rough and primitive conditions and for so little reclaim. Before I had finished I realized that I was preaching to a converted audience, for Marie Ney is a particular friend for whom they have as much admiration as I. But I

F

hope I persuaded them that what is true of her is likely to be true of others besides.

We had an excellent meal and spent a pleasant evening which was interrupted by only two air-raid alarms. The first passed unnoticed, but the second threatened to develop into something quite big, and we had to take cover.

When you go out of one of the Cathay flats or offices you are in the open air, for the various floors are just a network of bridges with no roof above them. You get from one floor to another either by the lifts, which don't work during Alerts, or by the stone stairway, which is in complete darkness on moonless nights.

We couldn't use a torch (that would have been a serious breach of the blackout regulations), and we'd have risked breaking a leg or two if we'd attempted to grope our way right down to the basement shelter. So we were content to squat on one of the lower flights of stairs. A lot of people think the stairs provide the best protection in any event.

We went up to the studio on the fifth floor for the poetry reading. The raid was over by then.

We found Peter Hume, one of the news assistants, looking very hot and dishevelled in the midst of a dramatic and impressive representation of the Governor's speech. This was in place of a recording which had been announced earlier in the evening but had not been broadcast for the simple but unfortunate reason that it didn't exist. No one had remembered to make it!

We had an hour's rehearsal, and I think Margaret did pretty well considering she had never broadcast before and at her first attempt had to tackle one of the most difficult jobs in broadcasting. There are very few actresses who have the vaguest conception of how to read poetry. Most of them turn verse into declamatory prose by all manner of trick pauses and deliberate failure to observe the lines. Margaret kept the metre very faithfully. Even if she hadn't done so, even if her performance had been abominably dull and inexpert, I wouldn't have minded much. She'd have served my purpose just the same ; for if her listeners weren't particularly enthralled, they know now that there's at least one white woman left on Singapore Island.

The failure to record the Governor's speech was symptomatic, perhaps, of the day's general confusion. There's still no definite news about the move to Batavia. Peggie has a theory there won't be a ship before Monday. I found her packing in a rather dispirited, lackadaisical manner when I got back to her flat after the broadcast. I think she's thankful that the decision of "stay" or "go" is out of her hands. But she's certainly not elated or even pleased at the prospect of leaving. No one with a heart could be, and Peggie is very conscious of the fact that there will be no chance of escape for many of the Asiatics whom she had known and liked during her stay in Singapore.

She's promised to take three of my most treasured books with her into safety. I don't suppose I'll ever be in a position to reclaim them, but it's good to know they'll be spared from falling into Japanese hands.

The members of the Batavia unit have been told for certain that they'll be travelling on some kind of evacuee ship and won't be allowed more than a limited amount of personal luggage. Clothes apart, they'll have to leave nearly all their possessions behind. So Peggie was in a very generous mood, while Eric and I watched her pack. She bequeathed us her canned-food stocks, her bottles of drink, and all her furniture, hangings, pictures, etc. She said we could have the flat if we continued to employ her *amah*. We agreed to the proviso, which was a weight off Peggie's conscience, for she had been in dread of leaving her *amah* unprovided for.

When we returned to Goodwood Park about 1 a.m. we were considerably enriched. . . .

Goodwood Park Hotel, Sunday, February 1, 1942.

I was awakened by the telephone bell. It was Margaret Robinson. She told me last-minute arrangements had been made for the Batavia unit to leave this morning. Would I inform Michael Miles, who apparently lived a few doors away from Goodwood Park, that he must be at Clifford's Pier by 10 a.m. at the latest?

I roused Eric and we dressed as quickly as possible. But Michael had already gone by the time we reached his house. Someone must have got there before us. We drove on to the Cathay. A string of cars and a huge van were parked outside the Mount Sophia entrance, the entrance to the flats and offices. A group of Asiatics stood lazily and silently by, while luggage, typewriters, dictaphones and packing-cases were being feverishly loaded, a look half of resentment, half of disdain, on their immobile faces. A few of the more energetic members of the unit were acting as carriers. I went into the Cathay to see if I could lend a hand. On my way up to the news-room I ran into several colleagues who had known nothing of the projected move to Batavia and who seemed completely bewildered. They asked me if I was going, and I couldn't help feeling glad and proud and exalted when I answered no.

This, perhaps, was a defence against my envy of those who were leaving. And yet, even from a material point of view, there were compensations to be had from staying behind. The cars outside the Cathay would soon be deserted by their owners. They would be taken as far as Clifford's Pier and then they would be ours for the driving away. The manner in which I acquired my Morris no longer seems in the least bit bizarre. Incidentally, the licence of the Morris is months out of date, but I don't think there's the remotest chance of my being had up on that account. I'm quite confident that the police have neither the time nor energy at this juncture to be concerned with such a minor breach of the law. So far as the ordinary routine of civilized life is concerned, we are already in a state of anarchy. Responsibilities like the guardianship of money and possessions, the observance of rules and conventions, which used to make up the sum total of our worldly worries, have slipped from us. All that matters now is the preservation of our lives and if possible our liberties. We are rich beyond the dreams of avarice, for we have come into a great inheritance of abandoned cars, flats, houses, furniture, food stores, etc., and for what we want we have no need to pay. But our inheritance is none the less made of the same stuff as dreams, and is only for fleeting enjoyment. A few days will decide whether Singapore is going to survive.

Margaret Robinson was standing sentinel outside Clifford's Pier. She said there'd been a hell of a rush and a muddle. Apparently she'd been on the 'phone since the early hours of this morning frantically trying to get in touch with the various members of the unit who had to be told that arrangements for their departure had suddenly been made. But, at any rate, she'd succeeded, for they were all collected now and I marvelled at their number.

Among them were W. R. Reid, the chief executive officer, and his wife; four of our six newsmen; Allan Rose, the senior announcer; and Michael Miles, one of his assistants; Weigall, the director of engineering; and Anderson, one of his assistants; the whole of the monitoring unit; the Dutch, Japanese, and Chinese units; and nearly all the permanent women members of the staff save Margaret Robinson herself. This was no skeleton staff. It was sizable enough and ubiquitous enough to run full-fledged programmes from Batavia. Last-minute muddle or no, the whole thing had been an amazing triumph for Eric Davis. He'd slashed his way through competition, opposition and officialdom to get his own way. Within thirty-six hours, in the midst of the great outrush, he'd secured more than forty passages and Dutch visas.

He was there now, looking very happy and energetic and debonair, in khaki shorts and a pair of canary-coloured stockings and a slouched trilby hat—supervising the completion of one job before getting on with the next.

A launch made several trips to the boat, which was anchored in the roads, and the five of us who had come to see the party off—Eric Robertson, Margaret, Johns, one of the surviving news editors, Davis and myself—helped to load it with baggage, office paraphernalia, food stores, blankets, pillows, etc. We went aboard ourselves on the last trip—our reward for so much hard work and so much hanging about.

The launch took us to a cattle-boat. I'm not sure what sort of a vessel I'd expected to find—but at any rate something a little grander than that. The members of the party who had preceded us were perched like birds on various corners of the deck and were already munching away at their first picnic lunch. I must confess they looked quite clean and comfortable, but I wager they'll be neither comfortable nor clean by the time they reach Batavia, for the boat must obviously be a slow one, and its sanitary equipment is of the most primitive kind. I didn't inquire how much cargo it was carrying, but I noticed a pig on deck, and I was told there were some cows in the vicinity of the two cabins below, which is probably the reason there was no zealous competition for possession of the cabins. But I'm convinced the cattle-boat will reach port safely. For how could it be otherwise with Allan Rose aboard? With Allan Rose, always something of a dandy, now dressed in a suit of impeccable white, securely enthroned on a hatch, eating sardines from a tin as if they were caviare off a golden plate, superbly impervious to the buzz of activity around him and the drama and tragedy of parting.

As a matter of fact, the parting itself was rather an anticlimax because it was so protracted. We, who had come aboard to wish our colleagues *bon voyage*, had intended to tarry only a minute or so, but for some reason we remained for nearly two hours. With so much time for reflection, the situation became stripped of all pretence, and it was impossible to indulge in meaningless and futile assurances about seeing each other again soon, etc. Equally, it was impossible to give way to unbridled emotionalism, so instead we were elaborately casual and carefree. We stood around and reminisced and revived old jokes and laughed uproariously. Our final good-byes were almost wordless and without fervour of any kind.

There had been a couple of air raids while we were still aboard, but when the five of us got back to dry land Singapore seemed as peaceful as any English town at the hour of Sunday luncheon. Clifford's Pier, which at our last sight had been strewn with all the trappings of departure, was now swept clean; the wide thoroughfare from which it leads to the sea was trafficless and floodlit by the sun, and the great buildings on the other side were closed and empty. We were alone, and all that remained to remind us of the hectic episode which had begun so suddenly and was now so abruptly at an end were the motor-cars—neatly parked, but in fact abandoned.

I was reminded of that afternoon nearly eight years ago when my father died —or, rather, I was revisited by a similar sense of loneliness as had possessed me then and an inability to visualize the future. It was a Sunday afternoon in August. My mother and I walked out of King's College Hospital into the sunlight. Nothing apparently had changed. Everybody and everything about us were exactly as they had been last Sunday and the Sunday before that and for as many Sundays back as we could remember. Tomorrow the shops and the offices and the theatres would be open, and another perfectly ordinary working week in London's history would begin. Only we were conscious of the fact that the end of an epoch had been reached and that the complexion of our lives would never again be the same.

Margaret had dutifully collected the ignition keys, but we decided to see to the salvaging of our colleagues' cars later. We were tired and hungry now. Davis invited us back to lunch at Mount Rosie, and we drove off in a procession, though we lost Margaret and Johns on the way.

We found Jeffries enjoying a solitary repast at the far end of the museum-like room. There's a secret transmitter in the cottage adjoining the Mount Rosie residence, and Jeffries is in charge of it at the moment, which means that he has to live and sleep with it. Davis's Chinese servant conjured up an excellent meal for us three intruders which we washed down with iced beer.

The telephone rang incessantly during lunch. Afterwards Davis announced his intention of taking a nap, and advised us to do the same, for he warned us there was a lot of hard work ahead. He said he'd be at the Cathay at half past five.

I went back to Goodwood Park. I stretched out full length on a *chaise-longue*. But I was unable to close my eyes or read a book or really to relax. As a matter of fact, the afternoon passed without a belligerent murmur. Nothing happened to shatter the lazy enjoyment which the day and the sun seemed to dictate. Perhaps the Japanese across the narrow strip of water on the mainland over there were likewise resting, were likewise in harmony with Nature. But I had no substantial faith in so pleasant a reflection. More likely they were toiling viciously and making fearsome preparations for the grand assault which must come very soon now—any day, any hour, any minute. The communiqué —published way back in December—announcing the attack on Hongkong Island has stuck in my memory. "Under cover of an intensive, twelve-hour artillery barrage the enemy succeeded in landing in force." I've a deep-rooted superstition that history will repeat itself here. We'll hear the guns booming relentlessly for twelve hours, and then we'll know that the antlike Japanese invaders have taken to their little boats and are swarming towards us. I dread the sound of those guns.

I was glad when the afternoon ended. The last thing one wants now is time for relaxation, time for thought, time to be alone.

Aubrey rang up to say he'd spent the morning seeing his family off, for they didn't get away yesterday after all. I asked him whether he intended to leave the Seaview, and he said he was considering it and suggested he might share my flat with me. I welcomed this proposal enthusiastically. Eric Robertson is going back to live at the Mount Rosie cottage tomorrow, and I am frankly fearful of nights at Goodwood Park alone.

Davis was extremely busy when I reached the Cathay, but there didn't seem much for me to do. Of course, tomorrow the programme schedule will have to undergo another drastic revision. It's been maintained today, despite the sudden depletion of staff, by the superhuman efforts of John Ilsley, who's been on the job since early morning reading news bulletins, announcing recorded sessions and improvising alterations both in the English and Asiatic programmes. Thanks to him, there hasn't been a breakdown in any of our transmissions, which is, I think, a considerable achievement, however makeshift the actual material broadcast may have been.

I wandered up to Margaret's flat, ostensibly to discuss the gentle topic of looting, actually for a drink and pleasant company, for by now dusk had fallen and I knew it was too late to launch an expedition for the collection of those abandoned cars at Clifford's Pier. Neither Margaret nor Mrs. N. seemed in the least alarmed by the present or fearful of the future. So far as they were concerned, they had no wish to be anywhere but in Singapore, and they did not believe, so they said, in the possibility of defeat, nor would they allow a mention of it in their presence. "Singapore is not going to fall," they kept repeating, and they talked half wistfully, half defiantly, of eating their next Christmas dinner in Kuala Lumpur. I had the feeling that their conviction, so vehemently expressed, was not really conviction at all but determination, and because of this I was chastened, and was ready to fall in with their mood. After all, why should we allow ourselves to suffer the humiliation of being terrorized by those brown and Lilliputian barbarians ? The military, so I'm led to believe, still take quite a rosy view of the situation. At a conference held on the day the causeway was breached one of their spokesmen stated that there would be no difficulty in frustrating enemy landing attempts and that, even if there were no diversion, Singapore could hold out for a minimum of three months. Of course, the military have been wrong from the word "go," and my instinct tells me they're wrong now. But the time has passed for any truck with common sense. For better or worse we're stuck here now, and the least we can do is to have faith in miracles.

Eric Robertson came in with some bad news. He announced that a thorough search of Michael Miles's house had unearthed no treasure whatsoever. Since Michael had positively stated there was a considerable store of liquor and tobacco to be had for the taking, Eric assumed that someone must have got in before him. He revealed, further, that Davis had decided to commandeer Peggie's flat, and that even now we were in imminent danger of losing our precious heritage of food stocks, furniture and two bottles of wine. I said that we must go and stake our claim at once. And we did.

I invited the two Erics to have dinner with me at Goodwood Park. We sat in the large, dimly lit, sparsely decorated dining-room and ploughed through a complete five-course meal.

A locally recruited Army officer, who says "stengah" more convincingly and drinks stengahs more copiously than any other Singaporean of my acquaintance, ambled up to our table to ask whether Carol had got away safely. When I answered yes, he proceeded to tell me in his slow, halting way that of the three ships which left on Friday two had been sunk and the third had been forced to return to port. Davis, who is easily made impatient, was an unappreciative audience of this bald and alcoholically protracted narrative. Afterwards he dismissed its author as a fool who had no notion of what he was talking about. I only hope Davis is right, but I can't pretend my mind was at peace when at last I went to bed.

Goodwood Park Hotel—Monday, February 2, 1942.

At a programme meeting this morning it was decided to close down transmissions at 10.30 p.m. instead of midnight. And, so far as I can judge, that's going to be the only apparent result of our depletion of staff.

Our two surviving news editors—Rowan Rivett, a young Australian journalist who arrived in Singapore not more than a month ago, and Johns, who's a Canadian—will have the toughest job, for until the Batavia outfit gets going they'll be responsible for every bulletin and commentary broadcast by the M.B.C., and in present circumstances, of course, a substantial decrease of our news output is not feasible. It was suggested that the leading war correspondents might be persuaded to take over some of the commentaries, and this seemed an excellent idea until we realized that there are only a handful of them left on Singapore Island—Yates MacDaniel, Harold Guard and one or two others. The rest, including those who sent back to America such crushing accounts of British negligence and incompetence, have departed with the bulk of the European women and children. For them, presumably, the story is over.

But not for Eric Davis, who was quite indomitable. He opened the meeting with an assurance that in two or three weeks' time the situation would be stabilized and we'd get back to our normal broadcasting schedule. I don't suppose he really believed a word of what he was saying. But at least he achieved his purpose of making us all feel good.

Davis favoured—and virtually ordered—the suspension of plays and features. But I'm obstinately determined to put on at least one play a week, for somehow the complete abandonment of my drama plans would represent a defeat which I just can't stomach at the moment. Some time ago I made a script of Alice Duer Miller's poem, *The White Cliffs*, for Marie Ney. It's the sheerest sentimentalism, but it has previously been broadcast with astonishing success both in London and New York, and I feel it would have a considerable emotional appeal in Singapore at this time, particularly as in my version I've taken pains to exaggerate its crudities by all manner of martial and nostalgic musical links. Anyway, I'm proposing to produce it, come what may, on Monday next. On the Monday following, provided we're not all prisoners by then and I can gather together a sufficient number of players, I want to do Patrick Hamilton's superb radio drama, *Money With Menaces*.

Of course, we're very hard up for actresses. So far as I can judge at the moment, we've only two. One is Margaret Robinson, who's the Admirable Crichton of the M.B.C. now, for besides having placed her histrionic services completely at my disposal she's become Davis's personal secretary, director of administration and I don't know what else besides. The other is Patricia Mills, who used to be the star of Kuala Lumpur's amateur theatricals and was for a short while, I fancy, on the professional stage. She's living at the moment with her husband, who is a captain attached to the Army Public Relations Office, in one of the Cathay flats. I've already lined her up to take Marie Ney's place in *The White Cliffs*. The cutting down of "live" material means a lot of extra work for little Victor Grosz, our Hungarian music officer, who has to fill in the gaps. However, he seems quite unperturbed. Grosz, small, dapper, smiling and industrious, is sometimes enchantingly vague, but he has a magical gift for burrowing into his collection of 10,000 records and producing from it, at a moment's notice, a musical hour or half-hour under such diverse billings as "Melodious Memories", "Symphony Concert", "Dance Marathon", etc.

Aubrey and I have gone back to being relief announcers, for we've only two full-time announcers left—John Ilsley and Andrew Carruthers. However, announcing in present circumstances is a much more exhilarating occupation than it was a couple of months ago. When I read the news at lunch-time today I experienced the thrill of saying, "This is Singapore." It was indeed a thrill. It was precisely the same kind of thrill as the B.B.C. announcers must have felt when they said "This is London" during the stupendous days of the Battle of Britain. "This is Singapore." Those three words are now a constantly repeated message of assurance to the world. If they cease to be spoken, the world will know that Singapore has fallen.

Both Aubrey and Eric Davis were persuaded at the meeting that Hudson must be kept on the air whatever else we sacrifice in the way of "live" material. Hudson is our ace broadcaster, and his voice is undoubtedly the best tonic for morale we've got. He's built up a large listening public for himself—both among the Europeans and English-speaking Asiatics—and he's regarded as completely trustworthy and sincere. Eric Robertson and I had a long discussion with him this afternoon. He seemed embittered and rather dispirited, though still aggressively determined to fight on. He pointed out that the Governor's broadcast had been generally derided because of its empty exhortation to bravery, hard work, etc., without any mention of Singapore's unsolved problems, that the Malayan Government was now utterly discredited and that no one speaking actually or seemingly on behalf of the administration could hope to influence popular feeling in the faintest degree. We agreed that in present circumstances the M.B.C. would serve a far more useful purpose as a public forum than as a Government mouthpiece, and we urged him accordingly to undertake a new series of talks in which he could voice the view of the people on every aspect of passive defence under the general heading of "Singapore Citizen". He said he'd do this provided we gave him our assurance that he would be allowed to speak with complete candour and would be subjected to no censorship of any kind. On our own responsibility we told him to go ahead, and he promised to be ready with an introductory talk for Wednesday evening. Afterwards Eric discussed the matter with Eric Davis and Robert Scott, head of the M.O.I. Far Eastern Bureau. They both endorsed our decision, so now we should have some fireworks.

Carter is still with us, and still banging out strips on his typewriter. He has enough strips completed for a full-dress "Malaya Newsreel" tomorrow evening, and he has plans for several other programmes besides. He is negotiating with the military authorities for permission to do a broadcast reconstruction of the story of that heroic Scottish regiment who fought the Japanese all the way down the Peninsula and whose battle-torn survivors—a mere handful—crossed the causeway with their bagpipes playing. I hope he gets permission, for now surely is the time, in the midst of so much apparent humiliation, to pay tribute to an episode of superb gallantry—comparable with any other in our history.

Nothing can deflect Carter from his job and nothing can put "Malaya Newsreel" off the air. Somehow we've got together a cast for tomorrow's show, and we had a rehearsal this evening. Andrew Carruthers takes Michael Miles's place as "your radio reporter"; Margaret portrays, among other characterizations, an Irish colleen and a Russian peasant wife; and Patricia Mills, Carl Lawson, Eric Robertson, the author in person and myself make up the remainder of a distinguished company. I told Margaret we ought to have a gay party in honour of her début as a radio actress. She welcomed the idea, but I'm afraid it is stillborn. A strict nine o'clock curfew has been imposed, and though as members of the M.B.C. we're exempt from it, restaurants and places of entertainment, if there are still any open (and I've no evidence that there are), must close down promptly. Those after-the-show suppers at Cyrano's or Raffles seem luxuries of long ago, and we look back on them as we look back on last week, nostalgically through a fog of superseding events.

Incidentally, ours are the only civilian cars on the road after curfew hour, and one is beginning to resent more and more the military cars which dash along with blazing headlights. For some unexplained reason the military are under no obligation to observe the blackout regulations.

I persuaded Eric Robertson to spend one more night at Goodwood Park. He says I shall see very little of him during the next few days, as he has several vital and secret missions to fulfil which will keep him away from the office. He is still immensely preoccupied with plans for our eventual escape, and is more mysterious than ever. We are both anxiously awaiting news from Carey, who allegedly has a supply of hidden tommy-guns at his disposal. Nothing has been heard of him since Saturday.

Goodwood Park looks bleak and strange, because no one I used to know lives there any more. Whenever I drive up to the place I have the absurd hope that I may find Jack has returned.

Goodwood Park Hotel—Tuesday, February 3, 1942.

I have had a cable from Carol. She's arrived safely in Batavia and is staying at the Hotel des Indes, though I gather she's likely to move on to Bandoeng shortly.

I've also had a cable from my old friend Derrick Sington, which must either have been dispatched a long while ago or have been composed with more feeling for economy than drama, for it contains just the one word: "Greetings". Being now in a cabling frame of mine, I've sent off reassuring messages ("Don't worry, am fine", etc.) to Carol and my mother and have answered Derrick as follows:

Thanks Greetings Stop Carol Java Stop Self unbowed dash almost.

To do Derrick justice, his cable was prepaid up to two shillings and fourpence, and though my reply cost roughly five times that amount it was good to hear from him. It brought back vivid memories of that early morning of August 25 when he and Stephen and Nadine Thomas came to see us off at Euston Station.

Margaret has miraculously provided me with two secretaries. But I'm embarrassed by my inability to find enough work for them to do. When I'm not an announcer most of my available time is spent either rehearsing Patricia Mills for *The White Cliffs* or sitting at the electric gramophone, which Jeffries has installed in my office, timing and cutting records for the various "presented record programmes" I'm due to broadcast. (A presented record programme, according to our definition, is a programme of gramophone records which tells a musically illustrated story and is linked by a specially written narration.)

In any case, I probably spend several hours of the working day sitting not in my office, but on the stone stairs. The Japanese bombers have abandoned their polite and considerate timetable which, generally speaking, used to allow Singapore the afternoons off. Air raids are pretty much ceaseless, and now the long-expected shelling has begun and has presumably come to stay. So far it hasn't amounted to much. In fact, the net result of bombs and shells, within my actual experience, has been mainly noise, for the enemy is still refraining from any serious attempt to devastate the town itself. Because of their supreme confidence, the Japs are probably intent on causing as little unnecessary damage as possible. But their restraint in this respect is not dictated by humanitarian motives, of course, and gives one no permanent guarantee of safety. They may suddenly lose patience—especially if we show any signs of fight—and the Cathay, Singapore's tallest building, which today stands unscathed, may to-morrow be in ruins.

Shelling—according to my first impression—is considerably more alarming than bombing. To begin with, one has no warning of it. It takes one completely by surprise, like a sudden thump on the back, and somehow it goes on taking one by surprise. Bursting shells have a sharper, more peremptory, more earsplitting sound than bursting bombs. One can't tell whence they come and where they are likely to land. It mostly seems as if they are headed straight for one. But one can't be certain—they may be miles off. So that when they start careering overhead one hasn't the faintest idea what to do—whether to dive under the table or make for the nearest shelter or merely to hope for the best.

We had our baptism of shelling this morning. About a dozen shells were fired, and two of them landed in Orchard Road, a few hundred yards from the Cathay. By the time we'd collected on the stone stairs, however, the firing had ceased. An optimist from the M.O.I. surmised it had been our fellows practising. But evidently it was Japanese finding the range, for early this afternoon the thing started in earnest and it has been going on intermittently ever since.

So now even an illusion that the war is remote has become impossible to cherish, and consequently there's virtually no life left outside one's work. Davis is rather like the commander of a beleaguered garrison. I think he's anxious to collect his whole staff under the Cathay roof. He has turned Peggie's old flat into the M.B.C. day and night headquarters. He and Aubrey alternate on twenty-four-hour shifts as duty officers, and one or the other of them sleeps there every night. The flat opposite is occupied by Johns and Rivett, with a spare bed for Eric Robertson when he needs it. Several other of the abandoned Cathay flats have also been commandeered for the M.B.C. staff.

Lunch is served every day in the headquarters flat for those who want it, and we've embarked on the fashion of a sort of directors' round-table tea-party after office hours. At today's celebration Davis said he intended to place his Mount Rosie residence at the disposal of tired and overworked members of the staff who needed a day or week-end of relaxation in peaceful surroundings! This was a characteristic Davis notion, but a little too Utopian. He hasn't been back in Singapore long enough to realize that the country on this island offers no better chance of escape from bombing, shelling, etc., than the town, and that rest is impossible while the belligerent orchestra is playing full blast. The thing one wants least and dreads most nowadays is having nothing to do but listen and wait.

So far I've resisted the suggestion that I make the Cathay my home. I'm reluctant to leave Goodwood Park for two reasons. First, because it's my last link with permanence, and though this strange, irresponsible, unpredictable existence which began two days ago has many charms, I haven't yet got over my instinctive longing for normality. And secondly, because I daren't wound the feelings of the Chinese servant who looks after my flat. I think he only began his duties about a week before Carol left, but he seems very devoted to my interests. He has remarkable qualities. He produces cigarettes, which are hard to come by, and matches, which are virtually unprocurable, by the carton, and invariably he anticipates my needs. He is brave, too. The worst raids do not deflect him from his work or rob him of his smile. He holds the Japanese in contempt.

Though he has made no mention of it, I fancy Carol's departure came as a shock to him, for now he watches my movements like a lynx, and he is obviously suspicious of that rucksack which I was obliged to fill with such peculiar odd-ments. He is not my servant; he is employed by the hotel. But I haven't the heart to bid him good-bye.

At the same time I'm considerably tempted to move to the Cathay, for I've a horror of isolation. When I'm alone I lose the sense of pride and adventurous-ness and exhilaration at still being in Singapore which I feel when I'm with other people and instead come near to the kind of panic which must overwhelm people who are marooned and foresee no chance of rescue. I'm spending tonight in Margaret's flat. She invited me back to supper after the broadcast of "Malaya Newsreel" which, incidentally, went off with great *eclat*. When eleven o'clock struck, and I had made no move to leave but was still firmly seated in the best armchair sipping a stengah, she was kind enough to suggest that it would be foolish of me to venture home now and that I would be much better off sleeping on a camp bed in the sitting-room. I'm afraid I didn't pause to consider whether she really wanted me to stay or to dwell on the fact that I was probably being a confounded nuisance. I accepted with alacrity. And now I'm wafted back to the good old days of the autumn of 1940, when it was the fashion in London if you went out to dinner to take your mattress with you.

Goodwood Park Hotel—Wednesday, February 4, 1942.

I awoke very early—not long after dawn.

When I stepped out on to the balcony of Margaret's sitting-room, which overlooks the harbour, I saw that in the distance the morning seemed beautiful and clear. But only in the distance. Immediately above, the sky was enveloped by a huge pall of brown-black smoke, which at first I mistook for a gigantic cloud. Whether it was the result of yesterday's bombs and shells or of our own scorched-earth policy, which rumour says we've already begun to implement, I'm not sure. But in any case it was considerably alarming. It made me fearful that soon the sun over Singapore will be permanently and completely blotted out.

I declined Margaret's invitation to breakfast, and hurried back to Goodwood Park. I was anxious to convince the Chinese servant, who is so plaguily on my conscience, that I had not run out for good. Rushed and unheralded departures have been so common of late that a night's absence is as likely as not to mean a permanent "flit", and I was determined to prove my innocence at the earliest possible opportunity.

I found the breakfast-tray already laid out on my return, and by its side the packet of sandwiches and an apple which I habitually take to the office with me for lunch. Somehow it was delightfully refreshing to be back in my own home again, especially as no air-raid alarm interrupted the familiar ceremony of bathing, shaving, changing into clean clothes, eating and reading through the morning's newspaper.

I've definitely decided to hang on to my Goodwood Park abode, which to my mind has infinitely more character and charm than any of the Cathay flats —I suppose because it houses nearly all my possessions. I've always loved possessions—not in a practical, miserly sort of way on account of their value or rarity, but inanely and sentimentally because of their association with things past and fondly remembered. I've never in my life thrown away a letter or even discarded a piece of old clothing of my own free will. Somewhere in London is stored away the tattered remainder of all the twenty-four shirts which my father gave me on my twenty-first birthday—a gift which only he could have conceived. And the spare bedroom of this Goodwood Park flat is now littered with the remnants of a vast dinner service which Carol and I bought on our honeymoon in Quimper and took with us in two packing-cases from England to Singapore. When we opened the packing-cases a few days ago we found that most of the gaily coloured plates and bowls and dishes were smashed beyond repair. The Japanese may have the trouble of throwing away the pieces. I won't.

The eventual loss of all my possessions at Goodwood Park now seems inevitable. But I can't bear to part with them voluntarily or a moment sooner than is necessary. And after all the price I'm paying in the form of rent is purely nominal. In theory it is ludicrously high, for it still includes all my own and Carol's meals. But I feel quite confident that by the time it is due for presentation at the end of the month I shall either be dead or a prisoner or a refugee disguised as a native fisherman in a sampan!

The highlight of today's events was undoubtedly Hudson's introductory talk to his new series, "Singapore Citizen". I don't for a moment suppose that anything so outspoken has ever before been broadcast from a government-controlled station. His was the voice of the people. He roundly attacked the administration. He condemned idlers both among the Europeans and Asiatics. Without direct reference to it, he ridiculed the Governor's speech by pointing out that it was folly to prattle about the example of London, Malta, Chungking, etc., when everyone knew that those places possessed fine shelters, whereas in Singapore the only protection against air attack was a few slit trenches and street-side drains. He rejected official excuses for failure to make civilian defence a reality instead of a mockery and said that it was not too late to begin now— that it was imperative to do so. He came forward with the concrete suggestion that shelters could be built by tunnelling into the hills. "If the Government say they can't get the labour for this," he concluded, "I'll guarantee to go out and get it myself."

In many ways this was by far the most exciting occasion in my experience of broadcasting from Singapore, for, apart from the intrinsic merits of the talk, I had an instinctive feeling while Hudson was speaking that his words were being listened to by a large public and were producing a tangible effect. I can't say the same of any other programme with which I've been associated. On the

a spectacular escape. I've always known him as a charming, intelligent, rather spare-looking, gentle-mannered man—an artist by inclination and a soldier only by duty and force of circumstance. Seeing him now apparently unchanged, my admiration for what he'd done was all the more profound because it seemed so out of tune with his nature and upbringing. For his part he was superbly British and casual about the whole thing. He was amused by his adventure, and that's why he talked of it, but he showed no inclination to dramatize or brag about it, nor did he expect special consideration and attention from others because of what he'd been through. He was not in the least sorry for himself. He'd been given a few days' leave, at the end of which he'd rejoin his unit. Meanwhile, he was recuperating in a large and comfortable house secluded on the top of a hill and reached by a long, snakelike drive. There were good food and drink to be had again and friends to be met with, and for the moment he was content. The future could look after itself.

At the directorial tea-party this afternoon Davis talked of the defence of the Cathay, which he's taking energetic measures to improve, for he's just been elected chairman of the Cathay Defence Committee. The present position is deplorable. Though passes were issued weeks ago, they have not been used, and the several entrances to the Cathay, which is one of the chief nerve centres of the British war effort in Singapore, are without guard of any kind. Davis has already formulated plans to block up all the entrances save one, which will be watched over by an armed guard, and I've no doubt that characteristically he will get things done in the minimum possible time. But it is an ironic commentary on events here that it has been left to a civilian, who has only been back in Singapore a few days, to institute elementary precautions for the protection of the Cathay building, which, incidentally, has an anti-aircraft gun on its roof, from spies and saboteurs. It tempts one to suppose that if the fate of Malaya and Singapore had not been left in the care of sleepy Colonial administrators and outmoded military pundits, but had been entrusted to young men of Davis's calibre—young men of imagination, initiative and resource—this tragedy, which is moving inexorably towards its ultimate curtain, might well have been avoided, or at any rate have been a tragedy clothed in glory. In the last few days there have been some small signs of improvement in the conduct of affairs, signs that the common-sense view which the average soldier and the average civilian here has always held and has consistently striven for is at length beginning to prevail. But I fear that in the present belated circumstances these signs amount only to vigorous, pathetically courageous kicks of a man on his back and in his death throes.

I called in for another drink with Jack on my way up to the studios. I think that even in the first thrill of having reached safety again he is well aware that his days of liberty or life are numbered, though he is obviously set on enjoying what few may remain to him. And yet only once did he show any indication of embitterment, and that was when he voiced his hatred of the Japs and of the madness and greed which prompted the Americans and ourselves to teach these ancient barbarians how to wage a modern war. While he didn't actually admit that the fall of Singapore was now inevitable, he made the point —so often made before in this war, but made by him from first-hand experience —that the finest army is powerless without adequate air cover and that the bravest soldier is incapable of standing up indefinitely to unrestricted dive-bombing. One knows, of course, that unrestricted dive-bombing has been the lot of our troops throughout the Malayan campaign. Jack says that during his whole time at the front he saw only two British 'planes in the sky. The Japs were able to come over and dive-bomb at will. Those who underwent this ordeal must have felt like unarmed men being shot at with a seemingly inexhaustible supply of ammunition. Of course they had to give way in the end— or die. Unfortunately, there are no grounds for believing that the position will be any healthier for them when the battle of Singapore begins. On the contrary, it is likely to be worse, for at the moment there is not a single fighter 'plane left on the island. All the airfields were bombed into uselessness by the end of last week, and such 'planes as the R.A.F. have at their disposal for our defence are now allegedly operating from a secret base in Sumatra.

The only solid hope one can entertain is that the battle of Singapore never *will* begin, that the Japanese won't dare to attempt a landing on this island; will funk crossing the Straits of Johore in the same way as the Germans funked a crossing of the Channel. A slender hope, I'm afraid. And yet tonight in the 8.30 news the dear old B.B.C., quoting a Japanese source, solemnly announced that the "mass assault on Singapore had begun". Is the mass assault, then, no more than the rather half-hearted air raids and intermittent shelling which we've endured today and yesterday? Is that the maximum offensive effort of which the Japs are capable? If so we can certainly take it. Oh yes, we can go on taking it indefinitely.

Unfortunately the B.B.C. did not attempt to define "mass assault" and seems to have no idea at all of what is actually happening in Singapore. Its announcement therefore could hardly have had a very reassuring effect on the majority of its listeners at home and in the Empire.

On me, however, the news acted as a momentary stimulus, and I felt almost buoyant during my evening of announcing at Thomson Road studios. But when I got back to Goodwood and lay quietly reading in bed, and there was not even the faintest murmur of bomb or gun, I knew I had been fooled. I realized then that the B.B.C. had been the victim of Japanese propaganda, and that I, out of wishful thinking, had fallen a victim secondhand.

No, the mass assault has not begun yet, whatever the B.B.C. and the Japanese may say. It will not begin, I'm superstitiously convinced, until we've endured that Hongkong prelude of a twelve-hour artillery barrage.

Goodwood Park Hotel—Friday, February 6, 1942.

So far as the mass assault goes, today has been no more fearsome than yesterday. The Japanese are still refraining from any unusual activity.

Most of my working hours were spent coping unsuccessfully with a situation which was worse than the number one star falling sick just before the first night. Hudson rang up this morning to say that owing to unforeseen circumstances he was obliged to postpone the second talk in his new series, which he was due to broadcast tonight, until Monday evening. It was useless trying to persuade him to change his mind, for obviously he had no choice in the matter. On the other hand, I couldn't doubt that a larger audience than ever would be waiting eagerly to hear him, and that in view of the unique ascendancy which he's acquired over Singapore's listening public it would be impossible to find an adequate substitute. I dallied for hours with several fanciful ideas, including an invitation to the director of A.R.P. to come to the microphone and answer Hudson. But in the end I abandoned them all as pointless or impractical. I handed over the quarter of an hour's programme allocation to the admirable Victor Grosz, contenting myself with a long and dramatically worded special announcement, which was designed to explain away our apparent lapse in good showmanship.

I hope it succeeded in its purpose. But I have an uncomfortable feeling that the chance for Hudson to consolidate his advance may never come again. In normal circumstances, of course, one wouldn't have been worried in the least by a mere three-days' postponement. After all, short postponements of broadcast programmes are the most usual, the most natural, the most inevitable occurrences. But, as we are living now—on the edge of the end—every moment is super-precious, and Monday seems a hell of a long way off. By then large-scale listening and even broadcasting itself may have become impossibilities.

We are living strictly in the present. While we live thus there is still time for new ideas, bold action, hard work, courage, laughter, enjoyment. And there is still time apparently for little irritants which, though they have nothing to do with the war or the Japanese, assume momentarily the import of disaster. I encountered one myself this evening. It so happened that Margaret, who hitherto has been suspiciously evasive whenever I've asked her about the fate of those cars which were left behind at Clifford's Pier, admitted to me that she had come into possession of a nice second-hand Hillman, which even now was parked outside the Mount Sophia entrance of the Cathay. In a fit of unrestrained avarice I promptly demanded the right to call it my own, and, deserting my trusted Morris without a qualm, drove it off to Thomson Road. Alas! I was soon punished for my faithlessness and greed. The Hillman moved only in fits and jerks and responded to its brakes with even more reluctance. On arrival I found that its radiator was belching steam and that both its front tyres were as flat as badly made pancakes. To someone as unmechanically minded as myself it was a total loss.

I entered the studio in a mood of impotent rage and dithering self-pity, which was none the less so engrossing that it made me impervious to fear or even thought of the Japanese bombers. A taxi to take me home again was, of course, beyond the realm of fancy, and it was only as a result of considerable persuasion and a full, humiliating confession of my predicament that Eric Robertson at length agreed to come to my rescue and I was saved from another mosquito-bedevilled night in the office armchair.

I had an hour or two to wait after I'd finished my evening's broadcast—a presented record programme of the early works of Noel Coward—and I occupied the time chatting with Scott, one of our volunteer part-time announcers who is an engineer by profession. His working day begins before seven o'clock in the morning, and he spends several evenings a week on announcing duty either at Thomson Road or the Cathay. In fact he's characteristic of those many European civilians in Singapore who certainly merit praise but have so far not been distinguished from the few who deserve censure.

Scott is a young man—in his early thirties, I should say. He told me that if he'd been able to follow his own choice he would have been a writer or a painter rather than an engineer. We discovered that we had mutual friends in London and perhaps had met each other before. He used to live in Chelsea, and we reminisced about the landmarks on the King's Road—the Classic cinema and the Chelsea Palace and the Five Bells. After a while we began to talk of the immediate future. Scott said that he did not imagine there was the remotest possibility of his being able to leave before the end came, but that he wasn't particularly worried or alarmed. He intended, whatever happened, to make a break for it, and he thought there was a very good chance of success. I fancy that in this respect his view of things is fairly typical at the moment. Most of us are resigned to the probability of Singapore falling, but we can't yet imagine ourselves actual prisoners of the Japanese.

Eric Robertson drove me back to the Cathay. Davis and Aubrey were both in the headquarters flat. Davis, in his shirtsleeves, with a half-empty bottle of beer by his side, was correcting the draft of a talk which he's due to broadcast on Sunday night. He handed it to me to read page by page. It's a brave and concise script. A lot of it is concerned with the present and future of the M.B.C. He describes the progress that has been made in the last year and points out that, although it has not been possible to make the service entirely Jap-proof, four transmissions in thirteen different languages are still being maintained and emergency measures have been taken to ensure that Singapore will never be blasted off the air. He pays tribute to the loyalty and devotion of the Asiatic staff. And he singles out for special praise the switchboard telephonists, who day and night during the past week of bombing and shelling have never missed a call. These girls, incidentally—Chinese Eurasians, most of them—do not work in an underground shelter. They occupy an ordinary room on the fourth floor of the Cathay building.

The theme of Davis' talk is a comparison between the London of 1940–41 and the Singapore of today. Davis is a cockney born and bred who believes there is no place in the world more beautiful than the Thames Embankment under the mist of an early autumn morning. When Davis left London late in October, 1940, he was immeasurably depressed, for he felt certain that the city of his birth was doomed to destruction. But when he returned a year later he found it more alive than ever before, and, though battered and shabby, purged of much of its silliness and class-consciousness. He believes that history will be repeated here. Singapore, he says, has always been misunderstood and unfairly maligned; but now it has the opportunity to prove its worth. And he looks forward to the days immediately ahead when the world will be obliged to acclaim the inhabitants of this "equatorial Sodom and Gomorrah" as "half a million heroes".

Is Davis sincere in his prediction? Does he really believe that Singapore is spiritually equipped to withstand a long siege with heroism? I think he has allowed himself to be convinced by his emotions, if not by his common sense. For he arrived very late on the scene, and casting around him now, can he doubt that many people here—both European and Asiatic—are made of the same unconquerable stuff as the Londoners who won their part of the Battle of Britain? If by some miracle this island should hold, then I suppose the story of folly and negligence in high places will be forgotten; the record of the idlers and the ratters will be overlooked, and all who fashioned a great potential disgrace in our history will be vindicated by the world's applause. But if in compliance with every argument of reason this island should fall, then I am afraid there will be no admission that in its last hours it harboured any heroes. The soldiers who fought so gallantly and so vainly, the little men and women—the air-raid wardens, the office workers, the doctors, the nurses, the ambulance drivers, and so on—who remained at their posts to the end without apparent hope of eventual salvation or reward will share in the general condemnation which critics will find so easy to fasten on to the military and civilian leaders and on to those European parasites who have already run away.

There are heroes in Singapore—if heroes in modern war are men and women of energy and intelligence prepared to place the guardianship of freedom before their own self-interest and their own self-preservation. In the last few days their number has been growing, even though they are still far short of half a million strong, and, as I've said before, they have begun to make their presence felt. I dare to believe that if the enemy is foolish enough to hold off his assault for another week or so they may yet have time to organize a people's defence of Singapore comparable with the defence of London or Moscow. But I dare not believe that such a chance will ever be allowed them.

Goodwood Park Hotel—Saturday, February 7, 1942.

Today has been exceptionally idle and hard to fill. I spent most of the morning arranging the music for *The White Cliffs*, which I'm rehearsing in the studio tomorrow and with which I really intend to go to town. I handed Victor Grosz a copy of the script marked with such brief stage directions as "nostalgic music", "dramatic music", "doleful music", "Elizabethan music", "cheering crowd", "sound of water", "Edwardian waltz", "pre-war ragtime", "post-war jazz", etc., etc., and he provided me in turn with a collection of twenty-four records from which I've now been able to extract suitable "links". The whole thing will be unashamedly sentimental. But somehow the mere contemplation of producing it, which at any other time I would doubtless have shunned, represents for me a much-needed emotional outlet. *The White Cliffs* is an American lady's declaration of a tender and critical love for England, and I suppose that my idea of ending it with a great swelling chorus of "Rule, Britannia" would be regarded by any normal man of taste as unpardonably meretricious or as a deliberate attempt to make fun of the poem itself. But at this moment the strains of "Rule, Britannia", introduced quietly at first and then brought to a terrific crescendo after the speaker has affirmed that in a world where England is no more she does not wish to live, seem to me entirely appropriate and extremely moving.

This afternoon, for want of something better to do, I amused myself concocting an imaginary programme for our last day on the air in Singapore. Such humour as the result possesses is perhaps too esoteric for permanent record. It begins with John Ilsley sounding the air-raid warning and includes among other choice items outside broadcasts of a naval bombardment, a land assault and a paratroop attack, two Victor Grosz musical specialities, the one called "Melodious Memories" and the other "Memories Melodious", and a talk entitled "How to Mend a Puncture", by Mrs. M. Robinson, being the first in a new series "Hints to Motorists". It ends immediately before the announcement of the blowing of the transmitters at midnight with a stentorian voice saying, "Here is a boat and this is Eric Robertson building it." The final item, apart from its implied recognition of the M.B.C.'s unofficial director of evacuation, is an elaboration of a joke originally coined by Aubrey, who, in view of Eric's chronic habit of never completing a programme until the last moment, once impersonated him as follows : "Here is the news, and this is Eric Robertson typing it."

When I looked at my completed work I thought that perhaps it was rather tempting Providence. However, I couldn't bring myself to tear up something on which I'd expended considerable trouble and I couldn't resist showing it to Aubrey and Davis at the directorial tea-party. Aubrey made one alteration which enriched the whole. In place of the Victor Grosz musical programme at 11 p.m. (that is, after the various outside broadcasts of enemy action) he put in recorded excerpts from *Madame Butterfly*.

The noise of gunfire, though distant, has been quite loud and insistent today. But already it has become as familiar to us as the sound of aeroplane or traffic, and therefore causes no more than casual comment. This evening, as we sat on the front veranda of Biron Fox's house, where Jack is still a guest, it did not deter us in the least from indulging in what was nearly a representation of European life at cocktail hour in peacetime Singapore. We chatted amiably and laughed a little and sipped exotic-looking drinks which were served to us discreetly and deferentially by a well-trained Malay servant. Our conversation only just revealed that we were fully conscious of the impermanence of the present and the threat of the immediate future.

There were about six of us sitting there, and I do not think it could fairly be said of any one of us that we had not worked hard in our separate ways during the past two months or had been unmindful of the seriousness of the situation by which we were menaced. And yet I suppose to a casual observer we would have appeared typical of those Singaporeans who have allegedly swilled whisky and pursued pleasure instead of making preparations to repel the enemy. I sometimes think that certain of the foreign newspaper correspondents who attacked British indifference to reality with such frenzy were in fact manifesting their subconscious envy of a quality of outward aloofness to danger which they themselves could neither master nor understand.

All we needed to complete the scene were a few decorative ladies. Or perhaps I exaggerate; for I don't honestly believe that peacetime Singapore was ever very richly endowed in that respect. Of course there are exceptions, but most of the really attractive women I have seen would not have come here but for the war, or rather the threat of war. I remember how glad I was to learn before I left London that Bunty was in Singapore, for though I had only met her once or twice, she represented a link with the aesthetic delights of civilization which I supposed I was leaving behind—Beauty and the Theatre. Bunty is, in any *milieu*, a very decorative lady. And so too are her three colleagues—Carol (whom modesty won't prevent me from specifying), Joan Tanner and Joan Reid. Together these four were known latterly as the glamour girls of Kranji, and are known now, I hope, as the glamour girls of Bandoeng. But I doubt the possibility of a quartet in the same class at a *Pahit* party of pre-war days. Sweet, indeed, are the blessings of adversity!

Jack is still very lame, and I don't suppose for a moment he will be fit to return to his unit for some days yet. He's had a cable from Bunty, with which he's obviously delighted, and though he misses her greatly it's a relief for him to know that she's reached safety. My feelings about Carol are the same. The future seems considerably less alarming now that I know I have only myself to think of. I told Jack how reluctant Bunty had been to leave without news of him, how the decision was forced upon her at a few hours' notice and how she planned to make her way to New York (where her child is living). But as a matter of fact he had never expected to find her still here. He had more or less lost count of time while he was in the jungle and, philosophically, had been prepared when he reached Singapore to discover it already in enemy hands.

Unfortunately, he still appeared bashful of monopolizing the conversation, and recounted only a few brief incidents of his journey through the Japanese lines. But these were sufficient to convince me that his description of it as a *Boys' Own* adventure story was entirely appropriate. Indeed, one can't think of it at all except in terms of clichés like "hairbreadth escape", "cheating death" and so on, for in fact he *did* have hairbreadth escapes and he *did* cheat death or capture. There was the time when a Japanese patrol approached within a few feet of him. He and his men took cover in the undergrowth. When the enemy soldiers passed by they were so close that he could have touched their boots, which, as if detached from their bodies, were moving robot-like immediately above him. And there was the time when he decided to sleep in hiding during the days and to venture along a railway line during the hours of darkness. The scheme worked out well enough for the first two nights. On the third night, however, which coincided with bright moonlight, he ran slap into a score or so of Japanese soldiers on bicycles. It would have been suicide to try to fight it out. So, ignoring the risk of a bullet in the back, he and his men, like hunted animals, made a wild dash down the embankment and back into the protective labyrinth of the jungle. The Japanese fired but missed by inches. "They're poor marksmen with a rifle," said Jack, "though with a mortar they're deadly."

As I had this little glimpse into his adventures I couldn't help wondering whether Fate will be so cruel as to allow him to fall a prisoner to the enemy in Singapore after his spectacular escape from Malaya. For—to permit myself another appropriate cliché—spectacular it certainly was.

I shall probably never know all the details, for he has been refused permission to broadcast. It is a great pity and a great waste of a good opportunity to put something worth while over the air. His is just the sort of story listeners want to hear and should be allowed to hear at the moment, and told at first hand by an experienced actor it would make first-class radio material from any point of view. However, I am not altogether surprised. Foolish as it may be, this refusal fits in nicely with the official policy of obstinate silence about the accomplishments of the British forces in Malaya which has persisted from the very beginning of the campaign. Apparently there's no chance even now of its being relaxed. The world, I suppose, will always be encouraged to believe that this, like Libya, is strictly an Aussie show until, of course, the time comes to apportion the blame.

The men for whom I feel most sorry are the so-called reinforcements who've been arriving by shiploads in the last few days. From their looks most of them are very young. They have had no previous training in jungle warfare and they have no knowledge of the kind of predicament into which they've been plunged or of the swiftly falling fate which will probably engulf them. They are, in brief, as lambs who have been led to the slaughter.

After dinner tonight, in the small candle-lit bar of the Goodwood Park Hotel, Eric Robertson and I talked for a while with one of the newly arrived Army officers. We gathered he was here on some kind of Intelligence job, for he told us that he was a Japanese linguist and knew a good deal about Japanese psychology. But his specialized knowledge had apparently given him not the slightest inkling of the gravity of the present situation. He seemed to imagine that he would have ample time to settle down at his leisure, and he was far more interested in discovering from us what there was to be done and seen in Singapore, and where were the best places to live and eat, etc., than in discussing the war's immediate future. We hadn't the heart to disillusion him. And indeed he must have been confirmed in his blissful, ignorant calm by the general atmosphere in

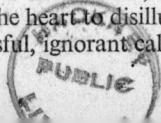

the bar of hearty, carefree, "here's how" jollity which was sustained, in particular, by Mrs. Q.

Who is Mrs. Q. ? She is the *grande dame* of the European women still left in Singapore. As a matter of fact there are far more European women left in Singapore than I supposed when the great exodus took place a week ago. There is Helen Dicksey, for example, who refuses point-blank to contemplate departure. There is Diana Stafford, one of the local belles who, deaf to the voice of prudence or self-preservation, bravely insists on remaining at her post as a volunteer nurse in the general hospital. And there is Mrs. Q.

I am not sure whether Mrs. Q. is doing or has ever done a full-time war job. I know that once when Carol and I were complaining softly, because the air-raid alarm had sounded and the service of our dinner had consequently come to a full stop, she shouted across the room that we had only ourselves to blame for the inconvenience of which we were now victims. "You should have your 'Makan' earlier," she admonished us severely. And she seemed incapable of understanding that our work usually prevented us from eating until late.

But Mrs. Q. is a loyal and staunch resident of Goodwood Park. Tonight she came striding into the bar, followed by three or four male attendants. In her loud, confident, commanding voice she shouted to the rather elderly Malay barman, "Give me the dice and I'll have a Kuala Lumpur."

Oh, God! Cecil Brown and all you others who have hated and despised this place and have not hesitated to say so, there, surely, is your epitaph for Singapore—"Give me the dice and I'll have a Kuala Lumpur." A few months ago it would have been nauseating. It would have been characteristic, illustrative of all that is worst in the European system here—the slothfulness, vulgarity, indulgence, false luxuriance, self-interest, indifference to humanity which made peacetime Singapore a fat and easy prey for any determined and well-organized foe. But now with the guns booming and the bombs falling and the enemy only a few miles off, across a narrow strip of water, and this hotel likely to become at any time a rendezvous for a Japanese picnic of murder, barbarity, loot and rape, is there not something absurdly, comically magnificent about it ?

One can no longer be nauseated. One can no longer be angered. One can only laugh.

Mrs. Q., I salute you. "Give me the dice and I'll have a Kuala Lumpur."

Goodwood Park Hotel—Sunday, February 8, 1942.

One's worst dread nowadays, as I've said before, is having nothing to do. Every minute has got to be filled somehow. So this morning, with no work of any kind awaiting me at the office, my reason was saved by a telephone call from Rowan Rivett. He asked me whether I'd be willing to supply tonight's five-minute news-letter in the "Calling the Allied World" series. I said I certainly would, and sat down at once to knock out a script.

The result of my labour was not very profound, for I don't flatter myself that I'm well cast in the role of news commentator. I said a good deal about Hudson's broadcast, and I was glad of this opportunity, for in my view Hudson's broadcast was representative of a revolt which deserves world-wide publicity. I described in general terms the spiritual change for the better which has become apparent in the last few days. And I ended with an unconditional affirmation that Singapore is going to hold. This, perhaps, was a minor breach of personal integrity. But it was justified, I'm sure. For to voice the smallest hint of lack of confidence in any kind of public announcement is no longer sensible realism but plain stupidity and defeatism.

As a matter of fact I'm still obstinately convinced that it never was sensible, at *any* stage of the war, to give Asiatic listeners the impression that the British were incapable of winning. In other words, defeats and shortcomings should not have been admitted, but either vigorously explained away or, whenever possible, concealed. All the official talk in communiqués of forced withdrawals, setbacks, disasters, ill-preparedness, etc., merely substantiated the main enemy propaganda lines, which were, in brief, (a) invincibility of Japanese arms and (b) no real volition or intent on behalf of the British to fight for Malaya and Singapore.

When I argue thus I am not stating any hastily formed views of my own. I am quoting the expert opinions of our Asiatic programme organizers, who told me from the word "go" that we were tragically mistaken ever to admit in news broadcasts—either directly or by implication—that the enemy was strong and that we were weak. And that is why I am still satisfied that Cecil Brown was rightly banned from the air. I do not think he was rightly banned because his criticisms as such were unjust or because his affronts to British susceptibilities were intolerable. I think he was rightly banned because he ignored the effect which his words would have on Asiatic listeners. So far as they were concerned, he was a prophet of doom—in fact he was tantamount to a full-fledged Japanese propagandist. Admittedly, our own authorities did not consider Oriental reactions very carefully. But Cecil Brown never bothered about them at all. He was interested only in serving up the news—hot and unvarnished—to the Great American Public, who, God knows, after Pearl Harbour, were not in a position to help very much.

I had lunch with Margaret in her flat at the Cathay. Her husband and Andrew Carruthers' elder brother, Nigel, were there—both on short leave from service with the Volunteers. We were served with an excellent dish of curried chicken and rice. I set about it thoughtlessly with a knife and fork and noticed too late that the others were eating it correctly, in the European Malayan fashion, with a spoon. I was so embarrassed that I refused a second helping —which shows that it is still possible to be bothered by minor conventions.

The afternoon was spent rehearsing *The White Cliffs* up at Thomson Road. Margaret helped me manipulate the four gramophone turntables which I needed for my music and effects, for there was no competent programme engineer on duty and I had to manage the M.B.C.'s archaic control board myself. It took us more than four hours before we were through, and it must have been a trying experience for Patricia Mills, who sat alone in the studio repeating the same lines over and over again. She was very patient, however, and didn't seem to resent in the least the continued interruptions which were caused not only by technical mistakes on my part but by a succession of air-raid Alerts. The climax came when an excited Asiatic roof-spotter dashed up the passage shouting, "The enemy is here!" For a moment we were seriously shaken, but, in response to some shrewdly directed questions, this alarmist explained that he had only meant to warn us that Japanese 'planes were immediately overhead. Obediently we adjourned to the nearest trench.

When we got back we were subjected to a further delay by the sudden and quite unexpected occupation of the control room's loudspeaker by Allan Rose, whom we had left enthroned on a cattle-boat hatch exactly a week ago. It seemed an age since I had last heard his voice, and I suppose that now it would have had for me a ghostlike quality if it hadn't been so loud and clear and meticulous and if its message had not been so extremely prosaic. It kept reiterating monotonously, "This is the Malaya Broadcasting Corporation calling in a test transmission. This is the Malaya Broadcasting Corporation calling in a test transmission." It was telling us, of course, in its own fashion—and I've no doubt that in the studio at the Cathay Aubrey and Davis were listening attentively—that the Batavia unit had arrived safely and was already prepared and equipped to take over its allotted share of news bulletins. But I am afraid that at this particular moment I didn't much care. I felt neither joy nor relief, nor indeed any emotion other than acute irritation that my rehearsal was being held up once again. I ordered the engineers to banish Mr. Rose from the control room, and after some show of protest they did as I asked. Thus we were able to proceed with what seemed at the time the most important business imaginable.

At its best the fashioning of entertainment has an all-engrossing quality which is the foundation, I fancy, of that noble tradition in the theatre—"The show must go on." While one's heart is fully engaged in it, one lives in a world apart. One is completely immune to the impact of events from outside, however significant they may be in themselves, and one's concentration cannot be disturbed. For that reason I don't think I have ever been frightened by bombings while I've been rehearsing or broadcasting at Thomson Road, and only once or twice has my attention wandered—and that has been because of my lack of interest in the particular programme and not because of the intensity of the particular air raid. For the same reason the greater part of my work in Singapore has been—and still is—an escape from fear, or rather a means of shutting myself off from fear. Fortunately, it is a form of escapism which is not akin to running away from issues which ought to be faced, and is therefore untainted by any sense of guilt. For I am now more than ever convinced that the continuance of our broadcast programmes is an essential part of the defence of Singapore, and this very conviction intensifies the all-engrossing quality of my job as a fashioner of entertainment.

The news that the Batavia unit has arrived safely is, of course, extremely reassuring. It means that it is still possible to get out of this place and live—and I must confess I had begun to doubt that in the last few days. It means that we have allies in a near-by land which is secure, at the moment, from sudden subjugation. It means a link with normality and with the outside world. It means a hundred-per-cent certainty that so long as an inch of Singapore's soil remains in British hands, the M.B.C. will never be silenced.

Yes, the news obviously has exciting significance, but I had no realization of it until after the rehearsal was over and we were on our way back to Goodwood Park. Nor did I realize until then that the guns were louder and more insistent than I had ever heard them before.

It is past midnight now and they have not ceased. Aubrey, who is spending the night with me, is as optimistic as ever. He says that we are obviously giving the Japs on the Johore mainland a hell of a pasting. I hope he's right. But I've a haunting fear, which I dare not speak aloud but cannot quell, that the enemy guns and not our own are making most of the noise, which represents the bombardment prelude before the mass assault begins. I calculate that the guns have already been in continuous action for more than seven hours. They thundered away during dinner at Goodwood Park and throughout the broadcast of my "Singapore Newsletter", when they must have been clearly audible to all our listeners in the Allied world, and while we were driving home again. If they do not become quiet within the next five hours, then the Hongkong parallel will be complete.

Earlier this evening the admirable and remarkable Chinese servant (I wish I knew his name) was instructed without previous warning to blackout the spare bedroom. He accomplished the task in less than thirty minutes with the aid of a few odd bits of cardboard and brown paper. Aubrey had insisted on it, since he likes to read half the night. Indeed, he cannot sleep at all otherwise.

Personally I have never bothered much about the blackout. I've been content to grope my way through the darkness into bed. I am not able to concentrate sufficiently to enjoy a book, and tonight I shall just close my eyes and pray for swift unconsciousness and hope that when I awake the guns will be silent.

The Cathay—Monday, February 9, 1942.

I don't know when the barrage finally came to an end. In my fervent desire for it to cease I had been conscious of it intermittently throughout the night and had slept badly. When I awoke this morning it was apparently over. Indeed, I might have forgotten my fears of yestereve if it hadn't been for a series of devastating explosions which began during breakfast. They lasted for about half an hour and happened at regular intervals of three minutes or so. They were so loud that when the first one came Aubrey and I made an involuntary dash for cover. Their very noise was like a sharp blow between the eyes, and even after we had grown used to them and knew that they were coming it was impossible not to be cowed by them.

Presumably one of the Japanese big guns was responsible. By the time we reached the Cathay the gun had either been put out of action or had ceased fire of its own account. There was quiet again, and the usual early morning air raid had not yet materialized. But none the less there was an obvious atmosphere of foreboding. I went up to the news room; Eric Robertson stood by Rowan Rivett's desk, reading through what I supposed was the ten o'clock news bulletin. He said good morning and nothing much else and seemed in no mood to converse.

Carter came in, looking very disconsolate. He explained that the broadcast on which he had set such great store—his tribute to the Scottish regiment—had been cancelled and that there was now small likelihood that it would ever be done. Then he added quite casually, as if the news in itself were only of subsidiary importance to the professional disappointment which it had caused him, "I suppose you know they've landed."

"You mean," I said, trying desperately to make him disavow what I really thought he meant, "you mean they've landed on that small island near by?"

"No, they've landed on Singapore."

I glanced at Eric for confirmation. He was holding a piece of paper. It contained a message which in a few minutes he would broadcast to the world. He read it aloud for my benefit. "Here is a special communiqué. In the early hours of this morning the enemy succeeded in effecting a landing in force . . ."

For the first time in this war I knew what it was to be really scared. I thought I had been scared on the night of September 1—the night following the Nazi invasion of Poland and thirty-six hours before Britain and France declared war on Germany. That was the first night of the blackout in London. I hated it. But the streets in the West End were as crowded as ever, and for most of the people it was a great game trying to grope their way to familiar landmarks which mistakenly they had supposed they could find with their eyes shut. The bars and the restaurants and the cafés, which had been hastily equipped with light traps, were refuges from the darkness. In a famous popular café on Piccadilly Circus, filled to overflowing, there was an atmosphere of exuberant, wild, almost hysterical cheer. Everyone was talking to everyone else, which is a habit Englishmen indulge in only at moments of supreme national crisis, as when the King dies or abdicates. A rumour circulated, while I was there, that the Nazis intended a surprise air attack on London and that the Luftwaffe had just crossed the coast at Dover. But this caused only excitement and no alarm. Most of the men were already in uniform, and were toasting each other from table to table. I suppose that the blackout and the mobilization and the inevitability of war represented a tremendous relief from the shame and uncertainty of the past year. But I had the impression that we were celebrating not so much the beginning of a new epoch as a return to the suddenly glamourized days of 1914 and that the morrow would bring disillusionment. Fortunately, that was the only occasion when the spirit of this war, which hadn't even begun at the time, resembled the hysterical spirit of the last.

I had been on a fruitless quest to join the auxiliary police. I got back to our flat in Courtfield Gardens just in time for the midnight news. Carol was there and my mother, aunt, brother and two acquaintances whom we had only met recently and would never see again but whose lives were at the moment completely interwoven with our own. At the end of the news a great orchestra crashed unexpectedly into "God Save the King". We all rose, and as we listened in silence it was impossible not to be deeply moved. I put off going to bed as long as possible. I knew that I wouldn't sleep a wink, and of course I didn't. My imagination ran riot, and childhood memories of Zeppelin raids, when the moon was full over London, became as vivid as if they were of yesterday. As a child I had the curious habit of thinking in colours. Every word that I spoke conjured up a particular colour in my mind, and the words belonging to my limited vocabulary of those days have retained their colour. Germany, of course, was black, and England was white. Germany still is black, and England is still white. Now I could see the 'planes lined up on the landing-grounds of that black land. I could see them take off and fly at great speed with their bombloads towards England. I could see them cross the coast at Dover, and, rigid and expectant, I awaited the first note of the sirens while I tried by rational and common-sense arguments to convince myself that my imagination was awry and that my fears were groundless, and when I failed I strained my eyes to detect the first signs of the dawn.

But I wasn't really scared then. And I wasn't really scared during those long nights a year later when the bombs screamed and thudded all around, and I lay on a mattress in a basement shelter, my whole mind concentrated on the next minute and not wishing to be disturbed from this aimless, gruelling occupation by speaking or being spoken to and not daring to go to sleep lest a bomb become my bedfellow, a complete victim of my imagination.

No, I wasn't really scared then, though I thought I was. I was scared now for the first time in this war. I was overcome by a choking, sickening fear—the worst kind of fear—the fear of the unknowable, the fear of something which can only be conceived in the fancy. All fear is a product of danger and imagination. We don't necessarily hand out medals to heroes, we hand out medals for heroic accomplishments. That is the best we can do. Real heroism is the conquest of fear in the face of danger, and when a man does a brave thing we have no means of telling whether or not he has a vivid imagination.

Strange to relate, the news came as a terrific shock, and that doubtless intensified the fear it wrought in me. It needed getting used to, for though my common sense had repeatedly warned me that Singapore was doomed to fall into Japanese hands, my fancy had never dwelled more than casually on what would happen to me when the enemy did arrive. Somehow I had contrived for the most part to remain aloof from the tide of events and to watch myself amusedly and unbelievingly trapped on this beleaguered island. Even during the past week the prospect of actually being taken prisoner by the Japanese seemed too remote for serious contemplation, and I had put it from me. But now suddenly and crushingly the fantastic had become real, and what already seemed ghastly in imagination might soon be ghastlier still in actual experience.

Fortunately I recovered my balance fairly quickly. For a while terror seemed to overwhelm me, and I could do nothing but wander hopelessly from room to room trying to find someone who would confess to being as scared as I was. I felt better after listening in the studio to the news bulletin, for Eric Robertson read the special communiqué quite coolly and impersonally and the Asiatic engineer at the control board was obviously unperturbed and ready to carry on to the end with his allotted work. I felt better still after ringing up Jack.

"Well, it's pretty bad," I began.

"Yes," he replied, "I'm afraid they're up to something. It was a rough night."

"I suppose you've heard they've landed?"

"No, I hadn't heard. When?"

"Early this morning, apparently."

"Is that official?"

"Yes, we've just broadcast a special communiqué."

"I'm afraid I missed it. Do you know *where* they've landed?"

"No, there aren't any details yet. Just said they'd landed in force."

"In force! Doesn't sound too good. Well, ring me up if you hear anything further, won't you, Giles?"

"Surely. I'll try and call round this evening."

"Yes, do."

If Jack, who has far more cause to be alarmed than I, could take it all so calmly, I decided there was no earthly reason why I shouldn't. But, paradoxically enough, my cure was completed by the morning's first air raid, which took place belatedly about eleven o'clock. Somehow the sirens and the anti-aircraft fire and the throbbing of the 'planes seemed so familiar and reminiscent of everyday life in Singapore that they brought me home to normality and enabled me once again to get outside of my fears and to recapture the comfortable illusion that whatever was implied in the imminent threat of enemy occupation was something belonging to the realms of fancy which couldn't possibly happen to me.

I went down to the Mount Sophia entrance hall, where Aubrey habitually takes shelter in an erstwhile display shop window. He sits cross-legged on a three-cornered ledge behind a glassless frame and from this vantage point surveys the milling crowd. He told me that Rivett had just returned from a Press conference with Major-General Gordon Bennett. Apparently enemy artillery knocked out all our beach lights save one, which promptly fused. The Japs then took to their boats and were able to land under cover of darkness. Bennett announced that he has succeeded in forming a defensive line. He believes, of course, that he can hold it, but unfortunately experience of what happened to our various defensive lines in Malaya does not inspire one with particular faith in this latest model.

The air raid didn't amount to much, and when it was over there was quiet again. As a matter of fact, today has been remarkable for its long periods of silence, which during the morning and the early hours of the afternoon were often so profound that I found it impossible to believe that this small island was actually a battleground. I remember standing with Aubrey by one of the Cathay balconies which commands a good view of the whole terrain up to the Johore Straits. I asked him where he thought the fighting was going on. He pointed to a place which didn't look more than a few miles off. He may have been right, for to be sure there were clouds of smoke drifting rather lazily skyward. But there wasn't so much as the sound of a rifle firing.

In the end I got through quite a good morning's work. At one point, while I was sitting peacefully by my electric gramophone, Eric Robertson looked in and said with becoming solemnity, "I don't want to be an alarmist, but I think I ought to warn you to be prepared for any emergency. It may be that we shall have to leave at a moment's notice. If you haven't got your rucksack with you, you should fetch it." "When?" I asked rather feebly. "Now," he said very firmly. "What, at once?" I rejoined with weak redundancy. "No, not at once," he replied with amazing inconsistency, and left me in a state of extreme perplexity.

There was another rather melodramatic interruption when Aubrey marched into my room looking pale and obviously distressed. "You've let me in for ten thousand dollars," he exclaimed. I stared back at him in amazement. "What on earth do you mean?" "Look at this."

He handed me a solicitor's letter which revealed to my astonished eyes that "A", one of our regular broadcasters, had complained that he was seriously libelled in a confidential inter-office memorandum which Aubrey wrote about him. Evidently this document, by some freakish, glaring and most unfortunate secretarial error, was enclosed in a note which I sent to "A" about a month ago. The strange thing is that "A" endured so great an affront in silence for so long, and during all the times he worked for us since my letter was sent never suggested by so much as a murmur that he had received the insulting enclosure. My ungallant suspicions tell me that now that Singapore is obviously approaching its last gasp, and "A" sees no more lucrative engagements in the offing, he has conveniently awakened to the startling realization that his feelings have been hurt and that he has suffered damage which he modestly assesses at ten thousand dollars!

Anyway, I was really very grateful to "A". He afforded me a most refreshing and richly humorous interlude in the tide of more alarming and serious events. I assured Aubrey that his inter-office communication to me was privileged provided no malice could be proved, and thereafter I occupied an entirely engrossing hour or more writing out a lengthy opinion and a draft letter of reply. I was considerably disappointed when I learned later that Davis intended to hand the case over to the corporation's legal adviser.

I took the opportunity at lunchtime of returning to Goodwood Park to fetch my rucksack. Carter and Hudson came with me, and we ate a picnic meal of sandwiches washed down by the remains of my gin and lime. Hudson was philosophical but apparently dispirited. He didn't attempt to disguise his opinion that the game is up. Carter, on the other hand, though appropriately solemn, was still able to talk quite enthusiastically of the future in terms, of course, of his own work, i.e. strips. His latest edition of "Malaya Newsreel" is ready for production tomorrow night.

God knows whether it will ever reach the microphone. Our programmes are now being run on a sort of hour-to-hour basis. We haven't instituted any kind of extra emergency schedule, but what we do and what we don't do depends entirely on the military situation of the moment. I gather that the Thomson Road studios are already menaced and may even fall into enemy hands tonight.

Early this afternoon the wildest and most optimistic reports were in free circulation. According to one rumour the Japs had been driven off the island by a brilliantly successful counter-attack and according to another the Americans had landed a relief force at Penang. But they were all brought to naught by the four o'clock communiqué, which said simply that in the face of continued enemy pressure our troops had yielded further ground.

Hudson produced another A.R.P. question-and-answer script for his talk this evening. It was the broadcast upon which we'd set so much store last Friday and which had had to be postponed. Now it seemed out of date, academic, almost irrelevant. However, to have cancelled it would have been pure defeatism, and though I didn't consider it worth dragging Hudson up to Thomson Road after dark, I made an advance recording of it in the Cathay studio with myself deputizing once again for Al Larson. Afterwards I invited Hudson to listen to a playback, but I'm afraid he couldn't have heard himself speak very clearly, for by this time it was five o'clock and the daily conversation with the Batavia unit was in progress.

We talk to Batavia to arrange programme schedules, etc., by means of an open broadcast in the form of a test transmission. In order to preserve a modicum of security we do not mention names, but simply refer to each other as "our listeners". The first actual news bulletin from Batavia was broadcast at lunchtime today, and it was something of a fiasco, for it announced that there had been no developments on the Singapore front for the past twenty-four hours other than artillery exchanges! We were, therefore, at considerable pains to find out the reason for this curious lapse, which had made the M.B.C. appear foolish before its listeners to say the least, and to ensure that it didn't happen again. Aubrey, who was our spokesman, addressed the microphone in a stentorian voice rather reminiscent of the first Earl of Birkenhead: "This is Singapore calling in a test transmission. Did our listeners hear the special communiqué which we broadcast at ten o'clock this morning?" There was a long delay and several pluggings of "Colonel Bogey", which is the Batavia call signal, before we got a reply. "Our listeners" then told us in a very roundabout way that they *had* heard our special communiqué; and so we were left to assume that the Dutch censors must have been at work. It certainly was hard lines on the general public, who have no means of distinguishing between what comes from Batavia and what comes from Singapore, and indeed no knowledge that such a distinction exists.

I went up to the headquarters flat for tea. Eric and Aubrey and Davis were there. Eric was more than usually taciturn, and there was no mention at all of his work as director of M.B.C. evacuation. Indeed, if plans for an exodus exist they are certainly being kept a close secret, for I have heard nothing of them since Eric issued his dramatic unofficial warning this morning, though the military situation is undoubtedly getting worse. Davis had lost none of his energy and none of his mischievous mastery, but he no longer made pretence of believing that the position was anything but hopeless or that there was a future for broadcasting in Singapore. He discussed in an amused, detached sort of way—the English way at its best, and most infuriating to those who can't understand it—the prospect of our being captives of the Japanese. "The most humiliating part of it," he said, "is that they'll probably force us to broadcast for them."

Afterwards Eric Robertson and I walked across to Rivett's flat for a rehearsal of "Malaya Newsreel". The rest of the cast—Margaret Robinson, Patricia Mills, Carl Lawson and Andrew Carruthers—were already assembled. Carter warned us to keep well away from the balconies, explaining that he'd been shot at by a native sniper earlier in the afternoon. I don't think Carter is at all the sort of man who likes to dramatize himself or to invent stories for the purpose of impressing other people. But I confess I found it hard to believe that a deliberate attempt had been made on his life or to accept the implication that it was now dangerous for a white man to show his face out of doors. I have been amazed by the calmness, or rather deadness, of Singapore City today. I have noticed no signs of excitement or turmoil or panic. The streets have been almost barren of people and traffic, and the shops, though they may have been open, have looked shut, like shops in any English town on a Sunday. I would have found church bells more appropriate to the atmosphere than guns. To me the whole place has seemed resigned to sleeping away the last hours of an old epoch before being plunged, however violently, into a new. But doubtless I have formed quite a wrong impression, for the others were undismayed by Carter's warning. According to Carl Lawson, quite a number of the native population have got hold of rifles and have been firing them indiscriminately.

The scripts were handed round and for two hours we solemnly rehearsed a performance which I don't for a moment suppose can ever really take place. Carter himself was delighted. One of his new "strips" deals, somewhat irrelevantly to the moment (he explained that "Sabotage ! ! !" was likely to run short and that he needed a "fill"), with a legend from the Scottish Highlands. He cast Margaret as the Heather Belle, Andrew as Willie, the love-sick swain, Eric as his friend, and myself as the wicked Laird. With the exception of Andrew, who is a real clansman, we failed ludicrously in our attempts to give even the vaguest impression of the Highland tongue. But Carter was blissfully unaware of our deficiencies. At the end of the second "read-through" his age-beaten, rather harassed-looking Australian face dissolved uncontrollably into a smile and he murmured, "One hundred per cent."

Pathetically make-believe as our rehearsal may have been, it determined me to go through with tonight's production of *The White Cliffs*. This morning Aubrey had instructed me to cancel it, but now I asked him to reverse his decision, and after some argument he gave in. I put the case to Patricia Mills and Margaret, who both agreed without hesitation to accept whatever risk the broadcast might entail ; and so, not altogether unalarmed at the possibility of running slap into an exploding shell, we set out on our journey to Thompson Road.

Alas ! It was all to no avail. On arrival I found a message awaiting me to telephone Davis immediately. The chairman was regretful but firm. "I'm sorry, Giles," he said, "but you'll have to return to the Cathay at once. I can't allow any women at Thomson Road tonight. The situation is too uncertain."

Back in the headquarters flat I listened to part of the evening's programme, which was a pretty ramshackle affair. For some reason the announcing was being done by one of the engineers, and he either forgot all about Hudson's broadcast or was unaware that it was due to take place, for at the scheduled time of 8.15 he made no mention of it, and nondescript music continued monotonously. I lodged a protest, of course, and eventually the talk came on at 8.45, after the B.B.C. news. But it would really have been better left unspoken. The announcement was bungled, and the recording was of such a poor quality that many of the words—not particularly pertinent in any event—were quite indistinguishable. In all it was a miserable ending—or rather petering out—to a series which once had had a great and lively significance.

It did more than depress me. It brought me face to face with the realization that my work in Singapore, menaced from the start, was now finished, or rather had been liquidated.

There is really no point in my staying here any longer. Apart from the heroic self-satisfaction of standing on the burning deck, I have no inducement to do so. And though I know that I shan't (and very probably can't) leave unless and until the official word is given, I don't disguise from myself that I would very much like to be off at once.

Is there really a sporting chance that I shall eventually get out of this place alive? My instinct tells me yes, without a doubt. My common sense tells me no, with one reservation. That reservation is my faith in Davis.

He has remained immune from the prevailing malaise of hopelessness. That is because he thrives on responsibilities, or, to say the same thing conversely, would be driven crazy by idleness. At the moment his responsibilities are many. They are mostly of his own seeking, and though not really belonging to him at all would never have been shouldered by anyone else outside the M.B.C. But what is more important, I am convinced he will discharge them to the full or, in other words, will achieve precisely what he sets out to do. He is quite fearless in his approach to problems and quite ruthless in smashing down opposition. He is no respecter of position. He has considerable personal magnetism, but while I imagine he is capable of charming a cheerless landlady into serving him with a drink after hours, he is not averse, when crossed, to being witheringly rude to a pundit. Everything he does—even little things—he does in a big way— with Cyrano's panache. And he has supreme confidence in himself and in the rightness of any cause he chooses to espouse. Indeed, to hear him answer the telephone is an unforgettable lesson in showmanship, salesmanship, or what you will. He says just the one word "Davis", but with such assurance and so impressively that one feels certain that the man at the other end, whether he has heard of Davis before or not, must be convinced that he is talking to a personage of almost regal consequence.

His responsibilities include the defence of the Cathay—but that is only a sideline. He has three main objectives, I fancy—the continuance of a broadcasting service of some kind until the last possible moment, the denial of all radio equipment and facilities to the enemy and the evacuation of the remaining members of his staff from Singapore Island. He can be virtually certain of success in the first, now that the M.B.C. unit which he sent to Batavia has begun operations. After some difficulty and a good deal of persuasion he has secured the co-operation of the military authorities in the second and the job is already under way.

It is significant, however, that before he set to work on them the latter had made no preparations whatever for the demolition or removal of radio transmitters. He has not mentioned the third directly, so that I have no idea what his plans are. There is a rumour that we may all be off before dawn, but I do not believe it myself unless the military position worsens considerably in the next few hours. I am convinced that Davis will make no move to leave until broadcasting from Singapore itself has become literally impossible and the last of our transmitters on the island has been blown.

But he has collected the majority of his staff under the Cathay roof and has instructed them to stay within call. He and Aubrey are sleeping in the headquarters flat. Johns, Rivett, Carter and Eric Robertson are sharing the flat opposite. Several other flats have been commandeered, and the half-finished studios on the basement floor have been transformed into dormitories.

For myself, I am preparing to lay me down once again on the camp bed in Margaret's sitting-room. Mrs. N. still says that Singapore won't fall. She tells me she had a long talk this afternoon with Hughie Fraser, the new Colonial Secretary, who assured her there was nothing to worry about. I argue that Mr. Fraser's words have unfortunately been disproved already by events. But she replies, somewhat illogically, that she knows that Singapore is going to hold. Poor Mrs. N.! She is, perhaps, the only one in the Cathay building tonight who still clings to the old illusion of hope, for even Margaret has abandoned her determination to gloss over the facts with brave words and fully recognizes now the uselessness of further pretence. Whether Mrs. N.'s refusal to admit defeat comes from obstinacy or courage, from self-deception or plain bluff, I'm not sure. But whatever the cause, and however foolhardy she may be, it is impossible not to admire and envy her steadfastness.

I have just finished broadcasting the nightly newsletter written by the editor of the *Free Press* and read by me under the new and original pseudonym of Horace Smith. The announcer said, "This is Singapore calling the Allied world. Tonight's newsletter is brought to you by Mr. Horace Smith." And then, with the double intent of disguising my voice (for, remember, I was Brian Golding at precisely the same time last night) and making it sound appropriately calm and realistic, I began as follows: "Good evening. In many ways this has been the saddest day in Singapore's history."

Surely an historic understatement.

The Cathay—Tuesday, February 10, 1942.

The last ten days have been for me immeasurable in terms of ordinary human existence. They are isolated from the years that have gone before, or rather are a lifetime in themselves. If this lifetime is real, then it must continue indefinitely. But if it is mere fantasy, it will suddenly dissolve. The one means imprisonment by the Japanese, the other emergence into the world of familiar things.

In my ardent hope and belief that it is the latter I have always willed this lifetime to end, and at moments have been panic-stricken by the thought of being engulfed within it. But now that release is in sight it is already beginning to take on the quality of a dream from which I am loth to awake, and I feel that if Destiny calls me to re-enter upon a humdrum existence I shall never be able to recapture its illusive charm or think back upon it without nostalgic longing.

Out of this lifetime today has been the longest and most varied in change of mood and events, and therefore seems like many days or months or years. If this lifetime is indeed a dream, then this morning I was deep in slumber but tonight am approaching the surface of consciousness.

A few hours ago I rang up Jack and told him that the position was now—so far as I could judge it—pretty well desperate, that our studios at Thomson Road had become untenable and that we were preparing to leave Singapore. I didn't actually say the words "preparing to leave Singapore". I used an ambiguous phrase, whose meaning was clearly understood by Jack, because it is a favourite and characteristic expression of a well-loved, mutual friend in London. I said, "We are sharpening our skates", and that, in fact, is more or less what we are doing. I couldn't tell Jack exactly when we would be off, or by what means, for I wasn't sure myself, and am still not sure. I only know for certain that it is no longer a question of *if*.

Jack asked me to ring him again as soon as I heard anything definite. I promised that I would, though I warned him that I might easily be obliged to call him to the telephone in the middle of the night. He said he didn't mind.

Davis must have made his decision to move some time during the afternoon. At five o'clock a very dramatic broadcast took place which, unfortunately, I was out of the way of hearing. It was the daily conversation with Batavia. Aubrey began: "This is Singapore calling in what may be its last test transmission. This is Singapore calling in what may be its last test transmission . . ." and then, using the prescribed formula, he asked Batavia to be ready to assume responsibility for all programmes from six o'clock this evening. There was a long pause before Batavia answered. Allan Rose was the spokesman. He said: "This is the Malaya Broadcasting Corporation calling in a test transmission. This is the Malaya Broadcasting Corporation calling in a test transmission. We would like our listeners to know that from six o'clock this evening we will be broadcasting a complete schedule of programmes. Our revised schedule is as follows . . ." He proceeded to read it out slowly and meticulously. Then, in a voice from which he could not entirely disguise his personal feelings, good announcer though he is, he added: "And may we wish all our listeners the very best of luck."

It must have been a moving moment both for those who heard the words spoken in Batavia and for those who received them here, and for the sake of dramatic appropriateness, perhaps, our service in Singapore should have ended then. But, as a matter of fact, programmes were still being broadcast from the Cathay studios throughout the evening, and may, for all I know, be resumed again in the morning. We still have one transmitter left to us, though the rest have been destroyed. It is the small, secret transmitter in the cottage adjoining the chairman's house, and we shall continue to use it for as long as we can. But the enemy is already uncomfortably near Mount Rosie.

Even now, while I am enjoying comparative security and freedom, I find it hard to believe that the Japanese are really on Singapore Island, and impossible to visualize them in occupation of familiar landmarks. Yet I'm told that they are probably not more than two or three miles away from Goodwood Park.

I shall probably never see my flat again. I went there after breakfast this morning to change—as hurriedly as possible, because I disliked the sensation of being alone. The Chinese servant had not neglected his duties. The place

H

looked as tidily kept as always, and when I left I took away with me a mental picture of my bedroom slippers placed neatly at the foot of my bed.

Outside the atmosphere of placid deadness seemed to me unchanged and undisturbed. There were still those same remarkable periods of silence, and the streets were practically deserted. I was rather surprised that I was able to get petrol for my car at the big garage on Orchard Road, for I had imagined that the pumps would be dry and that in any case there would be no one on duty to work them. A drunken Australian soldier, who tottered up to me when I was stopped by a traffic signal and demanded a "loan" of two dollars, provided the only evidence of disorder which came to my notice.

Back in the Cathay, Government officials were making bonfires of confidential documents. They stood miserably by while they watched the records of their work dissolve into thin smoke and drift away towards the great massive clouds of blackness from the burning oil storages and rubber go-downs which darkened the sky.

The emergency had obviously become more acute, and yet I was inclined to regard today merely as a prolongation of yesterday, and therefore did not suppose that there was any immediate likelihood of our leaving Singapore. In fact I was quite prepared to put on "Malaya Newsreel" this evening, and certainly had every intention of fulfilling my scheduled duty as announcer at Thomson Road, though I looked forward to it with considerable dread.

Admittedly there was quite a lot of talk about Eric Robertson's alleged plans for our evacuation. Some time during the morning John Ilsley asked me whether I had been allotted a place in one of the sampans yet, and when I told him that I had heard nothing at all definite about it he said that he had the chance to get away on one of the A.P.C. boats, and, with Davis's permission, intended to take it. I haven't seen him since, so I presume Davis must have advised him to make his own arrangements. Even now there is no certainty that we shall *all* be enabled to leave.

But for my part I was in a sort of dazed, wait-and-see frame of mind, and was so unprepared for any sudden move that I neglected to take the elementary precaution of drawing my money out of the bank. This was partly due to natural laziness and putting off till tomorrow, etc. But I didn't question there would be a tomorrow, and, folly of folly, when I learned that Andrew Carruthers was going to the bank and could do the job for me, I gave him no more than a small cheque to cash. The result is I'm now left with quite a substantial balance which in all probability I shall never be able to liquidate.

My only excuse for such ostrich-like stupidity is that I didn't really believe there was an official plan of evacuation and was inclined to dismiss all the talk about Eric's fleet of sampans as mere rumour. I still couldn't regard it with any seriousness. Davis certainly dropped no hint that our departure was imminent, and though he may have been deliberately secretive, I'm inclined to believe he had no sure knowledge himself at the time, for he instructed Margaret and myself to try and secure passages for two of the Chinese girl secretaries in the newsroom, and didn't suggest that our own getaway was even under consideration.

We set out immediately after lunch. The shipping office in question had recently been transferred from the centre of the town to a private house perched in splendid isolation on a small hill near the botanical gardens. It was quite a long drive there, and the nearer we approached the louder was the sound of guns and bursting shells. In fact it must have taken us as near the front line as it was possible to get, for when we arrived within a hundred yards or so we saw that the road was barricaded and we were halted by a sentry who told us —none too politely—that we would have to park the car and walk the rest of the way. I suppose he felt a natural resentment against civilians who were supposedly trying to save their own skins.

There was a queue outside the shipping office. Fortunately we didn't have to wait long, for Margaret had some acquaintance with the manager and was able to secure his personal attention. He listened to what she had to say, and then shook his head wearily. There wasn't a chance in a thousand of securing a passage out of Singapore. So far as he knew no more passenger ships were scheduled to leave. Of course, if he heard anything different he'd let us know. At the moment, with the best will in the world, there was nothing whatever he could do for us.

Obviously our mission had proved fruitless and there was no use pursuing it any further. But somehow I was reluctant to hurry back to the Cathay. I wanted to make believe that an emergency didn't exist and that this was just a fine and pleasant afternoon which good fortune had enabled us to spend away from the office. Margaret seemed disposed to fall in with my mood. We dallied to admire the green lawns and flower-beds; we strolled lazily down the pathway, and for a while, as two companions who rest by the wayside during a long country tramp, we sat on the sloping lawn and talked of this and that in a comfortably tired, relaxed and completely enjoyable sort of way. The spell of peace and carefreedom which we wove was only shattered by a particularly thunderous explosion.

The battle came very close to us on our return journey. We overtook some Australian soldiers who had obviously been fighting very recently at the front. They were a straggling bunch, scarred by defeat. They were tattered and be-grimed and they wore an expression of hurt and resentful bewilderment through which they said, without the need of words, that they still could not believe that what they had been through was true and were convinced that it should never have been allowed to happen to them. You had only to look at their faces to know that the fight was useless and that further resistance would be a sacrifice of brave and priceless lives to mere, intangible prestige.

And yet I still had a fancy to escape from reality while there was time. I suggested to Margaret we might have tea at Raffles and then go on to Jack's for a drink. She said she must first find out whether Davis had any urgent work for her to do. I suppose we got back to the Cathay about half past four. We haven't been out again since.

As it turned out, however, it was fortunate that we did return, for otherwise I should have missed seeing Carey, whom I had almost given up for lost. I was told that he had been looking for me and was now awaiting my arrival somewhat impatiently in the headquarters flat. I hastily summoned Eric Robertson, who was extremely keen to meet Carey again if only to find out whether or not the tommy-gun was available, and I also had a faint hope that by bringing them together at this juncture I might learn something concrete about the plans for our eventual escape. However, in the latter respect I was doomed to swift disappointment. As soon as we had done with an exchange of brief cordialities, Eric and Carey "withdrew", as actors in a melodrama, to renew their close and earnest study of that map of the channels through the minefields off Singapore. They spoke in whispers, so that I could not, even by straining my ears, overhear a word of what they were saying, and indeed I might well have imagined that no time at all had elapsed since their last meeting more than a week ago. Then, the conference over and the map rolled up again, Eric dashed off on a mission, which, so one could assume from his manner, was more secret and more urgent than any that had gone before. Actually it was to attend the final broadcast talk with Batavia, which I shall always curse myself for having missed.

Carey was wearing battle-dress. He looked tired and worn, but he had not lost the kindly, worldly, cynical smile which is so characteristic of him.

"Well, old boy, old boy," he began, "we're pretty well through."

"You think it's the end?"

"I'm sure of it."

"When will they be here?"

"Perhaps tomorrow, perhaps the day after. Friday at the latest."

"God!"

"You'll be all right. Eric's got the whole thing fixed."

"Yes, but it'll soon be too late. What are we waiting for? Why don't we go now?" And I started to pace the floor dramatically, simulating a show of frenzied alarm which I'm bound to admit I didn't really feel.

"Cheer up," said Carey, "you're not nearly as frightened as some of the others."

"I'm scared stiff—petrified. Have a drink?"

"Of course."

"What would you like?"

"What have you got?"

I opened the sideboard cupboard and pointed to an imposing array of bottles which I explained was all part of my honest loot, though falsely claimed by Davis as M.B.C. property. He chose a whisky-and-soda, and I poured out two stiff ones.

"How lovely."

"How lovely."

He said "How lovely" as Mac says it, slowly, deeply, thickly and ecstatically. It's Mac's favourite expression—in fact it's pretty well his only one. He uses it profusely and indiscriminately in almost every conceivable context—appropriate or inappropriate.

For a while we laughed anew at old, esoteric jokes, and reminisced about Mac. We wondered where he was now and what his eventual fate would be; what had happened to our other fellow passengers on the voyage from Sydney to Singapore which had ended only nine weeks ago. Then I asked him: "Are you coming with us?"

"I shouldn't think so. It depends when you leave, and I imagine there's no reason for your staying here much longer. I can't do anything myself, of course, until after the cease-fire order has been given. Then I intend to have a damn' good try at escaping. I know my way about pretty well, and I think I've at least a fifty-fifty chance of getting away with it. I certainly don't intend to hang around and wait for the little brown men to lead me off to a prison camp."

He said all this in a perfectly calm, matter-of-fact sort of way. And yet even then I found it impossible to believe that he was dealing with reality or that what he boasted he would do he might, in fact, be doing, not in the remote future, but within the next few days. I was still living in a dream.

He had to get back to his unit, and was already late. But I persuaded him to spare a few more minutes to meet Margaret, with whom he had had some slight acquaintance in Kuala Lumpur. We went down to her flat, only to find that she had not yet returned from her work. Her husband was there, however, and he welcomed us kindly, though he was busy packing his kit. He has recently transferred from the Army to the Navy Volunteers, and was due to join his ship this evening. (Presumably it is one of Singapore's small patrol boats. By good fortune it may even have been designated to take us out of Singapore. That was the rumour yesterday and this morning—started, I fancy, by Margaret herself.) Neither Carey nor I know him at all well, and for a while the conversation was slow and embarrassed. But soon our tongues were loosened by generous helpings of whisky, and when Margaret came in about half an hour later we had drunk sufficiently to forget all about the present discontents and Carey was telling a long and involved story about one of his favourite canine patients. Margaret had been working with Davis and must have been present at the talk with Batavia, but if she broke the news that we were leaving, I certainly didn't take it in. Carey had one more drink and then remembered that he really had to be getting back to the war.

"Look after my friend Playfair, won't you?" he said to Margaret. "I promised his wife before she left that I'd be responsible for him. And I expect you've realized that he's incapable of crossing the road alone."

Margaret said that she had realized it.

"Good-bye, Giles," he said.

"Good-bye," I said casually. "See you soon."

It was an inane remark. He looked at me in amazement. "You don't seem to realize," he said, "that this is a dramatic parting. There is no chance at all of my seeing you soon. In fact, it's quite on the cards that we shall never meet again."

I went with him to the lift, and said good-bye once more—this time with a better show of finality. But in my heart of hearts I thought Carey had overstated the case. I was still in the mood to believe that I would be seeing him in the normal course of events—either tomorrow or the next day.

Indeed, I was still so out of touch with reality that almost immediately afterwards, a trifle inflamed, I must confess, by alcohol, I had a royal row about a mere matter of professional etiquette. Margaret told me that she had to go and broadcast a talk. "What talk?" I asked, for no one had told me anything about it, and I was at once irritated and suspicious. She explained that a script had been prepared about a Singapore woman's reactions to the war and that she had been asked to read it. I protested that I was responsible for talks and that this represented a serious encroachment on my official prerogative, but before I had had time to question her in more detail she was gone.

I stayed behind with her husband to listen in. He agreed with me—whether out of politeness or conviction I'm not sure—that the script was outmoded and embarrassingly bad, and this added fuel to my indignation. Before the broadcast was over he had to be off with his kitbag, and to my shame I was too preoccupied with my own petty thoughts to wish him anything better than the most cursory Godspeed. I dallied for a little longer and then, my anger becoming minute by minute more self-righteous, I marched up to the control room.

"That's the worst talk I've ever heard," I said to Margaret as she came out of the studio.

"It was pretty awful, wasn't it?"

"Who arranged it?"

"Rivett."

"Well, it's really outrageous. He's no right whatever——"

"Why don't you tell him so?" she said consolingly. "I'll get him for you if you like."

She asked for Rivett on the house telephone and then, as if she were offering me a piece of candy, handed me the receiver.

I'd expected Rivett to wilt and apologize the moment he was charged directly with his crime. But instead he told me that what I'd just heard was a news commentary and not a talk, that it had been his programme allocation to fill exactly as he pleased and that I had better mind my own business. By this time it was too late for me to retreat, so in a pontifical bluster of words I thundered, "Please understand that so long as I am director of talks of the Malaya Broadcasting Corporation, no talk of any kind goes out without my permission." He slammed down the receiver.

I went straight to Aubrey's office. He was still at his desk, though by now it was past six and the light was fading. "Aubrey," I began, "I'm very angry. I don't think I've ever made any kind of fuss before, but this sort of thing makes it quite impossible for me to do my job." And I explained what had happened, urging him to take immediate action. He looked up indulgently. "I've no doubt you're angry, Giles," he said, "but, my dear chap, when we're preparing to blow up the station at any moment, when our main preoccupation is to get out of this place alive, and when it's extremely unlikely that there'll be broadcasting of any kind from Singapore tomorrow, it's really hardly the moment to worry about who is responsible for a talk and who isn't."

So at last I knew. So at last I came to my senses. We were leaving. The rumours had had substance after all. The decision had been made. We were leaving Singapore.

Of course, there was no more to be said. I had made a complete fool of myself. I was still suffering from a hangover of rage, but I was now thoroughly abashed. It was somewhat comforting to learn from Eric Robertson that Rivett had followed me into Aubrey's office a few minutes afterwards and had registered an even more passionate protest. He had alleged among other things that I was drunk (not entirely, I'm afraid, without justification) and that I was no fit and proper person to be included in an official evacuation!

Official evacuation is presumably the correct term, for I understand it has been negotiated by representatives of the Army Public Relations Office, with the Governor's approval, which Davis sought and obtained. But no one seems to have a much clearer notion than I of the exact means by which it is going to be carried out. Apparently space has been found on three naval vessels due to sail from Singapore either tonight or tomorrow morning. Eric Robertson, who has been entrusted with the actual arrangements on our behalf, does not yet know the names of the vessels or whether they are open lifeboats or battleships! He surmises they must be pretty small, for it has been made a condition that the men who go must be prepared to work their passage as deckhands or stokers. He estimates that there will not be room for more than eighty people at the most, and as the Ministry of Information and Censorship people have to be accommodated as well as the M.B.C. one can't feel completely certain that one won't be excluded in the end. The women have first claim on our allocation, of course, and after them the married men whose wives are still with them, and after them the technicians—engineers and linguists.

However, the offer of evacuation has been declined by a fair number of the Asiatic staff, who feel bound to Singapore by lifetime ties of home and family and have naturally no wish to venture, possessionless, into strange lands. It seems likely, therefore, that unless Eric's estimate is considerably too optimistic, the majority of those who wish to leave will be enabled to do so.

Among the Europeans, only Mrs. Nixon has refused to have anything to do with departure. Although she no longer pretends to have obstinate faith in Singapore's impregnability, she insists that it is her duty to stay behind with her husband, who is serving with the L.D.C. and who has no chance of escape.

Andrew Carruthers and I spent more than an hour trying to persuade her to change her mind. But we merely wasted our breath. We failed utterly. When we urged her to consider the feelings of her two sons in England, she said she knew that they would wish her to stay. When we suggested that in the end evacuation of women might be made compulsory, she retorted that she would never be coerced. And when we warned her that she would probably be separated from her husband by the Japanese, she said that she was willing to run that risk. Her decision was obviously made, and no argument, specious or potent, could deflect her from it. And yet I wish we had prevailed, not only for her sake but our own. For, while I believe her decision is a wrong one, I'm convinced now that it is born not of bravado but of calm and reasoned courage. Therefore it strikes sharply at the conscience.

There have been a series of conferences in the headquarters flat this evening, and although they have had the essence of urgency and drama, the atmosphere surrounding them has seemed to me more conducive to amusement than solemnity—perhaps because Davis himself has contrived to set an example of lightheartedness. On one occasion Eric Robertson stood by the door and, in a voice of mock solemnity, announced, "Mr. Jeffries and Mr. Barraclough request a word with Mr. Davis." Messrs. Jeffries and Barraclough (the latter, in the absence of Weigall, is the M.B.C.'s chief engineer) walked in purposefully. They are both tall, imposing-looking men, and they sat down side by side on the edge of the sofa opposite Davis, who was ensconced in an armchair. They had come to discuss a very grave matter—final plans for the destruction of the station and equipment at Thomson Road. But for some extraordinary reason I was irresistibly reminded of that episode in the first act of Drinkwater's *Abraham Lincoln*, when a delegation of venerable men call on Lincoln to persuade him to run for the Presidency. Consequently, the serious mission of our engineers at once struck me as being completely unreal and faintly comic.

It is a habit, and doubtless a fault, of mine only to relish those incidents of life, whether melancholy or gay, which I can translate into terms of the theatre. So that now I look back on this evening as on a number of disconnected scenes from an episodic play in which drama, comedy and tragedy are mingled, sometimes inappropriately.

Tomorrow—or perhaps tonight—the whole staff will receive payment in full up to the end of February, and for two hours before dinner Margaret and I helped Lucas, the accountant, put pay cheques into envelopes. I had not realized until then how large a staff the M.B.C. employs—250, including the drivers and the messenger boys. Some of the cheques seemed pathetically small, and I doubted whether their recipients would find an opportunity to cash them in any event. It is heartrending to think of the number of loyal Asiatics who will be left behind, jobless, to pick up the pieces of their lives as best they may. The horrors of modern war have come much closer to them than to the majority of Europeans, for, though statistically the damage to civilian property and civilian casualties as a result of air raids is very high, they have been mostly concentrated in the Asiatic residential districts, and no European who experienced the

London blitz would contend for a moment that in comparison he has ever had much cause to be frightened by the bombings. The Asiatics who have worked faithfully, bravely and uncomplainingly throughout the past nine weeks are the ones who have done so though their homes may have been wrecked and their dear ones killed. They are the ones, therefore, to whom honour is due in the greatest measure. But will honour ever be paid them? It seems now that all their steadfastness and heroism have been to no purpose, and that their only reward will be added risk of internment and persecution at the hands of the Japanese.

But to ponder very much upon the fate of those who must be left behind or upon the historic significance of events would certainly destroy all joy at the prospect of departure and might even, in a moment of revulsion, prompt one to reject the opportunity to escape. It would be mere hypocrisy to pretend that such thoughts have been uppermost in my mind, for deliberately I have kept them under. My desire to be out of Singapore is fundamentally so intense that I have excluded, in effect, all conflicting emotions. While I am only half conscious of the underlying tragedy, I am very much alive to the surface excitement. Consequently I am experiencing a sense of elation which, however selfish, is none the less so impressive that I want it perpetuated and am beginning to identify it with the whole of my lifetime in Singapore. It has a strained, mournful, haunting quality, but for me it has also something of a child's Christmas Eve or a schoolboy's last day of term.

However, it is already coming to an end.

Davis, who has now assumed complete control over our lives, has packed us all off to our respective quarters early, explaining that we must sleep while we can. The plans for departure are now complete in so far as they can be. Aubrey has made out three separate lists of the candidates, and according to Margaret, she and I have been assigned to the same boat, which is good news. I call it a boat, because after my course of instruction from Eric Robertson I picture it so—an open boat with iron rations sufficient for seven days. I've even a vague hope I may be in command. Margaret says that the odds on our being sunk are overwhelming. From a common-sense point of view she's right, of course, but I must confess the possibility of our meeting disaster after getting out of Singapore had not even occurred to me before, and I still have an instinctive conviction that once we sail our troubles will be over. Indeed, I look forward to the actual voyage with far less trepidation than I did to the crossing of the Atlantic last August.

In imagination the Cathay tonight seems like a fortress long besieged from which we are preparing to break out in a sudden dash for safety. If you look out of the window you can see the fires still burning and the sky alight with flames. But all is apparently quiet on the front. There is no sound of gun or bomb or 'plane. About the whole place is that awful silence which must be the prelude to the last, shattering attack.

PART III

ESCAPE FROM SINGAPORE

1

THAT Tuesday night was sleepless, as I had known it would be. We were drinking early morning tea long before the dawn, and later we stood on the balcony to watch the daylight break. There was a faint, liquid mist hanging over the harbour, and albeit the sky was still dark with smoke and the fires were still raging as though they were eternal like the waves of the sea, it seemed to me that Singapore had never looked more beautiful.

But the enemy was moving relentlessly forward. Our peaceful and melancholy contemplation was interrupted by the ring of the telephone bell. Margaret learned that some friends of hers, who live not far from the approaches of the town, had been ordered by the military to vacate their house, and were coming to her for temporary shelter. To ease the situation it was obviously incumbent upon me to take my leave, however young the day, and so without much enthusiasm I trudged up the stone stairs, still gloomy in the half-light, to the headquarters flat.

My discomfiture was increased by the fear of awakening Davis and Aubrey, whom I had supposed would be deep in slumber. However, I need not have worried, for I found them already dressed. They did not attempt to conceal their amusement at my dishevelled appearance; with a bundle of worn clothes clutched under one arm and a collection of hastily gathered wash-things under the other I must have looked like a lodger who had been turned out of his quarters in the middle of the night by an irate and merciless landlady.

Evidently our broadcast service had opened at the usual hour, for the radio was turned on and I heard Andrew Carruthers' voice dutifully announcing gramophone records. But I surmised without asking that no hitch had occurred in the arrangements for departure, and that we would be on our way in a few hours' time. Aubrey pointed out the good use to which he had put the back seat cover of my old Vauxhall. I had lent him this some days ago when he had requested the loan of a rucksack. Though he had been inclined to scorn it at the time, it was now bulging with necessaries, including, so he confided to me, a glass bottle of home-made lemonade and a packet of chocolate biscuits. I can't pretend it resembled very much the most up-to-date model in a hiker's equipment, but it certainly seemed every bit as good as Dick Whittington's bundle—except that it was tied together rather precariously with string and had no stick attached to it. By contrast, I noticed that Davis was the possessor of a new and rather handsome canvas grip.

I bathed, shaved and put on the tropical suit I had been wearing yesterday. I decided there would be time enough to change into my open-boat uniform later on.

Eric Robertson joined us for breakfast. He was dressed in a sarong, and I suspect, though I can't actually swear to it, that he had tried out the effect of an artificial tan to complete his disguise. I wanted to laugh outright. But he was obviously in no mood for ribaldry. He said that we would require at least a dozen bags of rice and some cooking utensils for our journey and suggested rather severely that I should be responsible for their collection. Somewhat to my discomfiture, Aubrey and Davis agreed.

Breakfast consisted of hot coffee, bacon and eggs. It was cooked as deliciously and served as efficiently as always by Peggie's Chinese *amah*, who, before the hour of lunch approached, would be left alone in the headquarters flat with only its inanimate trappings to remind her of the Europeans for whom she had worked until the very last, and with the enemy guns which had driven them away still thundering in her ears.

There was no sitting around when the meal was over. I hadn't much idea how to set about my quest of rice, but Eric had put me on my mettle and I didn't want to appear completely without resource in a crisis. So, on the assumption that where one impractical person would fail two might well succeed, I enlisted the help of Carter, who was prepared to assist in the job without monopolizing it and thus to cost me the minimum of face! Together we contrived to rifle a dozen pillow-cases from the various households under M.B.C. control, and then approached an Eurasian acquaintance of Carter, who had a one-room flat in the Cathay and kept an enormous sack of rice under his bed. This man did not intend to leave Singapore—indeed, he had no choice in the matter—but he was quite willing to bequeath us as much of his store as we wished, for, rightly or wrongly, he supposed that if we didn't take it the Japanese would.

The pillow-cases were prodigiously heavy after we'd filled them with rice, and we had to lug them upstairs two by two. We might have spared ourselves the trouble, for when the job was done Davis instructed me to arrange a general assembly of kit and personnel outside the flat of our Malay programme organizer on the ground (Mount Sophia) floor. He handed me a list of names, and said that everyone would have to be ready to leave not later than eleven o'clock and that I should warn them to get some sort of meal beforehand.

It was now about half past nine. I decided that the moment had come for me to change, for there might not be another opportunity. I took my rucksack into Davis's bedroom and with great deliberation extracted from it a rough, open-necked shirt, a pair of cheap blue shorts, a pair of khaki stockings which I'd borrowed from Carey, and a pair of stout golf shoes which I'd brought with me from England. These I put on in place of the comfortable, well-fitting, reasonably respectable clothes that I was wearing. I stuffed my notecase and a few other odd treasures into the pockets of my shorts, and I dropped my links and studs, albeit with a slight sense of guilt, into the rucksack before I refastened it. But I left the rest of my discarded garments lying in a heap on the bed and didn't attempt to pack them. Had I foreseen our actual conditions of travel, had I known that others of the party would be taking suitcases and even trunks with them, had I realized with what bitter regret I would think of my abandoned suit in the weeks ahead, I would never have been so foolish. But I had become so much a potential player in Eric's drama of the sea that I hadn't a doubt that my Spartan uniform was *de rigueur*, and that the transport of any personal belongings beyond the barest necessities was out of the question. Even later on, when I stood amidst a pile of normal-looking luggage at the place of assembly, I was still a victim of Eric's convictions. It is true I couldn't have returned to Goodwood Park even had I had a mind to do so. But I might have gone further than I did towards redeeming my folly. In fact, I only made two minor concessions to the reality of the situation. One was to rescue my brief-case and my bag of wash-things. And the other was to redon the coat of my discarded suit because someone suggested that otherwise I would be likely to get extremely cold at nights!

Mobilization proved a most exhausting and nerve-racking business. I knew that Victor Grosz was in the gramophone library, for he had been in-structed by Aubrey earlier to arrange the destruction of our ten thousand records. He did the job simply and well. I found him with his assistants picking up symphony concerts by the handful and hurling them to the floor, which was already littered with broken wax. It gave me intense pleasure to smash a couple of the larger records myself.

I knew that Margaret was in her flat playing hostess to the evacuees. And I knew that Andrew Carruthers was in the studio, for our regular morning's programme still held the air. But I had no idea where specifically to look for the others, and my only recourse was to search the entire building. It meant a desperate game of hide-and-seek, aided by Carter and Jeffries, whose help I enlisted. It meant chasing up and down twenty flights of stairs, for there was an Alert on and the lifts were out of action. And, worst of all, it meant making myself thoroughly conspicuous to those members of the Asiatic staff who were being left behind. They were mostly collected in the general office, which yester-day had been the scene of ordered work and was now just a room filled with disused office furniture. They were sitting around on the chairs and on the tables. They had nothing to do, but they had nowhere else to go. I hated to appear among them obviously busy and obviously with an immediate object in view. The little Eurasian girl who had been my secretary for the past ten days was there. She looked at me pathetically, in a hurt, uncomprehending sort of way. I avoided her gaze, because I couldn't think of a word to say. I felt like a vulgar intruder into a house of sorrow.

In the end we rounded up most of the people listed. But a few had been foolish enough to return to their homes, and I had no alternative but to rely on providence to guide their footsteps in the right direction. The telephone ex-change was now in a chaotic state, and to ask for a connection with a private number was a mere waste of endeavour.

By 10.30 the place of assembly, in its little recess, looked like a railway platform at a moment when the train's arrival is long overdue. All our party were obviously dressed for travel; some were strutting about impatiently, and others were sitting resignedly on their luggage.

We must have appeared a pretty miserable-looking lot, for the usual crowd of shelterers who thronged the Mount Sophia entrance hall stole occasional glances at us which seemed to betoken some curiosity, some scorn, but no envy.

The advisability of wearing my coat had recently been mentioned, and I was anxious to collect it while there was still time. But, having had so much trouble in bringing my charges together, I dared not leave them now in case one or more of them should suddenly be driven by impatience to disperse again. I was considerably relieved, therefore, when Eric and Aubrey turned up. Eric had abandoned his native disguise and was now dressed in a khaki shirt, khaki shorts and a tin hat tilted roguishly on one side of his head. He looked im-mensely efficient. He paused for a moment to survey us and murmured some-thing about the impossibility of accommodating so much luggage. Then he hurried on through the crowded hall, through the narrow lane between the sandbags and out of the Cathay's main entrance, which today was guarded for the first time since the war began—by two Malay soldiers with fixed bayonets and no ammunition.

Aubrey was now in charge of the assembly. I gathered from him that Eric had gone to reconnoitre, and would probably not return with the signal to leave for some time yet. So I decided it was safe to go off on my errand.

When I reached the headquarters flat it seemed already like a tomb. I was shocked to find it so, for half an hour earlier it had still been a centre of intense activity. Davis had been there, and Davis had been obviously the master of our destinies, engaged since breakfast in a series of conferences, interviews and long, important telephone conversations. Davis was still there, but he was no longer busy. He was sitting hunched up on his bed and was staring ahead of him into nothingness. He looked crushed and pathetically alone, like a beaten warrior who has at last been stripped of his power to resist and has been deserted by his followers.

I went to pick up my coat.

"Fools," he said as much to himself as to me, "they can't make up their own minds. The place is under machine-gun fire. It may be overrun at any moment. Yet they still refuse to allow the transmitter to be destroyed." And he buried his face in his hands.

There was no adequate answer I could make. I stood in silence for a while. Then he looked up and took off his glasses to wipe them and I noticed that his eyes were wet with tears.

At that moment I was suddenly overwhelmed by the full force of the tragedy which would make this morning forever memorable. I had been proof against it up to now, for my time had been kept well occupied and I had been buoyed up by excitement. Besides, for me it had had only slight personal significance. I had not been long enough in Singapore to regard the place as a home which had any claim upon my loyalty or affection. Although I was leaving behind nearly all my possessions, the majority of them and those which I valued most were associated in my mind with England, and in any case had no worth when set against the preservation of freedom. I was going out of jeopardy into safety. Soon I would in all probability be meeting Carol again and would be able to gather up the threads of my normal life. I had little cause, beyond a latent sense of shame, to be touched by regret.

With others it was different. Margaret, for example, who during the past few days had set a shining example of fortitude and cheerfulness and hard work, was this morning suddenly dispirited. When I went to call her to the place of assembly she seemed hardly to have the will to move.

Her *amah*, who was weeping copiously, and Mrs. Nixon, who was near the point of tears, were helping her get ready for the journey. She was leaving them, and her husband as well, behind. All that would be left to her of her home in Singapore were the few oddments which she was throwing carelessly into a kitbag. She was being pulled out of danger by the roots. And while I urged her to hurry, I realized that my mood was brutally out of touch with hers.

I knew now that for Davis, too, there was an acute personal tragedy encompassed within the larger tragedy of Singapore which engulfed us all, and I could understand it clearly because I had a small part in it myself.

In many ways Davis had personified the Malaya Broadcasting Corporation. He had been its pioneer as well as its chairman, and under his energetic leadership it had grown in less than two years from a small local station into one of the few sizable radio organizations of the Far East. In happier circumstances its future development might well have proved worthy of a lifetime's devotion.

Davis had returned to Singapore when it was already crumbling, and he had only done so, at such obvious and apparently unnecessary risk to his own safety, because of his deep concern for the welfare of every member of his staff. Perhaps he had been too busy in recent days to think much upon what its loss would mean to him personally. But now, his job done, it had crashed about him, and he was left alone amidst the ruins.

I was so deeply moved that I had lost control of my voice. I muttered "Bad luck" in a choked fashion, and walked away. Davis called me back before I had reached the door.

"Giles," he said, "you might ask Aubrey to ring me up when the party's embarked. He'll probably be able to get to a telephone without much difficulty. And I'd like to know."

I murmured my agreement automatically. But I was halfway downstairs before I realized the significance of what he had said.

I gave Aubrey the message. "Isn't Eric coming with us?" I asked.

"No," Aubrey answered, obviously distressed, "he's decided to stay behind—to settle things up. He daren't keep the staff here any longer in case the boats sail without us. And he won't leave until the order to destroy the transmitter has come through."

So I had been right, a day or two ago, in my assessment of Davis's three main objectives—the continuance of a broadcasting service until the last possible moment, the denial of radio equipment to the Japanese and the evacuation of as many members of the staff as possible. The first had been assured. In the end he was prepared to accomplish the other two at the expense of his own liberty.

2

We left the Cathay about midday. We were ordered to proceed to Empress Place, there to await further instructions. Aubrey asked all drivers to get their cars lined up outside the Mount Sophia entrance.

I didn't fetch the Morris. I had heard through Mrs. Nixon that its owner wanted it back, so I gave the keys to her and told her that it was safely in the car park with at least two gallons of petrol in its tank. Mrs. Nixon had just learned that her husband had got permission to live at the Cathay. "Aren't I lucky?" she said, and those were the last words she spoke before she wished Margaret and myself "*bon voyage*".

The cars were loaded with luggage. The passengers got in and we drove off in a procession, just as the Batavia unit had done ten days before. Margaret, Carter and I sat together in the back of a four-seater saloon.

There seemed no good reason why we had been directed to Empress Place. We dallied there uncomprehendingly for close on an hour, while enemy 'planes flew low over the Government buildings. The air raids this morning were well-nigh continuous, and were the most formidable since the attack on Singapore began. Exploding bombs and shells made a gargantuan noise and gave one the impression of being perpetually lashed and pounded. The periods of lull were considerably shorter and less frequent than the periods of apparent danger.

Someone got hold of the day's abbreviated issue of the Singapore *Free Press*.

Even to glance at it was painful. Across the front page was a banner headline quoting the Governor's last broadcast: "Singapore shall stand: it must stand." Inside there was a long account of an official plan, just announced by the Government, to build new air raid shelters for the Asiatic population! And so, posthumously as it were, Hudson had won his fight. It was the crowning irony.

When we were already feeling in need of lunch, Captain Steele, of the Army Public Relations Office, drove up on a motor-cycle and ordered us to reassemble at Clifford's Pier. We obeyed with alacrity. We had hopes now that our journey really was about to begin.

The censorship and M.O.I. people had arrived ahead of us. I noticed, much to my resentment, that they had brought with them not only a considerable amount of personal luggage but large packing-cases filled with papers, typewriters and all manner of office paraphernalia. How cruelly I had been deceived!

In all we were something above eighty strong, and I began to entertain a quite reasoned fear that there might not be accommodation for the whole party. We were, I think, a well-controlled crowd, but the calmest among us was one for whom there was no journey ahead. He was an Asiatic control engineer, who had assisted me in several programmes from Thomson Road during the past weeks. He had come now to see us off and wish us good luck. He was smiling and cheerful, and neither in his looks nor in his manner could one detect the slightest trace of bitterness. He was wearing a tin hat and had a rifle slung across his back, for he was still an active soldier of the L.D.C., though since this morning no longer a paid M.B.C. employee.

He set an example which, in the conventional fiction of the West, might well be described as the whitest of the white. And so, too, did another Asiatic engineer, who, though I was unaware of it at the time, had just assisted one of his European colleagues to destroy the transmitter at Mount Rosie while machine-gun bullets literally whizzed past his head. There was no journey ahead for him, either. But he had served us to the end, and his last, brave action in the course of duty had won a reprieve for Davis, who was now left free to make his escape from Singapore with the rest of us.

A small launch drew alongside. Eric Robertson was standing amidships, and with his tin hat still perched so jauntily on one side of his head he looked something of a buccaneer figure. As soon as the launch had been made fast he swung himself on to the stone steps which led from the water's edge to the pier. "Women without luggage," he shouted.

So the rumour that Margaret and I were to travel on the same ship was disproved, and we said good-bye. With one exception, the women embarked in an orderly fashion. The exception was an extraordinary-looking old lady upon whom I had never set eyes before and had not noticed among the waiting crowd. Her skin was white and taut and she had a long, eagle-like nose. Her large-sized feet were encased in even larger flat-heeled shoes, and her thin, spindly, shapeless legs in thick woollen stockings. She wore a costume more suited to Alpine climbing than the tropics, and her head was crowned with a man's old and battered homburg hat. Altogether she resembled a child's conception of a witch, though she was perhaps taller and tougher-looking than the average. You can lead a witch to her broomstick but cannot make her fly, and time after time she reached the last step, only to turn round and walk back again. She protested that she would not be separated from her husband—a sentiment easily comprehensible in a young bride, but coming from her it seemed pathetically incongruous.

How she was eventually coaxed aboard I am not sure, for I was out of the way of hearing, but she wasted many minutes of what seemed to us vital time, and it was creditable that no one lost his temper or even raised his voice.

"Ten men," Eric shouted.

I was standing advantageously at the top of the steps. Without appearing to hurry or to barge my way through I could easily have been among the first to reach the launch. What is more, my instincts prompted me to be off while the opportunity offered. But I glanced at Aubrey, who was just behind me. Obviously he did not intend to move, and I decided that as his second-in-command it would not look well for me to leave him. So I held back. Had I not done so, had my self-protective instincts overcome my sense of fitness, I would not now be at liberty to write this story. That first ship was ill-fated, and those of the M.B.C. staff who eventually sailed in her were Rivett, Carter and Andrew Carruthers, who was with his wife.

"Light luggage only" was Eric's third and last order, and we handed down a number of small suitcases and haversacks which we chose at random from the pile and without regard to whether or not they belonged to those aboard. As the launch pulled off, Eric shouted out the names of the other two ships, which was, at least, an assurance that we were not being abandoned.

In time we were joined by several stragglers. They included four women— Patricia Mills, who came with her husband, the wife of one of our engineers, and the wife and stepdaughter of another. Davis arrived, with Scott, head of the M.O.I. He was his old masterful self again, and his recent depression had vanished as if it had never been.

A second launch drew alongside. It was considerably larger than the first. It was crowded with Asiatic evacuees from an endangered, or already occupied, part of the island, and was piled high with all manner of old and pathetic-looking household treasures—tables, chairs, mats, carpets, vases, birdcages, and I don't know what else besides. No one seemed to know whether or not it was intended for us, but Davis, who had now assumed command of the situation, decided that we would be wise to take possession of it in any case, and so we set about the necessary preliminaries. We formed ourselves into a chain of coolies, and when we had finally unloaded the launch of its cargo we proceeded to load it with our own.

The whole business occupied perhaps an hour. But double that time passed before we eventually started on our journey. When we were all embarked we discovered to our confusion that the crew had disappeared. They had gone to take shelter, and though several emissaries were subsequently sent to treat with them, they could neither be bribed nor bullied into emerging from their retreat.

Of course they were hardly to be blamed. What good reason had they to risk their lives in order to assist the escape of a boatload of Europeans? The air raids, as I've said, were pretty well continuous, and were frightening by any standard. We were right in the middle of the target area, and the bombs were falling all around us. Normally they would have sent us scurrying for shelter. We defied them now, not because of a sudden onrush of reckless daring, but because danger is relative, and at the moment our instinct for self-preservation was dominated by our desire to be out of Singapore as soon as possible. Only once were we interrupted in our coolie work, and that was by a series of swift explosions which grew louder and louder. In a last, instinctive bid for survival we threw ourselves flat on our faces. When I looked up a great fountain of water was rising from the sea. Though bombs had come uncomfortably close to me before now, it was the first time I had actually seen one fall.

But whether the crew were justified or not, they had certainly put us in a most humiliating predicament. For all the good it had done us to embark we might just as well have remained on dry land. Here we were being rocked gently from side to side in a boat which was securely tied to Clifford's Pier. Barraclough went down to the engine-room to investigate the possibility of forming an amateur crew. He reported that the idea was impracticable.

The situation was eventually saved by a combination of good fortune and resource. Eric Robertson had returned. What had happened to his craft I don't know. I suppose that seeing us already provided for he had let it go. However, as if from nowhere, and for no good reason, a third launch appeared. Though it was obviously too small to accommodate so many passengers and so much baggage, Davis hit on the idea that it might be powerful enough to tow us. Someone who spoke Malay was deputized to open negotiations with the crew. After a certain amount of haggling the bargain was sealed in consideration of a cash payment of eight hundred dollars. The boats were lashed together, and in this eccentric fashion we pulled out of Singapore, with the sun beating down upon us and the tall, solid buildings by the waterside receding slowly into the distance.

Now that we were on our way I realized that none of us had the least idea what our eventual destination would be. Davis was giving each member of the staff hurried instructions. "I've made arrangements for money to be advanced on behalf of the M.B.C. in any part of the world where you are likely to land," he said to me. "If you find yourself in India, call on the nearest office of All India Radio. If you find yourself in Australia get in touch with the Australian Broadcasting Commission."

The air raid was still in progress, and we were passing several vessels which had been wrecked by recent bombings. Some of them were ablaze, and others were capsized or already half submerged. We drew alongside a rusty-looking hulk, which to my inexperienced eye seemed suspiciously akin to a tanker. Eric went aboard as our representative and returned some minutes later with the news that the captain was willing to carry twenty men on the understanding that they brought their own food with them.

Davis made the selection with Scott's concurrence. He picked those who had special qualifications and whose services were of the greatest importance to the war effort. Thus the M.B.C. engineers, Barraclough and Jeffries, went. Kalidas, our Indian programme organizer, went. The journalists from the M.O.I. went, and Scott himself. Though I think most people were naturally anxious to be named, I dreaded it, and, far from being downcast, as some of the others appeared to be, after the twenty had been chosen, heaved a sigh of relief. But I must confess I was motivated by poltroonery, not by courage. It happened that embarkation meant climbing up a rope ladder, a feat I had no confidence I could attempt without falling into the sea, or otherwise making a complete fool of myself.

We were now sufficiently depleted to transfer ourselves and our baggage to the smaller launch, which was towing us, and to cast the other adrift. As we pulled off we caught a last glimpse of our colleagues standing on the deck of that second ship, which, like the first, was ill-fated. Subconsciously, perhaps, I had recognized her rope ladder as a danger signal.

No one—not even Eric Robertson—could say for certain that the third ship was still in the harbour. I began to toy with the notion that in default of all else our present craft might be able to get us as far as Sumatra, and I suggested as much to Aubrey. I was an extravagant idea, of course, and quite impracticable, but the thought of returning, after so much exertion, to poor, flame-ridden, shell-torn Singapore, which still loomed ominously large in the background, was too sickening to be borne.

And then we began to gather speed. We had sighted our ship, but she was already on the move. Though we learned later that she was only circling round the harbour so as to avoid being a sitting target for the bombs, we thought now that she had set sail, and we were giving chase in all earnestness. Lucas, the M.B.C. accountant, who had some knowledge of Morse, was signalling her repeatedly on the steam whistle. For a while it seemed that she did not, or would not, hear, but at last she hove to and we drew alongside.

Once again Eric went aboard to interview the captain, and this time returned with the good news that we could all embark. We formed another chain to transport our baggage from the launch to the deck space aft, which was to be our living and sleeping quarters. My place was at the foot of the companionway, and as I staggered under the weight of trunks and packing-cases I looked in vain for my rucksack and brief-case to be handed to me!

Our ship was officially a submarine chaser. In fact, she was a converted merchantman, and, so far as I could see, mounted no greater armament than an anti-aircraft gun and a few depth-charges. She was small and shabby, but she was sturdy and friendly withal, and her crew gave us a most cordial welcome. Our quarters could hardly have been more primitive, but I am sure that none of us had ever been so glad to board a vessel in his life before. When the baggage was finally collected we could relax for the first time since early morning. It was four o'clock, and I realized that I was immeasurably tired, hungry and thirsty—most of all thirsty. Davis had evidently reached the same conclusion. He picked up a large tin of preserved fruit from one of our cases of food and pried it open. "Now," he said, "let's have a drink," and he handed the tin to me. Between us we drained it dry of juice.

3

The party which embarked on that third and only fortunate ship must have numbered about forty in all. Besides the M.B.C. staff there were four Army officers—a colonel, a major and two captains; the civil censors, Duckworth and my old friend, K. O. Fearon, with whom I had travelled from England to Australia on the *Themistocles*, and a few left-overs from the M.O.I. Patricia Mills, as the only white woman among us, received preferential treatment and was whisked off to live in splendid isolation in the officers' quarters. The two engineers, who had their womenfolk with them, were given cabins. And some of the older men were provided with bunks below. But the rest of us had to make do with the alfresco delights of the open deck. It was regrettable, perhaps, that we had not been warned to bring mattresses with us, though one fortunate man, an out-and-out rebel against the Robertson school of thought, of which I had been so ardent and misguided a disciple, had remembered to equip himself with a camp bed. Once he was kind enough to lend it to me for two hours of perfect bliss.

I

Our ship continued to circle round the harbour for the remainder of the afternoon and throughout the night. Apparently the other two ships adopted the same procedure, for on one occasion we drew level with the first ship and caught a glimpse of Margaret and Rivett leaning over the rail. We shouted at them, but they were just out of earshot. I wanted particularly to let Margaret know that we had her kit-bag safely with us.

In the twilight we stood around in mournful little groups and watched Singapore burning. It was a terrible, awe-inspiring sight, and I would like to have photographed it, though I knew that in any case it would never fade from my memory. It really did seem as if the whole island were alight, but at times great new sheets of flame would leap into the sky, and we would know that yet another store of incalculable wealth had been set ablaze and would soon be worthless.

When darkness came the red and yellow fires conjured up a picture of hell, and as we were only separated from them by a small expanse of water the ban on smoking struck me as being a rather unnecessary precaution. But, doubtless with admirable sense, the blackout was in fact very rigidly enforced, and though it was still not much past seven o'clock there seemed no alternative but to pass the hours that separated us from the dawn in attempted slumber.

If you are unlucky enough to enter an English prison and are in good health you spend your first three nights on a wooden plank. I had always imagined this somewhat barbaric custom to represent a deliberate inducement to insomnia. But four nights of actual experience taught me that it is possible to sleep on hard wood, provided you are tired enough. You don't sleep soundly or deeply, it's true. At intervals you become acutely conscious of aches and pains, and you have to stand up and walk about to get the stiffness out of your joints. You are never quite free—even in your dreams—of a longing for the morning. But, none the less, when you start the new day you feel moderately refreshed, so that you know you must have slept for some hours, at least.

The dawn is your alarm clock, of course, and it is also your permit to have the cigarette for which you've been yearning for the past eleven hours or more. That first smoke I had on Thursday was by far the most pleasurable of my life.

We had already set sail by then, and though no one had actually told us so it seemed obvious on reflection that we were bound for Batavia. There was no other feasible direction in which we could be going, and our ship did not carry sufficient coal to make straight for Colombo or an Australian port.

The voyage was obviously fraught with danger from air and submarine attack. And yet my instinct still assured me that we would come through without mishap. If I needed further grounds for confidence, they were supplied by the presence of De Trafford among our number, for this was his third escape from the Japanese. He had been working for the M.O.I., and had also been the M.B.C.'s film critic. He is a compact little man, with a tough-looking, rather humorous face and an engaging, forthright manner. He had escaped from Tokyo after being imprisoned. He had been in Bangkok on December 7, and had somehow managed to get back to Singapore. Now he was on the run again.

"I can't afford to be caught," he said. "There's a price on my head. They'd shoot me."

"And what would they do to me?" I asked.

"Well, you'd be considered an artist. They like artists. They'd make you broadcast for them."

"And if I refused?"

"They'd use what they call persuasion—torture, in other words. But don't worry; they'll never get me."

Lucky De Trafford, I feel sure, they must call him at the club.

We had only one scare. It happened about ten o'clock on the first morning out, though actually I didn't become aware of it until it was all over. I had been last in the bathroom, where we made some pretence of washing our hands and faces, and when I emerged I found the deck completely deserted except for one of our engineers, who was brandishing a rifle in a dangerous sort of way. In response to my frantic inquiries he said he hadn't the faintest idea what he was supposed to be doing, except that he had been ordered to stand by for action. I made a hurried tour of the deck in search of some other evidence of human life and eventually encountered Davis. "Where is everyone?" I asked breathlessly. "Fighting for democracy in the shelter below," he said.

We had been sighted by an enemy 'plane. It had dropped three bombs and one of them had landed within about a hundred yards of us. The 'plane was presumably on its way home now to report our position, and had we not been close to an inlet of one of the uninhabited Dutch islands, where we were able to lie in hiding, we might have had a very uncomfortable time. As it was, we didn't set sail again until the late afternoon, and the rest of the voyage was entirely uneventful.

Looking back on those four days, it is difficult to conceive how they ever passed. Men are resourceful, of course, and I have a memory of K.O. and three friends perched precariously in a square formation on the peak of the baggage pile, where they indulged in an earnest game of bridge with one excessively grubby pack of cards. Davis, who had to be busy or bust, introduced a daily news sheet. He monitored the bulletins broadcast from Batavia, and then with a great show of solemnity dictated his findings to the wife of one of the engineers, who happened to be a shorthand typist!

But, for the most part, there was absolutely nothing to do. We hadn't more than a couple of books between us. And we hadn't even sufficient seating accommodation to go round. The few available chairs, the camp bed and the ancient mattress which had been dug up from somewhere were all avidly desired, and in time we applied the old French proverb, "Qui va à la chasse, perd sa place". Once, when I had successfully occupied the mattress in Eric Robertson's temporary absence, he made a pathetic appeal to my better nature. "I did all the hard work," he said. "I carried through the arrangements. If it hadn't been for me you'd none of you be aboard this ship. I should have been offered a cabin at the least. Instead, I have been ignored. And now I'm not even allowed peaceful enjoyment of a mattress."

I had to admit the justice of his case, and reluctantly withdrew.

"Working our passage" consisted of spasmodic swabbings of the deck. When the order came most of our party obeyed with alacrity, and I, too, would have done so had it not been for my constitutional failure to get hold of one of the necessary implements with which we were insufficiently supplied. In consequence the tall, bearded young officer who was in charge regarded me as the worst kind of slacker. He would see me empty-handed and vacant-looking, and would mutter impatiently: "Come along, now. Get to it. No need to hang around doing nothing. There's plenty of scope for everyone." Eventually I worked out a defence against his reproaches. Whenever he came near I would place my hands on my knees and stare fixedly at the hose.

Very early one morning there was a call for volunteers to clean out the latrines. I'm ashamed to say I simulated deep slumber, and Eric Robertson followed my example. But I learned later that the colonel had acquitted himself manfully and had been in the forefront of the operations.

We had three meals a day, and though they were never very appetizing they kept us from feeling hungry. Breakfast usually consisted of tinned sausages, a mug of tea (which had oil bubbles floating on its surface, was sickly sweet, and tasted like no other beverage known to man or beast), and two ship's biscuits; lunch of some soup, rice or nondescript hash, tea and ship's biscuits; dinner of soup, rice or nondescript hash and, of course, ship's biscuits. On gala occasions there was a second course consisting of a *soupçon* of canned fruit. We used to line up with the crew at mealtimes, each of us carrying his own tin plate, spoon and empty fruit-can, which served as a mug. Then we passed by the galley in single file, where we were helped from a giant-sized pot. There was, of course, not enough cutlery to go round, and during the first day or so I was invariably among the unlucky few who had to wait patiently until others had finished. But latterly I learned primitive wisdom. Deliberately and with malice afore-thought, I stole a plate, a spoon and a mug from some unsuspecting person who was enjoying his afternoon's siesta, and I carried them away to a secret hiding-place.

Though, as I have said, we ate sufficiently, the longing for a change of diet soon became akin to acute hunger. There was a single tin of sardines left in our original food store, which had somehow escaped transportment to the galley, and there was an open wooden case filled with liqueur bottles which had been brought aboard by the exotically extravagant M.O.I. Aubrey and I cast many greedy glances at these gastronomic luxuries, and one evening gave way to base impulse. We decided on a sort of schoolboys' dormitory feast, and invited two or three others to join us in our conspiracy. We had hopes that thus we would be able to get rid, in pleasant fashion, of several tedious hours of the long, uncomfortable night. We squatted in a circle, and passed round first the tin of sardines, and then a bottle of "Grande Marnier", from which, in turn, we took generous swigs. By 7.30 we were all flat on our backs, praying for sleep to make us oblivious of the waves of nausea by which we were cruelly assailed.

In the circumstances we had every reason to be grateful for our food allow-ance. But drink was another matter. Apart from the tea, whose thirst-quenching properties were not particularly evident, we had to rely on a small, daily ration of rusty, lukewarm water from a pump, and there was seldom a moment when our mouths were not parched. I was always begging Aubrey for a sip of his lemonade, but, faultlessly generous in all other respects, this supreme favour he refused to grant. He said he was keeping it against an emergency—what emergency I could never comprehend, and long before we reached Batavia his lemonade must have been virtually at the boil.

My greatest joy was to go with Davis at six o'clock every evening to the officers' quarters on the pretext of listening in to the news. Patricia Mills would then take pity on us and would purloin a bottle of iced water from the refrigerator. The pleasure of drinking from that bottle can only be described as ecstatic.

Immeasurably refreshed, Davis would talk to me about the future. He had hopes that soon enough the M.B.C. would be re-formed and would operate, as a kind of station in exile, from some suitable base. In the meanwhile he had made specific plans for each one of us. He wanted me to go first to Australia, and, in default of hearing further from him, to proceed to the United States.

He wanted Eric to go to Chungking. And he wanted Aubrey to go to Rangoon. As a matter of fact, Aubrey himself regarded this plan as a little too Davis-like for his fancy. "Apparently," he told me, "I'm to call on the Governor, tell him that I'm an expert radio man and that I propose, therefore, to assume control of the Rangoon station. Eric seems to think it's all perfectly simple. But what if the Governor doubts my word?"

Davis had not made up his mind about his own immediate future. Perhaps he would go to Chungking or New Delhi or Washington. He would like, best of all, to be appointed head of the Broadcasting Division of the Ministry of Information in London. Then he would really be able to make some progress. He had dreams of a chain of Empire stations—a sort of Imperial network which would supplement or even supplant the B.B.C.'s centralized overseas service.

The news that fighting was still going on in Singapore appalled us. We, who had been there for three days after the landing, knew that further resistance was hopeless and a mere waste of lives. When Aubrey heard that the city itself was being shelled intensively, he went white-faced with anger. "It's scandalous," he said. "It means wholesale slaughter of the Asiatic population who have been provided with no adequate cover and have no means of defending themselves."

But our conversation was seldom serious and was mostly concerned with the immediate past. Already we were victims of that nostalgia from which I suspect that few of us have yet been freed or can ever be until the war is won. The fear and the danger and the grief were forgotten, and only the gay and amusing incidents were recalled; so that to hear us talk you would suppose that those last weeks in Singapore were stuff for delicate farce, not grim tragedy. But for us they were neither. They were a bitter enchantment, incomprehensible and intangible.

Our one source of present laughter was provided by an Australian seaman, who had somehow got aboard. He had a figure like a beer barrel and his every other word was an expletive. All his statements ended with the same simple conclusion, "Well, it's unprintable all period." He used to apply his expletives with equal force and gusto to friends and foes alike and to objects of his admiration and disgust, so that it was sometimes difficult to follow his line of argument. Thus while the Singapore authorities were unprintables, so too were the Russians. In the course of a long harangue he once said to be, "I usedn't to unprintable well hold with those bolshevik unprintables. But you've got to unprintable well admit they're unprintable good. Their unprintable system works, which is unprintable well more than our unprintable system does. The unprintables have done unprintable marvels. If the British unprintables had unprintable well learned an unprintable lesson or two from the Russian unprintables, unprintable it, we wouldn't unprintable well be in the unprintable mess we are now. Well, it's unprintable all period."

He looked at me for agreement. "Yes," I said feebly.

As the days passed, we began to look more and more unkempt. With the exception of little Victor Grosz, who had the curious but doubtless correct notion that the thicker his beard the kindlier would be his reception from his mother-in-law in Batavia, we all made a practice of shaving. But the remainder of our toilet was nominal. For no matter how diligently we washed our hands and faces they were as dirty as ever again within the hour. It was pointless to change one's clothing, and I could not have done so in any case. After a considerable search I discovered my brief-case buried beneath the pile of baggage, but my rucksack was nowhere to be found. Evidently it had been handed by mistake to someone on the second ship. By the laws of poetic justice only Robertson was as poorly off for belongings as I.

In the early afternoon of Saturday, February 14, we reached the roads off Batavia. Incredible though it seemed, our voyage was over, and we did then set about the task of making ourselves look as presentable as possible. K.O. kindly lent me a clean shirt and a pair of khaki trousers, and though both garments were by far too small for me, they were at least clean. I talked gloatingly of installing myself in a luxury suite at the Hotel des Indes. Eric, who had previously delighted my imagination with tales of packs of Jap submarines at work in the Java Sea, said that the Hotel des Indes would certainly be full, and that the most any of us could hope for was a room in a cheap boarding-house.

But, as it happened, we were both proved wrong. That night was passed in precisely the same fashion as the night before—on board. For hours we leaned over the rail and looked towards the heady delights of Batavia—a dream city if ever there was one. Sometimes it seemed as if we were on the move, but we were only describing a circle, and the harbour so close by remained as tantalizingly far away as ever. When darkness fell, and we were still lying at anchor in the roads, we knew that all hope of landing was gone.

"It's the wood again," said Aubrey.

And the wood it was.

4

Perhaps it would have been the wood for several more nights had not Davis taken decisive action. When it became obvious next morning that there was still no hope of moving into the harbour, he asked the captain for the use of one of the lifeboats. Such a request, coming from a civilian passenger, was unusual to say the least, and had it been made by anyone but Davis would doubtless have been refused. But, in fact, it was granted without demur. A lifeboat was lowered and Davis sailed away.

An hour or so later a Dutch patrol boat came alongside with instructions to take us ashore. We were not sorry to say good-bye to our ship, but we would never forget her and would never think of her again without gratitude and affection. As we pulled off some of us remembered to shout a heartfelt "Thank you" to the officers and ratings through whose skill and courage our liberties had been preserved.

Davis was at the landing quay, and it was obvious from a glance at his face that the news he had to tell us was not good. He called the staff together. "I'm afraid you can't stay here," he said. "I may succeed in getting past the immigration people, but there's not a chance for anyone else. The Dutch are very sticky at the moment. They'll let no one in who hasn't got a definite job to do. And I must warn you to be careful what you say. If anyone opens his mouth too wide, he'll be carted off to prison, and I won't lift a finger to get him out."

He then explained that two evacuee ships were leaving almost immediately, the one bound for India and the other for Australia, and that arrangements had been made for our embarkation. He made hasty division of us into an India party and an Australia party, placing Aubrey and Eric with the former and myself with the latter.

For Aubrey and me there remained the urgent problem of getting in touch with our families. Phyllis and the children were in Batavia, and could presumably be brought to the ship in time. But Carol was in Bandoeng.

"Where's she staying?" Davis asked.

I told him.

"I'll tell Reid to get her on the telephone," he said. "She can make it all right if she catches a 'plane."

We were bundled into an omnibus and driven to Tanjong Priok—to the same white and dusty Batavia docks I had left behind only ten weeks ago with such high hopes of the future. And there was the *Plancius* herself—the ship which had carried me to Singapore. She had looked tall and stately then, but now she was like a monstrous pleasure steamer. Anyone could go aboard her who wished. She was offering a free trip to Colombo, and already she was bulging with passengers.

She was obviously the ship for the India party, and they had no alternative but to embark and lose their identity amidst the swarming crowd of evacuees. They had every reason to be grateful, as it happened. But the hot bath, the comfortable bed, the meal *de luxe* to which they had looked forward so eagerly had now slipped away from them into the indeterminate future of days or weeks, and if their realization of this cruel fact blinded them to their good fortune they must be forgiven. They were certainly in no mood to understand that Java— so long regarded as a promised land—was at this moment the place above all others to be out of as soon as possible.

But what of the Australia party, for whom there was no ship in sight yet? They must have felt disappointment more acutely, for they had not even the stimulus of present action, however disagreeable. They dared not move, for they had been brought here under orders, as it were, and now they were left to hang around hopelessly like a band of itinerant salesmen whose wares no one wanted to buy but who had not a permit to go elsewhere.

Personally I was glad to know that for the moment embarkation was impossible. But then I was isolated in my feelings. I had worked it out that with the best luck in the world Carol could not reach Batavia until the evening, and all my thoughts were concentrated on what I should do if—as seemed most likely—we were required to embark before then. Should I, like some hysterical prima donna, urge a personal objection when so much larger issues were at stake? Or should I, on the other hand, sail without her and, weakly, allow myself to be carried off to a place of sanctuary while she was still in danger? In imagination both prospects seemed unbearable.

My only comfort was in Aubrey. He had not gone aboard with the rest, but sat firmly and disconsolately on his haversack, saying that nothing would induce him to move until Phyllis arrived. Selfishly, I hoped that she would never come, for then I would have moral support and Aubrey and I could set up a united front in refusing to leave.

But this comfort was shortlived, as I had known from the beginning it would be. Too soon a car drove up and Phyllis and the three Herbert sons, who are perhaps the most angelic-looking children this side of heaven, were inside, though almost submerged beneath a pile of belongings, some packed and some just carried. There was an excited shout, "Aubrey!", and he jumped up to meet them. There was a joyous family reunion and together they walked towards the *Plancius*, still luxuriating in those warm and intimate felicitations which follow a long parting, unexpectedly cut short.

The next few hours were for me the most lonely and miserable since I said good-bye to Carol in Singapore. My friends had gone aboard and there was no one in the Australia party with whom I had more than slight acquaintance. I was hot, sticky and dirty and acutely conscious of my unkempt appearance. I was possessionless and penniless, for it did not occur to me that in present circumstances the wary Dutch would be willing to offer exchange for Straits Settlements dollars. I was an unwanted evacuee, waiting around with nothing to do, for I knew not what, and always tormented by the fear that at any moment I might be ordered to embark on a ship which was possibly lurking somewhere out of sight and ready to set sail for Australia. The morning wore on and drifted into the afternoon. I grew hungrier and thirstier and more and more exhausted.

At the blackest moment, which was around three o'clock, there seemed no logical reason why food and drink should ever pass my lips again. But then one of our party, more enterprising than the others, revealed his possession of a few N.E.I. guilders, and after a little guilty indecision we said to hell with it all and went off for a belated lunch at a dockside café.

The meal, which consisted of a good round steak and a bottle of iced beer, was, of course, exquisite, and it put new heart into me.

When I returned to the drudgery of waiting I found that Duckworth and K.O. had arrived, also with the vain intent of embarking for Australia. They looked as forlorn as the rest of us, and said that no one seemed to have any knowledge of an Australian sailing. They suggested that I should refer the matter to Davis for his advice, which seemed an excellent idea and one which might have been put into practice a long while ago had we not been to all appearances marooned.

Reid drove up in a car laden with produce for the India party. He provided our first evidence that the M.B.C. staff already in Batavia had been busy on our behalf and that we had not been entirely forgotten. I explained the position to him and persuaded him to take me back to the landing quay, where I understood Davis was still hopefully awaiting news of the other two ships from Singapore.

Davis has enormous resilience and his moods change swiftly. Now he had lost his attitude of urgent severity, and was relaxed. He didn't seem in the least perturbed or even surprised by the news that so far there was no sign of an Australia-bound ship and intimated that we would just have to wait on events. When I suggested that in any case I would prefer not to leave without Carol he said that he agreed and that it was for me to make up my own mind. "So long as the India party gets off all right," he added, "it doesn't matter much. The rest of us will probably be able to slip through without bothering about the immigration people."

He told Reid something of the story of our last days in Singapore and mentioned the members of the staff who, in his view, deserved special credit— Margaret and Eric Robertson and the two engineers who blew up the transmitter at Mount Rosie and the girl telephonists who never missed a call. And then he talked of the future. "Aubrey doesn't want to go to Rangoon," he said, "so I've told him to return to England. Of course, we'll all be dispersed for a while—that's inevitable. But it's only a question of reorganization. There's still work for the M.B.C. to do even if we can't use the whole staff. Meanwhile, wherever you go and in whatever job you may be temporarily employed, you'll remain on our pay-roll."

As it happened, the Australian ship was just a myth, and having satisfied myself of this, I returned to Tanjong Priok. It was tedious to resume the pointless vigil at the docks, but there was no alternative. All through the afternoon I watched the continuous stream of passengers mount the gangplank of the *Plancius*. The ship had appeared already full to capacity this morning, but she was like a bottomless pit or a conjurer's trick-box, and seemingly could have accommodated the whole world if necessary. Once aboard, passengers were not allowed to disembark again, so that now one caught an occasional glimpse of familiar faces. Duckworth and K.O. were on deck. They had decided to abandon the idea of going to Australia and to make for Colombo while the chance offered.

Peggie arrived carrying a suitcase filled with an odd assortment of men's garments which had been hastily begged, borrowed or bought during the morning for the destitute men of our party. As no one else seemed to have the vaguest predatory designs on the suitcase or its contents, I promptly made them exclusively my own property. It gave me a feeling of renewed confidence to have some belongings again.

There wasn't time for more than a few moments' conversation with Peggie. It was a case of hail and farewell. Reid understood that Java's days were numbered, and before our arrival, which he had never believed possible, had already arranged passages for the women members of the original Batavia unit on a Melbourne-bound ship. They were due to leave for the port of embarkation in southern Java tomorrow, and Peggie, of course, was supposed to go with them. But now, on an impulse, she decided that she would prefer to join the India party, and so she added her name to the infinite passenger-list of the *Plancius*.

For hours and hours, so it seemed, I stood on the quay under the scorching sun looking up at the deck where Aubrey, Phyllis, Eric and Peggie had found a place in the front row. Occasionally I would take a stroll, but would always return to the same spot. And occasionally one of them would walk away but likewise would come back again. Though at intervals we exchanged shouts intended to be jocular, we just stood and looked for the most part with a sort of fixed grin on our faces. It was impossible to realize that we, who had hardly recovered from an experience which had brought us closer together than any lifetime acquaintance could, were now saying good-bye and would not meet again, perhaps, for months or even years.

Night threatened, and I was beginning to wonder how unfavourably stone would compare with wood as a resting-place, when a voice called me earnestly by name. I looked round, and there was Davis, and a few yards behind him Carol.

Usually the lowland Scottish in my blood precludes me from displaying any emotion in public and encourages me to affect the greatest indifference when I am most excited or most glad. But for this once my restraint was broken down. I ran to Carol and threw my arms around her and gave her a cinematographical embrace. Then I led her to the quayside and showed her proudly to our friends on the *Plancius*, and we all smiled and shouted a last good-bye.

We drove to the M.B.C. headquarters in Batavia with Davis. On the way Carol told me something of her own experiences. Only this morning she had given up hope that she would see me again, for she had heard a broadcast which allegedly came from Singapore, and she naturally had supposed that I was still there. She got the telephone message telling her of my arrival at lunch-time.

There was no 'plane available, so she hired a car. Bunty and the two Joans helped her pack and within half an hour she had started on her journey. All the way she shouted to the Malay driver, "*Lekas, lekas !*" (Faster, faster), while she was being driven through the twisting mountain road at breakneck speed, for she had been warned that unless she arrived before nightfall she would find me already gone. She covered the two hundred miles in just under three hours. And now she was here, at the end of a race which, as it turned out, need never have been run but was none the less dramatic.

The M.B.C. headquarters were part of a shipping office. There was a small, makeshift studio with a microphone, a sort of toy control board, and a gramophone which the announcer had to wind by hand. Programmes were still being broadcast from here on the Singapore wavelength, and when we arrived Allan Rose, looking as immaculate as ever, had just finished reading a very fateful news bulletin.

An hour or so later we were sitting at a large table in the dining-room of the Hotel des Indes. For the first time since my journey I had had a bath and had put on a complete change of clothes, which, though obviously ill-fitting and absurd to look at, felt none the less delectable. Davis was entertaining us and other members of the M.B.C. staff. He had ordered good food and good wine, and there were plenty of both to be had, for the Dutch had not yet recognized the word "rationing". This was indeed the dinner *de luxe* to which I had looked forward, and Davis said that he was giving it because he had promised it to me.

Everything I had wanted I had got. Every fear I had harboured had been set at rest. Carol was back with me again, and there was no flaw detectable in my good fortune. Yet it was impossible for me to abandon myself to enjoyment or even to feel entirely guiltless in my present exalted state when so many others, deserving much better, perhaps, than I, had fared so much worse. It was impossible to shut off my thoughts from those friends whose present fate, but for the grace of God, might have been mine.

Still less was it possible for any one of us, as we ate and drank, to make this an occasion for celebration. For how could we, of all people, rejoice now that Singapore had fallen ?

EPILOGUE

WHEN I was a boy I had, in common with many others of my age, a simple, straightforward ambition. It was to be Prime Minister of Great Britain.

Later, of course, I became persuaded, by reason of various mental deficiencies, notably a complete inability to understand the simplest economic problem, that I was ill-suited for the job. And so I lost my ambition. For a long time I was one of that abundant number who had no notion what they wanted to do or what particular objective they wished to attain.

But now I am blessed with a new ambition—as clear and straightforward as the old. It is to help redeem the pledge made in the last M.B.C. transmission from Batavia: "We'll be with you again . . ."

It may mean waiting until the war is won, but I am prepared for that. I shall then be able to explain to Jack how it came about that I was unable to telephone him. Jack is a prisoner now. He is among the seventy thousand whom the Japanese claimed to have made captive when Singapore fell. Very few succeeded in escaping after the capitulation. Carey was one of them. He got away, as he said he would, in a sampan.

Singapore is no longer news. The majority of the war correspondents considered its story already dead on the day the causeway was breached, and they went off to report happenings in other, more durable, theatres of war. But for us, who had a small stake in its survival, the story really began then, and it cannot end until our work has been resumed or, in other words, until British forces have driven out the Japanese invader. Nor can we regard kindly the cold predictions of those armchair theorists who close their eyes to the past—or regard it as all bad and all disgraceful—and talk grandly about the post-war status of Singapore. We certainly desire no return to the old Colonial system, with its "get-rich-quick-and-easy" appeal and its special attraction for family dunderheads and black sheep. But at the same time we have a debt to repay and a vengeance to exact. Let others arrange the final settlement. We shall not be content until the Union Jack is flying once again over Government House.

The M.B.C. was the first sizable British radio station to operate under fire. When it had to face that ordeal it was still young in experience, still understaffed and still woefully short of equipment. But at the end it had, like many other of Singapore's civilian organizations, far more cause to feel pride in its record than shame. It was administered during the nine weeks of war before Davis's return by W. R. Reid, its deputy-chairman. Reid's most treasured reminder of those days—which now seem so remote—is a telegram, dated January 23, 1942, which Davis sent him from New Delhi, for it contains the sentence- *Congratulate you excellent running whole station.* It is a little pathetic, perhaps, that he has no more recent and no more impartial testimony to his good work. But it is not surprising. Singapore fell, and those who deserved praise and recognition have shared the same reward as those who merited censure. They have all been left buried and forgotten beneath the ashes of a great defeat.

We know that, with the exception of Margaret and a few of the other women who were picked up by a passing yacht and brought safely to Batavia, the party on that first ship out of Singapore were taken prisoner by the Japanese. We hope that the party who went aboard the second ship are also prisoners, though nothing has been heard of them yet and we have no certain knowledge of their fate.   John Barraclough was among their number, and, thinking of him, my mind goes back to that New Year's Eve party at the chairman's house when he and Elizabeth Myers, one of Reid's assistants, became engaged.   They were married only a week or so before she was obliged to join the M.B.C. unit which was sent ahead to Batavia, and she has not seen him since.   Many other women in the same position as she—the wives of doctors, A.R.P. workers, L.D.C. men, Volunteers—are now enduring the agony of an indefinite separation with no news at all of their husbands.   It must be particularly hard for them to resist embitterment knowing that a sort of officially drawn veil has prevented the public from seeing the toil and self-sacrifice for the folly and inertia with which journalists—not noticeably those who cared to remain until the end—have identified the whole of civilian Singapore.   It must be harder still for the wives of the men in the armed forces, whose courage, though admitted, has been called vain and whose present fate is little better than oblivion.   For Bunty and Joan Tanner and Joan Reid, for example, who left Bandoeng after Java had already been invaded and eventually reached safety; for Bunty and Joan Tanner, whose husbands are now in captivity; for Joan Reid, whose husband went down with the *Prince of Wales*, Defeat, it seems, pays no dividends in glory.

We of the M.B.C. staff who survived death or capture are now scattered over various parts of the world—Britain, India, Ceylon, the United States, Gibraltar, the Gold Coast and Australia.   We have no longer any connection with each other.   We are serving different masters in different kinds of work.   But I like to think that we are still united in the feeling that we are but killing time, however profitably, until the moment comes when the engineer will be at his control board again, the microphone will be on its table, the red light will flicker and shine and the announcer will tell the world, "This is the Malaya Broadcasting Corporation . . ."

Perhaps by some ironic trick of fortune we shall be allowed control of the Penang station while a British army is advancing victoriously down the Malay Peninsula.   But, whatever happens, we must be there when Singapore is re-occupied.   We have promised as much to our listeners and to ourselves.   "We'll be with you again . . ." is the radio man's pledge to his public.   We spoke those words, and just as they are being honoured now in broadcasting studios throughout the Allied world, so eventually they must be fulfilled by us.

It is through no fault of Eric Davis that an overseas unit of the M.B.C. is not on the air at this moment.   He never lost hope, and his mind, which is like quicksilver, thought out various plans whereby our service might be continued.   But for once he was unable to have his way, and as it happened transmissions from Batavia petered out on Thursday, February 19, 1942—four days after the capitulation of Singapore.

On that same afternoon Carol and I embarked on an Australia-bound ship with an M.B.C. party which included W. R. Reid, Allan Rose, Victor Grosz, Michael Miles and John Ilsley, who had reached Java under his own steam.   With one or two exceptions the remainder of our colleagues had already left for India.   In the gathering dusk Davis came aboard to say good-bye.   He was staying behind to cover the war news for the B.B.C.   When he had learned that there was a C.B.S. man who proposed to remain in Java, he had decided that it was up to him to see that British as well as American broadcasting was represented.   Later he was informed that the C.B.S. man had made up his mind to leave after all, but he argued that this only provided additional reason for him to represent the B.B.C., for now British Broadcasting would have the field entirely to itself. It was a characteristic gesture worthy of his whole, heroic record in the Far Eastern war.

He did not linger long over this last parting. He was as restless, as energetic, as ever, and he wore the air of a man who has a mass of important business immediately ahead.

"Good-bye," I said. "I hope we'll meet again."

"Of course we will," he answered hurriedly, and was gone.

The voyage lasted ten days, and was, for the most part, undiluted misery. The ship was a 1200-ton coastal steamer, which for many years had plied in easy fashion between Singapore and Penang. It was in no sense ocean-going, and though the seas were never really heavy it rolled unmercifully and often stayed down on one side for so long that one began to entertain a genuine fear that it could not right itself again and must capsize. No one was more surprised when it finally reached port than the chief engineer, who confided in me that its hull was paper-thin; and indeed that it did so was a considerable feat of navigation, for the Chinese crew had been brought aboard more or less at pistol-point, and the Scottish skipper had no charts of any kind and had had to set a course by the stars.

We enjoyed the luxury of cabins, and we ate in a dining saloon, but water was very short and the food was nauseating. Eventually I gave up trying to eat it, and for hours during the days as well as after dark lay in my bunk in an endeavour to sleep away acute pangs of hunger and thirst and boredom. Hardest of all to bear, I think, was the sense of anticlimax. Several of our fellow passengers were war correspondents who had lost little and were now going on to new and exciting assignments. For us, who were more or less possessionless, there seemed no joy at all in the future.

Our last two nights were spent lying at anchor in the roads off Fremantle. On the second evening the Australian Customs officials came aboard and we were cleared for landing. But still there was no indication that we would ever enter the harbour, and I wished that Davis was with us so that he could command the lowering of a lifeboat or two. To add the final touch to our humiliating predicament we received official warning that we must be prepared for an attack by a surface raider. The first officer did not know quite what to make of this news. At first he ordered the women to the boiler room and the rest of us to action stations. Then he decided, for no good reason, that someone had played an unkind joke on him. He abused us all roundly for not keeping calm and ordered us to bed. The night passed peacefully, though for a while we were kept awake by his voice still raised in angry remonstrance at our conduct.

Next morning, after several indecisive and agonizing hours of hopes raised and hopes dashed, we weighed anchor. By a strange freak of chance we drew alongside the K.P.M. ship which had taken Carol and myself to Batavia. The captain invited us to have a drink, and we sat in the same place where less than three months or a lifetime ago we had enjoyed so many lazy hours in such civilized surroundings with Carey and Mac and others.

Ashore at last, we got into a handsome-looking station bus and were driven to Perth, which is a pleasant, sub-tropical country town whose ugly buildings are discounted by beautiful green lawns and gracefully decked parkland. We came to a halt outside a kind of parish hall. A middle-aged lady, wearing a large hat, stuck her head round the door. She had a buxom figure, and her face was round, florid and kindly.   When she smiled she revealed a row of very white and even false teeth.   "Well, well, well," she said, without pausing to survey us, and in the accent of her country, "here we are safe and sound.   Welcome to Australia, and now I expect you'd all like a nice cup of tea."

We had reached our haven, and for the first time we really felt like refugees.

APPENDIX

Note on the Malaya Broadcasting Corporation

THE Malaya Broadcasting Corporation was an organization set up by the British and Malayan Governments. It was charged with the responsibility of operating broadcast services for Malaya and the whole of the Far East. It had no connection with the British Broadcasting Corporation, nor was it an offspring of any parent body.

The word "Malaya" in its title, though not particularly grammatical, was used to distinguish its identity from its predecessor, the British Malayan Broadcasting Corporation Ltd., which was a private company operating a small local station.

The decision to set up a Government-controlled broadcasting organization in Singapore was taken before the present war began, but nothing effective was done in the matter until the Chairman, Mr. Eric Davis, and the Chief Executive Officer, Mr. W. R. Reid, arrived in Malaya—the former in December, 1940, and the latter in January, 1941.

The local station, equipped as it was with low-power transmitters, three studios and two subsidiary studios for Asiatic programmes, was the legacy of the new Corporation, and provided the only immediate facilities for putting into effect the instructions which the Chairman had received when he left London. Further, there was no trained assistance available other than the small staff of the local station headed by its manager, Mr. John Dumeresque. A skeleton executive staff was recruited in London, but, owing to transportation difficulties, etc., it reached Malaya only in dribs and drabs, and was not yet fully assembled on the day that the war with Japan began.

The vast enterprise of instituting a Far Eastern Radio Service which necessitated regular broadcasts in twenty-six languages and dialects was undertaken by the Chairman of the Governing Body, the Chief Executive Officer and the Director of Engineering, Mr. Danny Weigall, who arrived from England in March, 1941. Mr. Dumeresque left Malaya to take his leave in the United States, so that during most of the initial period even his advice and assistance were not available.

Thirteen months after the Chairman landed in Malaya, the M.B.C. was broadcasting on four simultaneous transmissions in thirteen languages; it was making ready large suites of studios in Singapore; it had altered and enlarged the existing broadcasting station; it had installed large transmitters and equipment which were almost ready for use; it had recruited and trained locally a staff of some 290 individuals—mostly Asiatics. These facts may give some indication of what was accomplished. The fact that the Chairman's aim was not fully realized before the transmitters and equipment had to be destroyed and the staff dispersed may be regarded as one of the tragedies of the War in the Pacific.

The Governing Body of the M.B.C. was as follows:

Chairman: Eric Davis.
Official Nominee of the Colony Government: The Honourable W. H. Weisberg.

Unofficial Nominee of the Colony Government : The Honourable E. N. C. Woollerton.

Far Eastern Representative (Imperial Government) : R. H. Scott.

Administrative Representative (Imperial Government) : Sir George Sansom.

The majority of the M.B.C.'s executive officers and the positions which they held have been mentioned in the pages foregoing, but it should be stated here that a most important job was carried out with conspicuous ability by E. A. Kennard, who was News Director. With one exception—Sze Chu Sian, who was Chinese programme organizer—the chief members of the Asiatic staff either elected to stay in Singapore or were subsequently taken prisoner by the Japanese. For obvious reasons their names have not been disclosed.

THE END